D1600342

America's First
Network TV Censor

The Work of NBC's Stockton Helffrich

Robert Pondillo

Southern Illinois University Press
Carbondale and Edwardsville

2/3/11
ww
$ 37. 50

13   12   11   10   4   3   2   1

Library of Congress Cataloging-in-Publication Data
Pondillo, Robert, 1951–
America's first network TV censor : the work of
NBC's Stockton Helffrich / Robert Pondillo.
    p. cm.
Includes bibliographical references and index.
ISBN-13: 978-0-8093-2918-2 (alk. paper)
ISBN-10: 0-8093-2918-2 (alk. paper)
ISBN-13: 978-0-8093-8574-4 (ebook)
ISBN-10: 0-8093-8574-0 (ebook)
1. Helffrich, Stockton, 1911–1997. 2. Television broad-
casting—United States—Biography. 3. Television—
Censorship—United States. 4. National Broadcasting
Corporation, inc. I. Title.
PN1992.4.H42P76 2010
384.55092—dc22
[B]   2009028248

Printed on recycled paper. ♻
The paper used in this publication meets the mini-
mum requirements of American National Standard
for Information Sciences—Permanence of Paper for
Printed Library Materials, ANSI Z39.48-1992. ∞

To Edie and Mac

Contents

Acknowledgments   ix

Introduction: Context and Beginnings of TV Censorship   1
1. Stockton *Who*?   13
2. The Early Years   33
3. The NBC-TV Program Policies Manual   55
4. Sin, Sex, and TV Censorship   73
5. Gagging the Gags   99
6. TV Violence   122
7. Postwar Racial Discourse   142
8. Of Truth and Toilet Paper   161
Conclusion: A Prescient Vision   190

Notes   203
Index   245

Acknowledgments

$\mathcal{I}$ am deeply grateful to my many mentors on this book project. Without their guidance and support, it would have been impossible to complete. My thanks to Kristine Priddy, Kathy Kageff, and Karl Kageff at Southern Illinois University Press and the several thoughtful readers who looked over earlier drafts of this book. Many thanks also to my sharp-eyed copy editor, Mary Lou Kowaleski; her thoughtful suggestions on improving or clarifying my manuscript enhanced the book in myriad ways. Also my gratitude to James L. Baughman, Jan Buechner, Brian Deith, Don Downs, Lew Friedland, Jim Hoyt, Lynn Schroeder, and Stephen Vaughn, all at the University of Wisconsin–Madison. A special heartfelt thanks to my friend Susie Brandscheid for her singular act of kindness on my behalf.

I send my gratitude as well to the dozens of thoughtful researchers who readily helped me in my journey, especially those at the State Historical Society of Wisconsin at Madison; Library of Congress, Washington D.C.; Catholic University, Washington, D.C.; and Museum of Radio and Television, New York City; and Michael Henry, Library of American Broadcasting, University of Maryland–College Park, and the extraordinarily kind J. Fred MacDonald in Chicago.

This work would not exist without the kind assistance of Stockton Helffrich's children, Jackie Austin and Richard Krauser, and his lovely wife, Maxie Helffrich. I am indebted to Helffrich, the central character in this book—indeed, we all are. Why? Because he kept notes. Copious notes—literally thousands of them, eleven years of them—on just about every program, script, and commercial advertisement he viewed (and often censored) at the network. Helffrich left more than a thousand typed, single-spaced pages, over 225 individual commentaries called Continuity Acceptance Radio/Television, or CARTs. He and his battery of "continuity editors" (another way of saying "censors") considered the appropriateness of just about *everything* noteworthy that paraded before NBC-TV cameras from 1948 through early 1960. His work offers not only a portal through which to gaze at TV's foundational times but also another way to access and understand the postwar world and how far TV today has progressed or stayed the same.

Portions of this *book have been* adapted from his previously *published* articles, as well as unpublished scholarly convention papers and academic presentations: "Cleavage Control!" *Television Quarterly* 36: 2 (2006): 53–57; "Saving Nat 'King' Cole." *Television Quarterly* 35: 3/4 (2005): 8–16; "Racial Discourse and Censorship on NBC-TV, 1948–1960." *Journal of Popular Film and Television* 33: 2 (2005): 102–114; "Chicago TV's Winter of Violence: 1952–53." *Television Quarterly* 34: 2 (2004): 24–29; "You Can't SING *THAT* on TV!'" *Television Quarterly* 33: 4 (2003): 62–67; "Rod Serling's 'The Censorship Zone.'" *Television Quarterly* 33: 1 (2002): *34–43;* "A 'Legion of Decency' for Early Television?" *Television Quarterly* 33: 2/3 (2001): 16–21.

My thanks to the following for allowing me to quote from their papers and correspondence: Joseph Atmore, Dolores Jackie S. Austen, Richard Krauser, the State Historical Society of Wisconsin at Madison, the American Catholic History Research Center and University Archives, the Catholic University of America, and the United States Conference of Catholic Bishops.

Thanks also to William Clotworthy, NBC-TV's chief censor during the 1970s, and Fritz Jacobi at *Television Quarterly* for their support. Cheers to Anca Rieza and Jennifer Wright for their superior editing skills. Gratitude as well to my Middle Tennessee State University honors students and my fine graduate assistants Anton Bates, Joe Fewell, Tori Harris, and Shannon Hickman. I'm also most grateful for the sustained backing of my wonderful colleagues Clare Bratten, Chris Harris, Bob Kalwinsky, John Omachonu, Jan Quarles, and Bob Spires, my department chair, Dennis Oneal, and my dean, Roy L. Moore. On the home front, hugs to my son, Macallan Currie. When I began this project, Mac was five years old. I completed its final draft two months after his sixteenth birthday.

I wish to extend thanks for the steadfast encouragement of my father, Albert M. Pondillo Sr., the support and kindness of the late Norton Urness and Virginia Urness, and the unwavering confidence of my brother, Albert M. Pondillo Jr., my hero and role model. I also wish to acknowledge my deceased mother and grandmother, Adelaide and Annie Peluso, respectively—two great women who inspired me to always pursue excellence and follow my heart. May their spirits forever guide me.

Finally, none of this would be possible without the unflagging support of my wife, Edie. She was there during the many highs and lows of this project and in times of discouragement and triumph. Although personal incertitude often plagued me, Edie never doubted. For that and her unqualified love, I am indeed blessed and eternally grateful.

*T*he 1950s were an anxious time for American television. While the fifties were undoubtedly an era of inventiveness and imagination, early television was also beset by, among other things, technical limitations, advertiser pressure, audience complaints, special-interest-group carping, government scrutiny, and a large dose of self-imposed censorship. Every nascent network—ABC, CBS, DuMont, and NBC—had offices of "Standards and Practices" or "Continuity Acceptance," euphemisms for censorship departments. And although bowdlerization, redaction, and expurgation are not usually associated with a time of "flourishing achievements," America's first network TV censor—Stockton Helffrich—used such methods of suppression as tools of creativity.

TV Censorship's "Golden Age"?

Many scholars of television history consider the years 1948–60 as network TV's golden age. The notion of a golden age comes from Greco-Roman mythology and was first used in the mid-sixteenth century to define what scholars celebrated as the apotheosis of classical Latin poetry (roughly 75 BCE to 14 CE). A golden or utopian age is always romanticized as a special time of first, flourishing achievements and novel creativity. Censorship, on the other hand, is most often seen as a dark domain of repression and deletion, a realm of restraint, of controlled expression. So how can TV censorship have a golden age? Although the notion seems like an oxymoron, it is not pretzel logic. TV's early postwar years were heady times when television forms and ways to censor them were literally being invented.[1]

The most productive way to understand what animated Stockton Helffrich's censorial behavior is to see his work in dialogue with the cultural attitudes and social mores of postwar America. Therefore, throughout this work, I strive to contextualize Helffrich's notions of censorship against the sociocultural Zeitgeist of the 1950s. The book, then, is not a comprehensive or comparative history of postwar TV censorship embracing all the major networks. Instead, it is a tightly focused, specific, and explicit analysis of early television censorship at one network, NBC-TV, based on the copious notes and more than a decade's worth of written reports by chief censor Stockton Helffrich. Every chapter concentrates upon and often draws explicit distinctions between the public and private behaviors of 1950s America. Only occasionally are references included to twenty-first-century episodes and attitudes, and only when I think appropriate.

The early television industry followed censorship models from radio and film that are abundantly clear. This chapter expands upon that notion and also tries to show how TV broke with some of those models and practices. Why? Because TV *was* different than radio and movies. No other consumer technology had achieved such wide acceptance and cultural diffusion in so short a time. It should be remembered that from 1934 to 1947, television was seen by only a few thousand people and mostly on the east coast. Within a decade, TV was being watched by more than thirty million people; this is a near 90 percent rate of diffusion. It took electrification of the United States more than sixty years to achieve that rate. It took the telephone more than fifty years and radio more than thirty to attain the same rate of adoption and dispersion. A communication technology with so much popularity and acceptance is bound to impact the nature of a culture—especially a culture like ours, squeamish about sex, language, drinking, and other moral behaviors—and, indeed it did. And with such impact came industry self-censorship. To be sure, if early network television did not strive to police itself, the government would have done so. Certainly, Helffrich and NBC-TV kept a wary eye on Federal Communications Commission (FCC) rules and other government regulations as well as sponsor-sanctioned censorship in programming, and occasionally in this book, their intersection is mentioned. But this work is not nor is it intended to be a specific treatise on TV censorship provided by legal or regulatory rulings. My intention is more specific: To focus and elaborate on how, when, what, and why Helffrich and NBC-TV self-censored its product and to draw some connections to the larger social and cultural implications of that behavior.

As I write these words in 2009, TV finds itself moving away from another restrictive cycle. Many contemporary pundits point to singer

Janet Jackson's 2004 Super Bowl breast bearing as ground zero for the roaring "comeback" of American media censorship in the early twenty-first century. But perhaps it was not Jackson who reopened Pandora's censorship box in 2004 as experts claim. Maybe it happened in 2003 when Bono—lead singer for the Irish rock group U-2—said, while gathering an award on live television, "This is really, really, fucking brilliant."[2] Perchance it was in 2001 when Florida-based disc jockey "Bubba the Love Sponge" (real name Todd Clem) discussed on the air what it would be like to have sex with cartoon characters.[3] Or possibly it was any time from 1990 to 2000 when "shock jock" Howard Stern offered listeners on-air farting contests and features like "Lesbian Dial-A-Date."[4] The point is: censorship did not made a sudden "comeback" in the early twenty-first century, because it never made a definite "go away" in any century. It is a perennial phenomenon that often blossoms during times of high cultural anxiety.

Readers, I am confident, will see parallels in television programming restrictions in then and now. Readers will also note a continuing, fear-driven tautology—such as, children must be protected from TV portrayals of sex, hyperviolence, and coarse language because American values are at risk. That has been exceptionally durable trope since the early days of commercial television. But there are others, particularly seeing female breasts on TV in any context and of any species. In 1958, for example, fearing many would find cartoon udders too explicit for home viewing, censors only permitted cows drawn wearing *skirts*.[5] And when one ciphers in the hoopla raised by the Janet Jackson episode, it is clear that exposed milk-secreting glands of any kind—and apparently on any mammal—have been a real and continuing source of social anxiety for American television.

It is my hope this book helps readers make a little more sense of TV industry self-censorship today by examining its postwar (or golden age) roots. And to that end will ponder the copious work of the nation's first network television censor, Stockton Helffrich.

Network Radio and Censorship

In 1934, NBC radio established its Department of Continuity Acceptance in order to maintain "good taste" in radio programming. Janet MacRorie, its first continuity-acceptance director, had the final word on what would be broadcast over the network. She and her staff scrutinized all program scripts and ad-agency copy to make certain each was free of "obscene or off-colored songs or jokes [and] language of doubtful propriety." Although "Negro" music (i.e., jazz) was studiously avoided by NBC, even music by so-called crooners like Rudy Vallee and Bing Crosby was considered profligate by many moral guardians.[6] Boston's Cardinal William Henry O'Connell told his Catholic congregation that he considered crooning, "bleating and whining, with disgusting words, the meaning of which is a low-down source of sexual influence."[7]

By 1939, NBC programs were prohibited from talking about suicides or describing homicides on the air. Demeaning or ridiculing public officials was banned. In children's programs, parental authority was sacrosanct, but NBC also proscribed horror shows, the use of vulgar or profane words, stories of torture, kidnapping, or morbid suspense or hysteria. Any program that described a medical operation, sexual disease, or advocated mercy killing or capital punishment was also strictly taboo.[8] Advertisers of the time could not use fictitious testimonials, false claims, or references to their competitors. Therapeutic or personal-hygiene products (deodorant, toilet paper, mouthwash, and the like) were verboten and repeatedly turned away. MacRorie censored any nostrum or elixir that promised miracle cures for a given ailment, and she refused to broadcast those ads that explicitly dealt with bodily functions—laxatives, hemorrhoid ointments, hair restorers, or depilatories.[9]

Sexual radio content was almost nonexistent, and even atomized words were scrutinized for double entendre. For example, memos flew back and forth between Hollywood and New York City analyzing the word *screwy*. MacRorie finally accepted it as a synonym for *unbalanced* proclaiming it had "no other secondary or suggestive meaning [when] used in that connection."[10] The use of gay humor was also on MacRorie's hit list. She felt the comedy of many NBC radio comedians—Jack Benny, George Burns and Gracie Allen, and Bob Hope—too often relied on jokes about "effeminate gentlemen or sex-perverted characters."[11] MacRorie and other NBC executives insisted all "female gentlemen" jokes had to be excised.[12] Moreover, according to Douglas Craig, the mere mention of sexuality of any kind was "too culturally challenging to be tolerated on a network that aspired to enter every American home." For that reason, divorce was mentioned only "when portrayed in an unattractive way," and birth control issues, although widely discussed in the culture at the time, were "unpalatable and even offensive to vast numbers [and a] subject . . . not yet ripe for introduction . . . [in]to the homes of America." Both NBC and CBS also banned jokes about prohibition for its duration. And even though the Eighteenth Amendment was overwhelmingly rejected by American society in 1933 with its repeal, NBC was still hesitant to broadcast drunken characters in comedy or drama as late as 1937, especially forbidding "any scene involving drunken women." As Craig observed, "part of the network's conception of entertaining the public was to avoid offending or shocking it"; such was accomplished through the censorious cultural politics of "good taste."[13]

Jewish Radio Humor

During the 1932 season, a host of new radio personalities burst upon the scene, among them Benny, Fred Allen, George Jessel, Burns and Allen, and Ed Wynn. Vaudevillians all, they "participated in the 'new humor' brought by immigrants to the vaudeville stage."[14] Theatrical historian Albert F. McLean Jr. characterizes vaudeville humor as "more excited, more aggressive, and less sympathetic than that to which the middle classes of the nineteenth century had been accustomed." The vaudeville stage comics, McLean reveals, would employ varying levels of vulgarity (also known as "jasbo," "hokum," and "gravy") to milk a joke for laughs—although, he notes, early-twentieth-century vaudeville was consciously targeting a middle-class family audience and moving away from the notion of hard burlesque. Vaudeville management, therefore, constantly censored comics for using indelicate language and joking about taboo subjects.[15] Irving Howe writes that *Jewish* vaudeville comics and comediennes were especially drawn to "dirty" or vulgar material.[16] While it is true many funnymen, funnywomen, and their writers were Jews who brought new ideas to radio from vaudeville that often shocked sponsors (and moral guardians), the bald assertion that Jews were more "drawn" to vulgarity than other races should be rejected as a racist generalization or perhaps the ravings of a self-hating Semite. There is considerable evidence that many top Jewish radio comics, who would do vulgar material at dinner parties and charity benefits, refused to repeat such jokes on the air for fear of offending listeners.[17] Such disturbing discourse is nonetheless productive in exposing religious and cultural prejudice as another locus of 1930s radio censorship.

Censorship of the time relied upon how radio "gatekeepers" (i.e., the sponsors, ad agencies, or network) imagined the audience (quite conservative) in relation to how radio artists conjured it (more liberal). The tension was found at the gap between these twin perspectives. When an on-air talent conceived of listeners, he or she may have seen them enjoying his or her artistry, play on words, or some hypocrisy exposed by the humor, but the gatekeepers imagined just the opposite: Words were bogeys offending the listener, scaring away potential sales, and creating ill will for the sponsor. In many cases, entertaining an audience on the radio and selling them something were often two opposing missions.

Amos 'n' Andy

Twin problems plagued black actors and creative talent during the emergence of network radio: an abiding culture of racism in the United States, and the commercial system of American broadcasting itself. The advertisers' fear of using African American talent in anything but traditional racial stereotypes—such as, "Coon," "Tom," or "Mammy"— was rampant. The "Coon" character used fractured speech and was portrayed as lecherous, conniving, lazy, indolent, and slow of wit; the "Tom" or "Uncle Tom" was racially stereotyped as the submissive black whose existence gave reassurance to white audiences that there were forces of reason at work within the black community; the "Mammy" was depicted as an overweight black woman, colorful of speech, quick to anger but full of love for her babies (be they black or white), and a great cook and kitchen servant. Such racist characterizations were not only heard on radio but also reinforced in film, theater, recordings, print, advertising, and music of the era.[18] Frank Silvera, a black actor of the era, wrote: If Pillsbury "were pushing Negro talent . . . the next thing you know [its product] would be branded as 'nigger flower' and [no one would buy it]." Newscaster Chet Huntley made essentially the same observation when commenting on the dearth of news coverage in the black community: "I presume that the reason for less Negro news was due to sales resistance. Sponsors would probably fear boycott of their products." This fear of alienating bigots and segregationists is found in early television as well. For example, some southerners claimed that

Coca-Cola was "the drink of the Negro" and insisted its commercial be removed from "white" television shows. Many other advertisers also "readily asserted that they could not afford to have [what they manufacture associated as] 'Negro products.'"[19] This is not to say that blacks went unrepresented on the radio for they did not and were indeed featured in some of the most popular (and most racist) programs on the air. For example, Eddie Anderson's portrayal as Rochester van Jones, Jack Benny's valet; the maid Beulah Brown on *Fibber McGee and Molly* (who was actually a white *man*, Marlin Hurt); Ruby Dandridge as Geranium the maid on *The Judy Canova Show*.[20] Radio inherited such stereotypes from American stage minstrelsy of the 1830s when white comics rubbed burnt cork and boot black on their faces, donned nappy wigs and garish costumes, and mocked regional, black dialects. Michele Hilmes also acknowledges blacks as "'permanent immigrants' always arriving, never arrived." James Baldwin similarly wrote that black folks showed white America "where the bottom [was]."[21] It was not until *Amos 'n' Andy*, one hundred years later, that racist minstrel comedy was welcomed as viable genre for nationwide commercial radio.

Anthony Tollin, billed as a "noted broadcast historian" and author of brief, popular booklets on early radio shows, declared the *Amos 'n' Andy* program "was not about race." Rather, he says, its "plots revolved around the age-old themes of love and money, and *Amos 'n' Andy's* romantic and economic woes struck a universal chord with depression era America."[22] While it was true the plots inaugurated and adhered to "situation comedy" formulas, to claim *Amos 'n' Andy*, American radio's first and longest-running hit show,[23] was not about race seems incredulous. *Amos 'n' Andy's* text and subtext were all about race. However, in a scholarly review of *Amos 'n' Andy* scripts, Hilmes (and others) found the most vicious racial humor was, indeed, avoided.[24] Nonetheless, the characters created by white actors Freeman F. Gosden and Charles J. Correll were that of Amos Jones and Andrew Brown, two black men, and Hilmes argues both characters were created "solidly in the [minstrel] tradition of . . . 'Jim Crow' [or 'Uncle Tom'] . . . hardworking, sincere, yet superstitious, and none too bright . . . (Amos;) 'Zip Coon' . . . lazy, devious . . . manipulative . . . given to womanizing and dubious financial schemes (Andy)."[25] Although both Amos and Andy seem to live in an all-black world with its own social strata, white characters infrequently appear, and there are never episodes where either black character deals with racial hatred, discrimination, segregation, unfriendliness, or injustice—all of which were constant cultural conditions for American blacks both before and after the Civil War. *"Amos 'n' Andy*, therefore, bore very little relation to *anything* authentically African American,"* asserts Hilmes, "owing its surface 'blackness' only to the imposed racial identity of its characters. . . . [The program's] central theme [was] cultural incompetence linked to race."[26] It is further argued that the large immigrant audience the show attracted used *Amos 'n' Andy* as a social barometer—a sort of measure their American acceptance—a level above black people, and below which these immigrants must not fall.[27] Toni Morrison wrote that through the new social tensions of the roaring twenties and the beginning of World War I, "immigrant populations (and much immigrant literature) understood their 'American-ness' as an opposition to the resident black population."[28]

Afraid advertising revenues would be lost if programming offended political bigots and segregationists, radio did little to change the culture of the nation by challenging old social narratives. It was thought mass audiences of the time would simply not accept authentic portrayals of black men and women on the air, and such programming was anathema to advertising agencies and their clients. While true the very structure of commercial radio had a direct and deeply censorious effect on what would be broadcast, it would be too easy to blame market-driven broadcasting, advertising, and advertising agencies as responsible for continuing racist stereotypes. To be sure, each was part of the problem, but to assume the medium could have changed the hearts of Americans at this juncture attributes radio much more pervasive power than it had. It also disregards an entrenched racist history in the United States and assumes those in industry, advertising agencies, and broadcast management had the cultural vision (and unusual courage) to push for social change. Such was not the case. Almost from the beginning of telephony, radio was conceived as an entertainment medium; it was not broadcasting's job to directly influence political change or cultural politics.[29] Moreover, radio was never a reflection of the times as was and is often claimed. Instead, it was a sanitized, deodorized social construction of it and a cost-effective way for large corporations to advertise their wares nationally. A new mainstream social dialogue would eventually be heard and enlightened ideas on race broadcast but not before the beginning of World War II. It would take a generation for new cultural attitudes to ferment. Media narratives on race would not radically change until the coming of the American civil rights movement in the late 1950s and early 1960s—although J. Fred MacDonald notes World War II had "a salutary effect upon the image and position of blacks in American broadcasting. . . . [T]here arose . . . an awareness of the paradox of fighting against a racist enemy abroad, while practicing segregation and exclusion at home."[30]

Sexual Censorship

Sunday, December 19, 1937, marked the date of the first network radio apology. On the previous Sunday, the slightly risqué and controversial film-star Mae West had offended the sensibilities of religious leaders and other moral guardians with her "artful" reading of a radio sketch. West and ventriloquist Edgar Bergen along with his wooden alter ego Charlie McCarthy (whom West, in her salty style, called "all wood and a yard long") were involved in a sketch that apparently insulted thousands of network radio listeners and prompted calls for more federal censorship of radio.[31] It was the infamous "Adam and Eve" sketch that caused the controversy; West portrayed Eve, Don Ameche played Adam.[32] In this satire on the ancient Garden of Eden story from the book of Genesis,[33] West, as Eve, asks the "palpitatin' python" (played by Bergen) to retrieve the forbidden fruit, "right between those pickets." The snake gets stuck in the fence, and West encourages him to "Shake your hips," and, once the snake slides through, seductively groans, "Nice goin', swivel hips. . . . Mmm, oh I see . . . Get me a big one . . . I feel like doin' a *big* apple."[34] Elizabeth McLeod called the sketch "possibly the bluest ten minutes the [NBC] Red Network ever aired."[35]

The *New York Sun* crowed the broadcast had hit "an all time low in radio." Thousands are said to have written and phoned NBC protesting the show as "vulgar" and "sacrilegious."[36] *Variety* acknowledged, "Radio is badly scared and will lock the barn door."[37] Chase and Sanborn, the show's sponsor, officially apologized to NBC for the error. NBC responded, "We share with you the regret you express. . . . [O]ur interests are mutual in giving the American public wholesome entertainment and we will intensify our efforts to that end."[38] An editorial headline in the *Catholic Monitor* announced, "Mae West Pollutes Homes." And the

Catholic Legion of Decency openly discussed the viability of launching a campaign to clean up radio. Iowa U.S. Senator Clyde Herring proposed a board of review for radio. The FCC began an investigation, and its chairman, Frank McNinch, declared the sketch "offensive to the great mass of right-thinking, clean-minded Americans." Dr. Maurice Sheehy, a professor of religion at the Catholic University, tagged it "indecent, scurrilous, and irreverent. . . . To have this lewd and filthy take-off on the Bible's Adam and Eve was a disgrace."[39] Sheehy's statement was also read into the *Congressional Record*.[40] Bergen went into hiding in Palm Springs, and according to his daughter Candice, "the show's ratings went up two points."[41]

West biographer Marybeth Hamilton takes a contrary view of the Adam and Eve sketch in saying it was not that controversial. It was, she hints, religious muscle flexing and politicos of all colors sensing a "can't lose" issue, jumping on the moral bandwagon. Hamilton points out after the broadcast, Paramount Pictures seeking to capitalize on the publicity of "scandal"—always good for business—released West's *Every Day's a Holiday* film early to bad reviews.[42] It seemed the questionable sketch caught only limited audience interest for the film.[43] The "huge" public outcry, according to both trade and mainstream press, was orchestrated by the Catholic Legion of Decency and other religious groups. Ever concerned about pleasing sponsors and diffusing government regulators, the networks simply sacrificed West and made of her an example. Mae West was banished from appearing on any future NBC programs and was not heard on radio again for the next thirty-seven years.[44]

Fred Allen

Radio comedian Fred Allen always seemed to be in hot water with the NBC network because he liked to ad-lib. Performers going off script meant a loss of the tight control over which radio network and their continuities departments insisted. Allen was not the only radio comedian who went with the moment and ad-libbed on the air—Eddie Cantor was notorious for it, as were Burns, Benny, and Crosby.[45] However, as Allen biographer Alan Havig speculates, because Fred Allen was "NBC's only major comedy performer to broadcast from its Radio City headquarters in New York, by the late 1930s his spontaneous remarks attracted close[r] network scrutiny."[46]

The NBC Continuity Acceptance Department, Program Standards division required its editors to review all copy and continuities at least *two days* prior to the broadcast. Moreover, NBC reserved the right to make the final cut on any questionable dialogue.[47] The NBC line censor assigned to the Allen show, Dorothy Kemble, explained in a 1938 memo to her boss Ken R. Dyke: "Adlibbing on the part of our comedians is probably the most difficult problem that NBC encounters. . . . Some portions of the [Allen show] Master Copy bore little or no resemblance to what actually went over the air. . . . There have been cases where particularly dirty jokes were made out of seemingly innocent ones."[48] In addition, Janet MacRorie, director of NBC's Continuity Acceptance Department, was not fond of Allen's off-the-cuff remarks and even suggested a meeting with the advertising agency that sponsored and controlled the show, Young and Rubicam,[49] as a way to silence him.[50] A clearly frustrated MacRorie wrote that her department "politely begs and cajoles [ad] Agency representatives to persuade their talent, namely Fred Allen, to refrain from . . . libel, derogatory reference, vulgarity, cross-[plugging of products] as may have been encountered in the script before."[51]

The events of April 1947, referred to as *"l'affaire Allen"* by *New York Times* critic Jack Gould, are vintage Fred Allen.[52] By the late 1940s, Clarence L. Menser, an NBC programming vice-president (whom Allen labeled a "petty tyrant"), replaced MacRorie.[53] Havig describes Menser as a "conservative old-timer who [held] fast to the policy . . . that gags about NBC on NBC are strictly taboo."[54] Menser said he would pull from the air any radio comics "who think they have the right to say what they want."[55] Havig picks up the story from there:

> Allen's show of April 13, 1947 went over . . . time. The network, employing standard policy, cut the program short. . . . [O]n his next show . . . Allen offered a different explanation . . . His story, which was aimed at Menser[,] . . . alleged that a network official accumulated all the seconds and minutes cut from the [ends] of comedy shows for his own vacations. Menser had rejected the routine prior to airtime; Allen read the lines anyway. Menser cut the program from the air [for twenty-five seconds].[56]

Response was swift against NBC and Menser: The American Civil Liberties Union accused the network of stifling free speech, other NBC comics rushed to defend Allen in the press, listeners wrote nasty letters, and media comments were particularly cheeky against network management. But the real blows came when the show's sponsor, Standard Brands, angrily defended Allen's right to free expression, and the J. Walter Thompson agency declared it would invoice NBC demanding compensation pro rata for the portion of the show that had been paid for but not permitted broadcast.[57] Embarrassed NBC President Niles Trammel replaced Menser with Dyke, apologized to all concerned, and said he looked forward to any jokes or sketches that Allen may write in the future satirizing top management. Then, as a joke, Trammel asked Allen to accept the position of honorary vice-president of the network. With the tables turned, Allen refused, not finding the offer very funny. The choice of Dyke as new censorship chief, however, was a brilliant move that Allen applauded. Dyke worked to liberalize the standards code and used a consultative, talent-inclusive management approach with his creative writers and performers. "For the first time," Allen told a reporter, "my relations with [NBC] script censors have been pleasant."[58]

This incident with Fred Allen and NBC management illustrates the tension between radio talent and network officials and the balancing act it took to keep the program process intact. Dyke's method is similar to those used at NBC-TV by a young man Dyke himself mentored: Stockton Helffrich, America's first network television censor.

1. Stockton *Who*?

*T*he period known as "the fifties" (roughly 1947 to about the assassination of John F. Kennedy in 1963) was an anxious time in America. It was a time of promise and peril as the Cold War raged, and nuclear annihilation was a distinct possibility—indeed, *Newsweek* reported, "By 1952, 1953, or 1954, the Kremlin may be ready for a major war."[1] There were whispers of clandestine Soviet-directed fifth columns—the enemy within—eating away at the moral foundations of the republic. Catholic Bishop Fulton J. Sheen, an iconic figure of the 1950s, often repeated British historian Arnold Toynbee's observation that "sixteen out of the nineteen civilizations . . . decayed from within."[2] Could that decay happen in America? Some said not only it *could* but it *was* happening here, and the godless Communists were the prime suspects. By the early fifties, Communists, real or imagined, seemed just about everywhere, around every corner, under every bed. And by then, something else seemed just about everywhere: television.[3]

As this new technology insinuated its way into U.S. homes—often co-opting entire rooms and changing eating and sleeping habits—Americans at once celebrated television and were a bit wary of it.[4] By 1955, it was a brave new TV world populated by legions of writers, producers, directors, actors, singers, dancers, comedians, sales executives, managers, affiliates, commercial sponsors, and hosts of censors. It was these men and women (but mostly men) who decided the appropriateness of television programs during this time of heightened anxiety in America. This story is about one such censor; it is an account of America's *first* network TV censor, NBC-TV's Stockton Helffrich (pronounced HEL-frick). Do not let his aristocratic-sounding name fool you, Helffrich was a middle-class fellow from Yonkers, New York, who paid his way though Penn State University during the twentieth century's Great Depression. He is quite possibly one of the most significant people from early television that you never heard of.

Although this is indeed Helffrich's story, it is also an historic sketch of his time, for without noting some of the era's reinforcing ideological discourse—what American postwar culture saw as "common sense"—Helffrich's censorship may, at first blush, appear quite curious. One has to frequently remind oneself that Helffrich and the others who developed and implemented television standards in the 1950s were trapped in their time's ideological treacle—what the noted Italian Marxist Antonio Gramsci labeled *egemonia*, or hegemony (i.e., the invisible, dominating influence of power). Media theorist Fred Inglis calls it the "heavy, saturating omnipresence of the way things are."[5] In every age, each person finds him- or herself caught in that era's own sticky set of commonsensical beliefs. These viscous, everyday values invariably point a society toward a certain cultural calculus, a kind of collective logic that reinforces thinking, believing, and behaving. By understanding postwar Zeitgeist, one may better make sense of Helffrich's impulse to suppress one idea or image over another. Besides, it is near impossible to grasp a period's inflection of censorship without a coterminous investigation of the historic milieu that prompted it. And examining a nation's social taboos can teach what it morally values, what power institutions it protects, and what sociosexual discourse it permits between genders, among lifestyles, and within age groups. It may also offer a glimpse at the ominous fears that lurk in that nation's communal soul.

Helffrich kept notes for eleven years on almost everything he viewed—every program, script, and commercial advertisement, all of which he often censored at the network. "Continuity Acceptance/Radio and Television," or CART, is the name he gave his writings, which from 1948 to early 1960 graded the acceptableness of almost all programming worth mentioning on NBC-TV. This opening chapter, then, acts as a brief introduction to the main historic actor, Stockton Helffrich, as well as a cursory impression of the fifties.

Although there is abundant literature on censorship of social expression, from Federal Communications Commission (FCC) regulations and Supreme Court rulings to First Amendment issues—and this book does not avoid touching upon some of them—the legal/regulatory aspect of censorship is not its thrust. Instead, the work is limited to the many cultural issues Helffrich's media guardianship addressed. His work offers another lens to better see the era and nascent TV industry. Although Helffrich's work has been invoked in scholarly treatises of the recent past, no one to date has done an exhaustive study of both his far-reaching CARTs and his life in post–World War II America. This book seeks to fill that void in scholarship and examine what Helffrich did to change the content of early television within the corporate broadcasting structure.

Early Days

Helffrich took responsibility on November 26, 1947, for program and commercial-message acceptability at NBC-TV.[6] By the next autumn, from his second floor office at Rockefeller Center,[7] Helffrich began writing memoranda concerning the TV network's programming "continuities"— a term borrowed from radio, suggesting the continuous and uninterrupted flow of all that was heard and seen on the network. The notion of *continuity* also suggests a certain sameness or durable uniformity in programming: entertainment with its sharp edges removed and, so, a safe haven for commercial messages.[8] It is unclear what occurred in the period *after* NBC-TV's Continuity Acceptance Department took control of network television censorship, but *before* the earliest CART memo was written (i.e., from late November 1947 to September 21, 1948—the date of the first report). There is no explicit documentation by Helffrich on this eleven-month gap. One might speculate, with NBC-TV's New York flagship, WNBT, programming only twelve hours of television *a week* in 1947—little of it sponsored—that simply not enough was happening on which Helffrich *could* report.[9] Moreover, the relatively scant number of TV receivers, spotty programming schedules, and three-and-a-half year federal government "freeze" on television construction permits and licenses (from 1948 to 1952) made it difficult early on to attract national advertising dollars—although sponsors and ad agencies experimented with television and were enthusiastic about its future potential.[10]

Helffrich's memos, originally read only internally, over time were routinely quoted in industry press and mainstream media. Moreover, Helffrich became a sort of minicelebrity, appearing on NBC-TV programs like the *Tonight Show* with both Steve Allen and Jack Paar and doing speaking engagements around the nation. He was without question a public-relations force for the infant commercial-television industry.

NBC-TV censors—about three dozen men and women stretched across the contiguous United States—while under the supervision of Helffrich, showed abundant restraint for the often astonishing and contrarian social images, advertising, and ideas seen and heard on postwar television. Some students of American popular culture might be surprised to learn that early network censors worked more with scalpel than hatchet in censoring TV content. Although Helffrich was less inclined to cut dialogue from drama than comedy, in both genres he would more often advise and guide producers by using subtle persuasion and negotiation, engaging them in dialogue rather then making unilateral cuts. This surprisingly collegial approach to early censorship helped influence the television forms of today.

In the 1950s, NBC television-network censors worked hard to "protect" viewers from what they and others saw as intolerable societal vices. Their decisions may seem as black and white as the television pictures that were then being broadcast. But if one looks deeper at the culture of postwar America and considers the exigencies of the time, one learns NBC-TV censors took a measured approach to their work. Moreover, as later chapters show, in areas like the depiction of mental illness and matters racial, NBC-TV through Helffrich took a clear leadership role. That notwithstanding, excised from the crepuscular flicker of early television screens were disingenuous commercials, "dirty" humor, "indecent" language, women exposing cleavage or limb in dresses cut too low or too high, and any reference to sex or couples occupying the same bed without having "one foot on the floor."[11]

As motion pictures and radio had before, postwar television offered xenophobic views of immigrants, sexist innuendo, near exclusion of African Americans (except for racist stereotypes), and an assumption that 1950s-era programs like *Ozzie and Harriet*, *The Donna Reed Show*, or *Leave It to Beaver* reflected "real" American families. The TV images and narratives from *these* shows were rarely censored, yet they no more reflected reality than a funhouse mirror, its wavy surface designed to warp most images, amplify some, and not reflect others at all. That is because television programming is not the stuff of reality but an ideologically based social construction of it with political, economic, and cultural implications.[12] So, too, television censorship is a cultural creation, a "social process," writes sociologist Heather Hendershot, "through which the politics of class, race, gender, violence and other potentially 'problematic' issues are deconstructed, reconstructed, [and] articulated."[13] In addition, early television brought mass consumption and worship of the consumerist lifestyle to a hyper level with the use of image, sound, and motion to intrigue and attract potential buyers.

A Cultural Centerpiece

Television was powerfully intriguing to postwar America, evident by the television-set–buying boom: more than 6,300,000 were sold per year from 1950 to 1959. Over twenty thousand sets were purchased *each day* by 1956—that's one TV set about every five minutes.[14] By decade's end, a phenomenal 87,000,000 televisions were plugged-in to nearly 44,000,000 TV households; 86 percent of Americans viewed over five hours of programming per day. No other electronic technology to that degree had achieved such diffusion throughout U.S. culture in so short a time.[15]

As the number of television sets grew so did a ground swell of public opinion calling for regulation of the broadcast industry. In 1950, for example, there was a pubic outcry to establish a federal censorship board to keep a wary eye on TV because of its "pedigree." Nascent television was associated with low culture; it was seen as transient, popular, and attracting the wrong kind of people.[16] Many of the first television sets were installed in East Coast taverns so that fans could watch boxing matches and professional baseball. The 1947 World Series, for example, televised by NBC in New York, was seen in Philadelphia, Schenectady, New York, and Washington, D.C., by about 4 million people—3.5 million of whom watched in corner saloons and neighborhood bars.[17] At taverns showing the series on TV, business went up 500 percent, and in New York during the games, Broadway box offices suffered a 50 percent slump.[18]

Early television programming kept its lowbrow taint because it continually featured popular spectacle like professional wrestling and roller derby. Gritty, unsophisticated, ethnic sitcoms also populated early television schedules. Programs like *The Goldbergs* (about a working-class Jewish family, set in the Bronx), *Life with Luigi* (concerning an Italian immigrant, set in Chicago), *The Honeymooners* (centering on a working-class New York City bus driver, set in Brooklyn), and *Amos 'n' Andy* (featuring stereotypes of conniving and simpleminded African Americans, set in Harlem)[19] each had a large following. And Milton Berle, a vaudeville comic who specialized in slapstick, dressing in women's clothing, insults, and one-line jokes, was television's first superstar. Television historian Steven D. Stark relates, "Less urban audiences couldn't stand Berle's brand of humor, as measured by a 1954 survey, published in *Variety*, which showed Berle's program drawing a 1.9 in Charlotte, North Carolina, compared to a 56.3 there for *Death Valley Days*." Stark also points out, "Berle was too fast, too urban, and too Jewish to be broadly acceptable. His demise thus foreshadowed an important development: as television's soul moved from New York to Hollywood, the medium began to portray the typical American as conforming to a suburban, white-bread ideal."[20]

Without a doubt, television's early programs were heavily urban focused and clearly ethnic. Then within a few years, television was criticized for being *too sophisticated* for its audience. Matthew Murray, Lynn Spigel, and William Boddy have each written that New York–produced television became "excessively adult" for the tastes of many viewers[21]— referring to television shows that featured women in low-cut evening gowns, "lewd" comedy, and shows centering on mayhem and violence. In 1952 testimony before the House Subcommittee on Interstate and Foreign Commerce, ABC newscaster Paul Harvey compared television's offerings to an airborne scourge, calling it "a nonfilterable virus" that was "contaminating an awful lot of fresh air."[22] Harvey singled out Jewish comedians (like Berle) as sort of a later-day Typhoid Mary. On that point, media historian Lynn Spigel comments, "[T]he disease Harvey particularly feared was the spread of Semitic cultural traditions into the hinterlands."[23] Religious and secular pressure groups brought more tension to the television-programming equation, as did educational and noncommercial activists. Their position was that radio had been "lost" to program sponsors and ad agencies, and the activists lobbied to avoid repetition of that loss to television.

The Cold War

Politically, it was the age of the Truman Doctrine, alignment of the United States against Communism in Greece and Turkey in 1947, and the creation of the North Atlantic Treaty Organization in August 1949 to curb Russian expansionism. The much-publicized prosecution of the Alger Hiss espionage case was tried in 1949, too, and the same year brought the confession by eleven leaders of the American Communist Party for advocating the violent overthrow of the U.S. government. By January 1950, the United States had severed its diplomatic relations with Communist China and witnessed a massive commitment of American troops to Korea. The Russian spy trials of Julius Rosenberg and Ethel Rosenberg began at the outset of the 1950s and concluded with their state execution in 1953. Citizens and politicians alike were clearly frightened of this so-called second Red scare, and postwar America's social compulsion was to reconstruct a romanticized, stable, nuclear-family unit in response to the Cold War.[24]

Censorship of television programming—consistent with radio, motion pictures, and printed material before it—was based on perceptions by pressure groups, government, and broadcasters of the identity and composition of the audience. These groups often imagined the viewing public as a monolithic mass, possessing similar life experiences, religious beliefs, and moral values. Accordingly, contemporary thinking held that television without boundaries would disrupt the ideals of parental, family, civic, and church authority. It was believed that such a disruption would contribute to the internal collapse of the United States. The collective common sense said that if the family became "softened" by too much materialism and uncontrolled or "perverted" sex, it would be easy prey for infiltration by Communists. If America fell, went the bromide, it would fall from within, since the organizing center of American values was constructed as "the family," that unit had to be protected from the corruption of sin and sexual chaos. Television with its violence, "suggestive" jokes, alleged perversions, and recurrent images of sexy, scantily clad women was an unmitigated pathway to the destruction of the heart of home and was, therefore, suspect.

The work of historian Elaine Tyler May found assumptions of gender containment and fears of sexual perversion a dominant motif of the postwar era as well: "According to the common wisdom of the time, 'normal' heterosexual behavior culminating in marriage represented 'maturity' and 'responsibility;' therefore, those who were 'deviant' were, by definition, irresponsible, immature and weak. It followed that . . .

[those] who were slaves to their passions could easily be duped by . . . the communists."[25] May also offers some persuasive survey research supporting her argument that the nuclear family of the 1950s—with its stay-at-home mother and working father—was "glamorized, professionalized . . . eroticized" and emblematic of U.S. superiority over the USSR.[26] Such logic appears to have permeated postwar thought, along with a general sense of ennui that the United States might be losing the cultural, economic, and educational edge to the Communists. A 1954 opinion poll asked, "Do you think the time will come when we can live peacefully with Russia, or . . . is it only a matter of time until we have to fight it out?" Only 16 percent said we could live in peace with our sworn enemy; 72 percent replied that a third world war was the only way out.[27] In other grim polls, 75 percent feared American cities would be bombed in the coming war, and 19 percent anticipated the next war would bring an end to humanity.[28] When accepting his 1950 Noble Prize for Literature, William Faulkner remarked, "Our tragedy today is a general and universal physical fear. . . . There are no longer problems of the spirit. There is only the question: When will I be blown up?"[29] At the start of the Cold War, the government, concerned about the possibility of civilian population panic, distributed 55 million palm cards with detailed instructions of "things to do after the first Soviet missiles strike."[30] *Time* magazine wrote of the coming of nuclear-bomb shelters, with prices ranging from $13.50 for a "foxhole" to a $5,500 for a deluxe underground sanctuary fully equipped with toilets and telephones.[31]

But for all of those who saw the Soviets threatening, others behaved as if they had already won. The FBI and its director, J. Edgar Hoover, worked to root out the Red menace in public and private spheres because Communism, said Hoover, "was an evil and malignant way of life . . . that eventually will destroy the sanctity of the home . . . [That's why] a quarantine is necessary to keep it from infecting the nation."[32] Much of the government's rhetoric dovetailed with the virulently anti-Communist mission of many religious groups, especially the Catholic Church. As early as 1937, Pope Pius XI issued an encyclical saying, "[C]ommunism is intrinsically wrong and no one who would save Christian civilization may collaborate with it in any undertaking whatsoever."[33] Cardinal Francis Joseph Spellman from his New York pulpit saw "communist conquest and annihilation" on the horizon, declaring there could be no security "until every communist cell is removed from within our own government."[34] U.S. Senator Joseph McCarthy called for a "moral uprising" to defeat the godless Communists, whom he saw as "the enemies within."[35] Of McCarthy, long-time *New York* staff writer Richard H. Rovere commented, "[N]o man was closer . . . to the center of American consciousness . . . [W]hatever is illiberal, repressive, reactionary[,] . . . anti-intellectual, totalitarian, or merely swinish will for some time to come be 'McCarthyism,' while to . . . other[s it is an eponym that] means nothing more or less than a militant patriotism." Fulton Lewis Jr., radio commentator and prominent McCarthyite of the era, said, "To many Americans, McCarthyism *is* Americanism."[36] Even mainstream politicians from both parties like Robert Taft and Adlai E. Stevenson saw Communism infiltrating the nation's social infrastructure. Stevenson said the scourge was already in "our schools, colleges, business firms[,] . . . labor unions and . . . the Government itself." Taft declared soviet agents had permeated labor, publishing, teaching, and Hollywood "to influence those who were in authority to take a soft attitude toward communism."[37]

A Pious Renaissance

The transitional years of the 1950s, according to sociohistorian Alan Ehrenhalt, were times of limited choice, conformist standards, and behaviors arising from conscience. In this remarkable time of conformity and unexpected postwar prosperity, which saw the beginning of the three-martini lunch, suburban living, the Cold War, and the so-called baby boom—by 1957, a baby was born every seven *seconds*[38]—Americans seemed to be losing many of their old reference points. Ehrenhalt sees the postwar era as a time of "rapid and bewildering change: nuclear tension, population explosion, the creation of a new world of the suburbs, the sudden emergence of prosperity and materialism that scarcely anyone had expected and few knew how to handle. The people who lived through this change looked for anchors to help them cope with it all, and found them, however imperfectly, where people normally look for such things: at home, in church, in the rituals and pieties of patriotic excess." These were the people that found their life's anchors "in the familiar places: family, religion, and patriotism of the hokiest and most maudlin variety . . . in the Holy Name Society[,] . . . in Bishop Sheen and Walt Disney."[39]

A periodic religious revival was also happening in America following World War II, partly because of the perceived Communist threat but also because of the new world order wrought by the war and America's prominent place in it as a superpower. Regularly, on high school and college campuses, nationwide "religious emphasis" weeks were held;[40] New York's Fifth Avenue Presbyterian Church began a telephone service called Dial-A-Prayer;[41] even the Ideal Toy Company marketed a doll with flexible legs that could be bent to "kneel in a praying position." The company said they manufactured the plaything in response to "the resurgence of religious feeling and practice in America today."[42]

At Dwight D. Eisenhower's 1953 inaugural parade, "God's Float" led the way featuring pictures of various churches and synagogues and the phrase *Freedom of Worship* written in giant Gothic letters.[43] It was also the time of Eisenhower's presidential prayer breakfasts and his assertion that democracy could be defined as "a political expression of deep and abiding religion"[44] and that "recognition of the Supreme Being is the first and most basic [manifestation] of Americanism."[45] Historian J. Ronald Oakley found Eisenhower made "frequent statements about the importance of faith and the close ties between Christianity and Americanism in a country battling against godless communism."[46] Government bureaucrats and lower-level politicians also attended their own frequent prayer breakfasts, as did pious business executives across the nation. Roadside billboards announced the Roman Catholic Family Rosary Crusade's popular slogan "The family that prays together, stays together."[47]

In addition, certain religious leaders were given prestige and high visibility as the nation's moral caretakers. Citizens responded quickly to the evangelistic crusades of Billy Graham, Norman Vincent Peale's mass call to the power of faith, and Bishop Sheen's popular television program in which he, too, frequently equated Christianity with Americanism.[48] This was the decade in which a majority in the U.S. Congress approved (without debate) stamping the phrase "In God we trust" on all U.S. currency (as well as on an eight-cent red, white, and blue postage stamp), and inserting the words "under God" into the Pledge of Allegiance.[49] U.S. Senator Ralph Flanders of Vermont even made an unsuccessful attempt to amend the U.S. Constitution proclaiming, "[T]his nation devoutly recognizes the authority and law of Jesus Christ,

Savior and Ruler of Nations, through whom are bestowed the blessings of Almighty God."[50]

Clearly, God and morality were dominant cultural motifs at mid-twentieth century, and belief in religious faith was key to access the Almighty and fight the Cold War.[51] As religious scholar Robert S. Ellwood notes, talking about God and sin was "fashionable" for just about everybody in the early fifties; when polled, 99 percent of Americans said they believed in God. Edward R. Murrow's radio program, *This I Believe*, was heard by over thirty-nine million people a week and eventually became a syndicated newspaper column. Popular magazines like *Good Housekeeping* and *Life* did lengthy articles and "double issues" devoted entirely to the beliefs of Christianity. It was in this socially segregated, politically paranoid age of abundant, expansive affluence, the coming of interstate highways, growing suburbanization, and hyperreligiosity that commercial television made its debut.[52]

In 1958, researcher Hilde T. Himmelweit wrote, "Every new medium of communication has in its time aroused anxiety—the cinema, the radio . . . even reading. Now it is the turn of television."[53] From its inception, television was perceived as having a liberal, secular, humanist bias, and by midcentury, it was alternately described as spectacle,[54] intruder,[55] and menace.[56] It was argued that television, like radio before it, was a social force that could easily short-circuit existing norms by bringing sex and crudeness directly into the sanctum sanctorum of the unsuspecting family. Many thought this new technology could undo moral teachings and American values, and sow the seeds of violent revolution. Or so some thought at the time. As shown in coming chapters, Helffrich's early CART reports reveal little of the angst and psychic discomfort historically associated with postwar America. Undoubtedly, many citizens lived with a certain anomie and neurasthenia during the era, but as Oakley correctly points out, most "were more concerned with enjoying the fruits of a great economic boom that was transforming American life and ideals."[57] A majority of U.S. consumers were *eager* to spend the $150 billion they had saved during the war rather than contemplate McCarthy, Communists in government, or even the evils of television programming—at least for any length of time. Americans' lives were now centered on the personal acquisition of things and property. New-car sales vaulted from seventy thousand units in 1945 to near seven million in 1950;[58] likewise, as a result of rising incomes, abundant credit, and low-interest GI loans, affordable homeownership in new suburban tract housing increased 44 percent for urban working families.[59] Photographer Barbara Norfleet offers her personal recollection of the era's ethos: "[P]ostwar America was a privileged interlude. . . . A perfect lawn and my neighborhood get-togethers were more important to me than the Korean War, the invention of the transistor, or Jack Kerouac and the alienated Beats. . . . History says the mood was intensely optimistic during this postwar period, and it was—at least for the white middle-class. . . . People knew their place [and] were not disturbed by inequalities. . . . It took the sixties to get me involved and . . . even think about racism and poverty. . . . .[As long as t]he cold war fed our prosperity, [w]e were incredibly passive. . . . *We complained but did nothing.* . . . We buried our anxiety about the bomb and the end of the world."[60] The nascent NBC television network, consonant with chief censor Stockton Helffrich's CARTs, reflected that cultural passivity. Not surprisingly, NBC-TV appeared most concerned about finding commercial clients, placing advertising, and developing a viable television-programming schedule than with presenting shows that challenged social norms. In this way, early commercial television and the postwar ethos were ostensibly symbiotic.

Caught in a Cultural Paradox

Although a certain overall passivity was evident in postwar culture, there was also a sense of social melancholy, an uncomfortable feeling that the nation was adrift, moving further and further away from its traditional ethical and moral moorings. Something was wrong, and someone or something was to blame. Television was an inviting target, easy to finger for the many "problems" religious fervor and anti-Communist paranoia encouraged.

As the number of television sets grew from less than 2 percent of total U.S. households in 1948 to nearly 90 percent ten years later, the public's call for government regulation of programming and commercials also increased exponentially.[61] Guy LeBow, a television personality of the early era, reported that some of the problems television programming had with its viewers included, "Blue jokes, busty girls and sight gags that concentrate[d] on breasts, buttocks and legs. Double entendre jokes.

. . . Lots of lap-sitting, ass-pinching, tit-touching. Bosoms galore in plunging necklines. . . . [D]irectors of wrestling matches [even] ordered crotch shots for female fans." R. D. Heldenfels, a television historian and journalist, tells of a Los Angles "watchdog group" claiming far too much violence existed in children's programming over the course of one week. The outraged group reported that between 6 and 9 P.M., the count was "91 murders, seven stagecoach holdups, three kidnappings, 10 thefts, four burglaries, two cases of arson, two jailbreaks and a murder by explosion . . . [and] a suicide, a case of blackmail, many instances of assault and battery, and 'numerous' instances of drunken brawls."[62]

One needs only to read transcripts of the several U.S. House and Senate hearings on television to hear the Pentecostal zeal with which many politicians spoke of "cleaning up TV." U.S. Representative Thomas Lane of Massachusetts said in 1951 that the federal government "must step into this mess and clean up the house of television so that its occupants will not track any more dirt into our homes."[63] In 1952, U.S. Representative Ezekial Candler Gathings of Arkansas demonstrated in the halls of Congress a bizarre "hootchy-kootchy" dance he reportedly saw on the television show *You Asked for It*. He next attributed the wave of "panty raids" by college students to the influence of this kind of show and urged Congress to control television because "competition is keen and great financial stakes are involved, making it difficult for the [industry] to properly regulate [itself]." It was the Gathings's resolution that precipitated the 1952 congressional hearings regarding television. The congressman said an investigation was needed "to determine the extent to which . . . television programs . . . available to the people of the United States contain immoral or otherwise offensive material. Or place improper emphasis upon crime, violence and corruption."[64] These were the same concerns expressed by most religious groups about early television programming, the Catholics foremost among them.

Catholics and 1950s Television

In Catholic religious circles, there was ambivalence toward television. Some prelates seeking to cast a wide net on a "broadcast congregation" saw television as an "electronic pulpit," and because television came directly into the living room, others saw an opportunity to reinvigorate the nuclear family. *America*, the Catholic weekly newspaper, printed, "The

American home has been 'breaking up' for a long time. Television could become the great magnet drawing family and neighbors together."[65]

Although many clergy praised television programming, the overwhelming tenor in published reports was sharply critical. The National Council of Catholic Men wrote, "Dad has been replaced by a television set."[66] Ministers complained that video viewing depleted church attendance. "Vulgarity and immodesty" in programming convinced many religious leaders that television is "Hell's pipeline into the home."[67] Francis J. Haas, bishop of Grand Rapids, Michigan, likened TV to "an intruder . . . [who] like any other sex promoter . . . should be removed to a place where he can do no harm."[68]

The early 1950s were difficult years for the Legion of Decency (LOD), the Catholic Church's monitoring body for motion pictures. For thirty years, the LOD exercised a powerful censorship over Hollywood motion pictures. From 1933 to 1963, film producers changed scenes, excised dialogue, and reconfigured movie trailers and promotional ad copy in order to meet the LOD's moral standards. At its height, the legion claimed that each week twenty million parishioners learned from the Catholic pulpit movies to patronize and those to avoid.

Because of changing social mores and the U.S. Supreme Court's 1952 ruling in the so-called Miracle Case,[69] the legion's grip over movie morals was loosening, and television was acknowledged to be superseding the cinema in social and cultural influence. This development prompted ecclesiastical leaders to advocate extension of LOD oversight to television. This way the legion could now extend its influence as moral watchdogs of broadcasting "under penalty of sin" for the perfidious.[70] Indeed, many prelates considered the monitoring and regulation of the nascent television medium to be the prerogative of the Catholic Church. Cardinal Spellman warned that "a man's home is no longer his castle, for the locked door no longer keeps out the trespasser. . . . The moving picture has moved, indeed—it has from a limited number of theatres to millions of private homes where . . . horrors add to the infamy of the massacre of innocents."[71] By January 1951, reports surfaced that priests in the metropolitan New York area were "advising their congregations on the television shows considered [morally and ethically] unacceptable" and encouraging the laity to boycott the products manufactured by sponsors associated with those programs.[72]

For the better part of the 1950s, the Catholic Church, through the National Catholic Welfare Conference (NCWC),[73] debated the concept of categorizing television programs similar to that of the Legion of Decency's classification of films. The National Council of Catholic Men (NCCM) was a federation of organizations of Catholic men and was an arm of the NCWC. This was no passing idea. The plan was an outgrowth of a resolution adopted at the 1950 convention of the NCCM that called upon the television industry to take steps for its own regulation. At the NCCM's 1951 annual meeting, another resolution passed, asking that a pledge be made by broadcasters *and* the viewing public to avoid unwholesome television programs.[74]

As Archbishop Richard J. Cushing in Boston criticized television comics like Berle, Ken Murray, Jerry Lester, and others as "fools . . . because they permit themselves a momentary weakness to cater to the laughter gales of individuals with a perverted sense of humor,"[75] the debate on television content raged in religious, educational, and political circles throughout 1951 and 1952. At their annual conference, Catholic teachers voted for the formation of a Legion of Decency to "clean up" the "off-colored" television programs available to the young, and recommended a survey "to determine how much time children spend with TV."[76]

Again, Congressman Lane, citing "hundreds of complaints from constituents, particularly parents and educators," called for an FCC–administered federal censorship board to clean up television "before it ruins itself and debases everybody with whom it has contact." Lane said television programming "seems to be plunging down to the primitive state of nudism and the manure pile." The U.S. Senate Judiciary Committee on Internal Security began closed hearings on "Communist influence" in the broadcast industry as well. *Variety* reported that the "House Committee on Un-American Activities had planned to look into radio and TV" but deferred to the Senate inquiry. At the same time, again reacting to constituent and Catholic pressure, U.S. Senator William Benton of Connecticut introduced a "bill to establish a National Citizens Advisory Board on television which would report to Congress and the FCC on television program performance."[77]

In 1949, the Television Broadcasters Association (TBA) discussed drawing up moral regulations, but the idea was subsequently abandoned on the assumption that video was still in too much of a development stage to be subjected to stringent laws. The TBA instead circulated copies of the Hays office production code to help guide local broadcasters.[78] By July 1951, both the National Society of Television Producers (NSTP) and the National Association of Radio and Television Broadcasters (NARTB) began work on writing separate and specific codes to "clean up TV programs." The NARTB set up five "program standards committees" and "a reviewing body" to interpret the yet-to-be-written standards and commissioned a nationwide viewers survey to evaluate television. The television producers offered a litany of proposed religiously responsible dos and don'ts—for example, do not glamorize "sin or wrongdoing," "evil should never be presented alluringly or attractively," the law of the land "must be upheld," "high types of characters" should be held up for admiration, and "story lines that affect life for the better" should be presented. These guidelines would "all [work] toward creating a better knowledge of life and living, and to develop good conscientious thinking . . . aimed toward the improvement of mankind." The debate continued, and near summer's end, the *New York Times* reported the NCCM was now "studying plans to set up a system of classifying television programs similar [to] that used by the Legion of Decency for rating motion pictures."[79]

A Legion of Decency for Television?

The idea of containing immorality on television deeply resonated with the Catholic mission. Based on past success at controlling movie content using the LOD, there was serious talk—and even some action—by the Catholic hierarchy that television could be brought in line as well. The Archdiocese of Chicago, for example, had already developed its own TV code and proposed a "diocesan Television Review Board," as did the Archdiocese of Los Angeles. However, the idea of homegrown policing was abandoned for another more encompassing concept. Father D. J. Masterson of the Chicago Archdiocese suggested a National Television Review Board: "The task, of course, would be an enormous one. . . . Television has to be checked every day, all day long and when you have a number of channels it means watching each one of the channels and all of their programs." There was discussion of using "bedridden veterans in . . . Service Hospitals" to watch television "all day long" looking for and noting any moral infractions. Astonishingly, the unseemly idea met with approval from both the cardinal and auxiliary bishop of Los Angeles and was sent to Monsignor Howard J. Carroll, NCWC general secretary. As NCWC liaison to the NCCM, Carroll was to share the suggestion with others at the NCCM—the group still pushing for a television rating system that would put economic pressure on the sponsors of television shows the Church concluded were morally bankrupt.[80]

In 1956, reports surfaced saying the Revlon Cosmetics Company— sponsors of the successful (albeit eventually doomed) game show *The $64,000 Question*—was working on another TV project tentatively titled *The Most Beautiful Girl in the World*. Word of such a program continued the heated debate for a TV morality code. The show was to be patterned after the annual Miss America Pageant in Atlantic City and was to be a combination quiz show-beauty contest with a $250,000 prize awarded "to the contestant who manages to overcome a series of 'mental and physical hurdles.'"[81] The Archbishop of Philadelphia, Reverend John F. O'Hara, was incensed over the news, as was New Jersey priest Father Tom Chapman: "This will probably be a weekly . . . pulchritude contest, channeled into our homes. Perhaps you can interest the [Church] hierarchy in the matter. . . . The fear of a boycott of [Revlon] products by decent Catholic girls and women may give them pause in their commercial exploitation of sex."[82] Plans for the program were eventually scrapped. Instead, Revlon put its advertising money into *The Arthur Murray Show*, a program in which a husband and wife, clad in formal attire, taught dance lessons to home viewers. It is not clear if the Catholic complaints were the reason for Revlon's timidity, but Monsignor Paul F. Tanner commented to Archbishop O'Hara, "I would like to believe [pressure from] the Councils . . . had something to do with the change of heart."[83]

Talk of a Legion of Decency for television appeared to have died down for a time within Catholic circles, but an encyclical by Pope Pius XII started it anew in 1958. The pope had promulgated a statement to the Italian bishops regarding television in January 1954, but an earnest debate on the issue did not begin in the United States until four years later. In the papal encyclical, referred to as the *Miranda Prorsus* (or unquestionable, infallible conclusion), the pope reminded the faithful that "evil and moral ruin" had come from motion pictures and now, via television, the same "poisoned atmosphere of materialism . . . frivolity [and] hedonism . . . can . . . be brought into the very sanctuary of the home. . . . [L]urid scenes of forbidden pleasure, passion and evil" would "undermine and bring to lasting ruin a . . . healthy personal and social upbringing." The pontiff had contempt for the concept of creative expression and found "groundless . . . the pretend rights of absolute freedom of art" because by "safeguarding" the family living room from television, "higher values [were] at stake." The basic recommendation of the encyclical was that a national office be established for radio, television, and films, with the purpose of coordinating and promoting Catholic activities in these fields. The business of this proposed office would be to provide guidance and encourage higher standards for the preservation of Christian morals in secular films and broadcasting, to support Church-based media productions for the dissemination of the Catholic doctrine of salvation, and to advance the Catholic use of radio and television.[84]

On April 21 and 22, 1958, a television study meeting was called by the Episcopal Committee for Motion Pictures, Radio and Television "to determine the most suitable and acceptable [way] of implementing the aims and objectives of the Papal Encyclical as they apply to television in the United States." After some discussion, the bishops voted that nothing be done immediately on the question and that further study of taste and morality on television was certainly required. The meeting was adjourned after only one hour and forty minutes of discussion on the *Miranda Prorsus*. After nearly a decade, the issue of a TV morality code—a Legion of Decency for television—had come to an end.[85]

Pope Pius XII died on October 1, 1958—a little more than six months after the bishop's television meeting. This is not to suggest that had Pius lived there would have eventually been a National Catholic Office of Film, Radio and Television or a television morality code. But perhaps if the Catholic hierarchy would have acted swiftly in the late 1940s or early 1950s before the NAB had developed its TV Code Authority, before the television-producers' code, before local television stations (like WTMJ in Milwaukee among others) wrote their own codes (as did some neighborhood Catholic parishes), and before the major television networks penned new standards-and-practices guidelines, then, it is arguable some form of Catholic belief–based morality code may have been tolerated at the network level for a while. Even the early idea of the preproduction screening and editing of concepts and scripts (à la the Legion of Decency) may have found a censorious home—at least temporally—as television programming was being invented. But it did not happen, exposing as myth the widely held conviction of a fascist papacy. Clearly, when Pope Pius spoke, declared, or commanded, not all in the chain responded with slavish obedience. It took years to debate the Vatican's encyclicals, layer upon layer of Catholic hierarchy and numerous laity had to be informed and involved, and political maneuvering was common. It is no wonder nearly a decade passed, and no formal Catholic code on morality was developed.

Television's Commercial Motives

The lack of a Church-ordained code for television does not suggest that there would not have been a sizeable television audience for pornography or the profane at midcentury. Had such shows been easily available, viewers would have watched. However, explained sociologist Ehrenhalt, "because there were sanctions against ['indecent programming'] being shown . . . someone in a position of authority—in this case, a censor—[had to step] in to overrule the market and declare that some things are too lurid, too violent, too profane for a mass audience to see." In other words, postwar television was less free-market driven than it is today. That singular notion is key to understanding how censorship operated in the days of early television. Ehrenhalt points out that at mid-twentieth century, there was a clear "array of social institutions that stood outside the grip of the market and provided ordinary people with a cushion against it."[86] Implicit in his analysis is that broadcasters' interests were being soiled by their own commercial motives. This appears to be one facet of the most fundamental issue of the period. While a market-driven economy represented Western democracy, victory over totalitarianism, and common American individualism, a more traditional society was still suspicious that unbridled commercialism would lower the morals and taste of the common rabble. Still, the dominant ideology of the era held that one could not be against commercialism, which was like being against progress, so the television industry regulated itself by answering only to the American public and cultivating its support. "There is obvious conflict and contradiction in such a plan," comments cultural scholar Matthew Murray. "The ordinary citizen is mature, decent and informed, but cannot be trusted to make moral choices."[87] The audience was simply too naïve to make its own virtuous choices, so it needed someone or some group to determine morality in television programs. It could be done by anyone except the government. But if not some democratically chosen government board, who was qualified to negotiate with censorship groups and sit in judgment on questions of television propriety? Normative conceptual beliefs of the era suggested that business regulate its own house. Television broadcasters endorsed such a notion because of its compatibility with radio's structure—a network-based, sponsor-supported economic model, labeled the "American System" twenty years earlier in a speech by RCA/NBC Chairman General David Sarnoff.[88] In this address, Sarnoff equates American capitalism and broadcast-network profits with freedom and better programs, as opposed to state-run European broadcasting, which he calls "propaganda" and links with totalitarianism. (The prevailing NBC attitude at that time was one of left-handed semantics: commercializing culture constituted poor taste, but infusing it with commerce was commendable!) Moreover, in the early 1950s, many telecasters were struggling to recoup their financial investments in the new medium and regarded programming that appealed to minority interests (and produced no revenue) as wrong-headed.[89] Given this tension among morality, programming, and commerce, TV broadcasters began to realize that the issue might be avoided entirely if offending words and images could be cut or in some way toned down. Hence an equation was drawn between the public interest and certain kinds of programming.

The first corporate manager chosen by NBC-TV to judge and certify that their shows adhered to strict standards of "good taste," protected the moral welfare of the citizen-viewer, and benefited the public trust, was Stockton Helffrich. It was believed he, for reasons the remaining chapters will examine, possessed the wisdom and qualifications to decide the appropriateness of programs for a vast and diverse television audience.

2. The Early Years

Stockton Helffrich began his professional career at NBC six months after earning his baccalaureate degree in English from Penn State University; he was twenty-two years old.[1] Helffrich would remain at the network for twenty-seven years working as: a script reader, script division, 1934–35; assistant manager and then manager, script division, literary-rights division, 1935–42; manager, radio/television Continuity Acceptance Department, 1942–55; and director, Continuity Acceptance Department, 1955–60.[2] His first big break came in November 1933 as a page for the NBC general-service staff.[3]

NBC pages were more than just well-dressed lackeys. Pages managed desks on various studio floors, answered phones, and relayed messages to top radio actors and executives. Helffrich was among the original group of young men selected to wear the distinctive NBC page uniform. He was a member of the first class of "The Long Blue Line."[4] Early NBC pages were required to dress in a distinguished, dark-blue, double-breasted uniform that featured six brass buttons, gold braids worn on the right shoulder, epaulettes, circular gold markings at the base of the sleeve, and white flannel trousers. These original NBC page uniforms were based on the ones worn by the U.S. naval ensigns.[5]

The 1930s were growth years for the NBC network, just completing its first seven years and already moving from its headquarters at 711 Fifth Avenue to massive new studios at Radio City. The contemporary "broadcast metropolis" was situated next to the corporate headquarters of its parent company, the Radio Corporation of America (RCA), in Rockefeller Center. Reporter Samuel Kaufman of the monthly magazine *Radio News* describes the enormous art-deco radio facility as "[t]he world's largest and most modern broadcasting studios . . . Covering some 400,000 square feet of floor space, in an 11-story wing of the RCA sky-scraper, the new NBC studios embody the most up-to-date broadcasting ideas." Helffrich was on hand at the network's gala seventh-anniversary party and inaugural broadcast from Radio City on November 15, 1933.[6]

Within weeks, Helffrich transferred from the page staff to the more desirable tour-guide coterie not because of his erudition or charm but by virtue of his height; NBC had more guide uniforms ready for long-limbed young men rather than short. Besides, there were worse activities a freshly minted college graduate could be doing in New York City during the peak of the Great Depression, and acting as a studio docent to a daily bevy of mostly female guests came easily to Helffrich. However, some of his contemporary associates clearly did not have Helffrich's finesse or sense of maturity. During an NBC tour, one wag remarked to a group of young women, "Alright, ladies, hike up your girdles, we're headed to studio 5-C." Upon hearing such indelicacy, Helffrich admonished his colleague and organized a committee to write an NBC manual on tact, setting down specific standards of how to properly deal with the genteel public. It was the first set of guidelines he would write during his network tenure but not his last—Helffrich later went on to help craft or update the censorship rules for both NBC radio and television. However, his initiative in organizing and composing this early guidebook brought him to the attention of corporate management. Within six months, Helffrich received a raise in pay and the title of script reader, joining the script division under NBC radio's Continuity Acceptance Department directed by Janet MacRorie and later Clarence L. Menser.[7]

Social Awakenings

Born on October 23, 1911, the youngest son of a Yonkers stockbroker, Helffrich grew up with all the amenities of a middle-class, turn-of-the-century American youth. As he came of age, though, it was clear Stockton was different than his four older brothers and his all-business father. The Helffrich's were a well-to-do, registered Republican family, neither wealthy nor terribly political. Since only Charles, Stockton's father, worked outside the home, the Helffrichs' lifestyle rose and fell with the turbulent stock market of the age. Stockton was a sensitive young man, less athletic, more studious, more socially aware and outspoken than his four older brothers.[8]

During the Great Depression, young Helffrich personally felt the cruelty of the times. His father lost his Wall Street job and eventually his life, dying from complications from a paralyzing stroke after the stock market crash of 1929. Helffrich watched as his family's possessions were put into storage or sold at auction. The family's fortune continued to dwindle as economic times worsened, and, through move after move, the Helffrich homes got smaller and smaller. Watching his father consumed by worry and overwhelmed with debt, Helffrich vowed never to take the path of business (or finance) as a career—a decision encouraged by his always-supportive mother, Clara Eleanor. Instead, young Helffrich, with his "beautiful hands and perfect penmanship," exhibited a sensitivity and love of the written and spoken word and a flair for the dramatic. In college, he was drawn to the study of literature with dreams of becoming a writer. Certainly, his new NBC job was a good starting place because, as a tour guide, he could make important connections in the growing broadcasting industry. His foot firmly in the door and earning a whopping seventy dollars a *month* as part of the general-service staff, Helffrich thought it was just a matter of time before he was "discovered."[9]

Tour Guide and Artist

Going to work everyday at the Rockefeller Center complex was always thrilling for Helffrich. One day, as the Christmas holidays approached, he decided to sneak over to the RCA building's main entrance to see if he might catch a glimpse of Diego Rivera's massive and controversial mural project commissioned by Abby Aldrich Rockefeller and John D. Rockefeller Jr. Helffrich. Many others thought it strange that Rivera—a world-famous, free-spirited artist and a self-avowed Communist—would accept a commission by the Rockefellers, the apotheosis of capitalism, a family obsessed with the appearance of virtue and restraint. Yet, for a brief moment in the midst of the agitated 1930s—the so-called Red decade—Rivera and the Rockefellers shared the limelight. Their improbable association would soon unravel, bringing about one of the biggest art scandals of the early twentieth century. The "battle of Rockefeller Center" as Rivera liked to call it left both parties bruised—and the lobby of the RCA building without a memorial to a socialist vision of life.[10]

Helffrich heard work on the controversial mural had stopped during the summer of 1933, and that the center's management company had whitewashed the unfinished painting making sure no one could see it. The theme of Rivera's venerable mural was: "Man at the Crossroads Looking with Hope and High Vision to the Choosing of a New and Better

Future."[11] It featured opposing views of society, capitalism on one side and socialism on the other. As an outspoken leftist, the Mexican painter tapped into the American political elite's growing fear over the upsurge in Depression-aggravated radicalism and the growth of the Communist Party. Upon checking, Helffrich discovered the mural had not been merely painted over but covered with canvas and shaded to match the adjoining blank wall. Perhaps one day, he and others would get to see the reason for the commotion, but such was not to be. In February 1934, Helffrich learned a dozen fifty-gallon oil drums were found near the RCA building entrance. Inside were the ruins of Rivera's mural. The art had literally been chiseled from the walls on orders from the center's management team, the Todd Corporation. It seemed John D. Rockefeller Jr. did not approve of the portrait of Vladimir Lenin that Rivera had added to the mural and thought it "Red propaganda to further the doctrines of Communism."[12] The incident was an outrage as well as an education for Helffrich. If social change was to happen, he realized, "it had to be done slowly, methodically, and, most likely, underground."[13]

The Union Settlement

During the day, Stockton donned his uniform and was transformed into a sharp-dressed NBC guide. At quitting time, however, the lanky, six-foot-four-inch Helffrich would leave the glitter of Rockefeller Center and take a nickel subway ride to Harlem.[14] There on the gritty East Side of Manhattan, he took classes at the Union Settlement Association, one of New York City's oldest settlement houses. Between 1890 and 1929, over two hundred thousand people arrived in East Harlem, most as new immigrants and others trying to escape the desperate, over-crowded conditions of urban life. An array of citizen-immigrants settled there—Jewish, Italian, German, Irish, African—and racial hatred ran rampant. Settlements were social oases that taught adult education and Americanization classes, provided schooling for immigrants' children, organized job clubs, offered afterschool recreation, and initiated public health services. The notion of "settling" among the poor or immigrant classes was based on London's Toynbee Hall, the world's first settlement house, which encouraged college-educated men and women (or people of means and influence) to live in poverty-stricken neighborhoods providing daily services. In 1895, six years after Jane Addams opened the doors of Hull House on Chicago's West Side—arguably America's most famous settlement house—the Union Theological Seminary founded the Union Settlement Association in New York City. The settlement first operated from a brownstone on 96th Street, but within a few months, it had outgrown its original space and moved to larger quarters on East 104th Street. Helffrich, though socially sensitive, was not first attracted to the Union Settlement to do good works; he came for art classes.[15]

Radical Education

Helffrich, who expressed himself best through words and poetry, initially patronized the settlement to take advantage of the creative-writing courses offered and eventually found himself acting in community theater sponsored by the Union Settlement and funded by the Works Projects Administration (WPA). In 1936, Helffrich had a part in the settlement's presentation (not the original, professional production) of "proletarian playwright" Clifford Odets's celebrated 1935 drama, *Waiting for Lefty*, a powerful plea for labor unionism. Suggested by the New York taxicab drivers' strike of 1934, the play used flashback techniques and "plants" in the audience to create the illusion that a spontaneous strike meeting was occurring. The effort was a success, and, afterward, Helffrich even considered pursuing an acting career, but something deeper and more significant happened to him: his participation in this play and frequent visits to the Union Settlement awakened Helffrich's social conscience.[16]

Traveling fewer than four miles from his job at the resplendent Rockefeller Center to the squalor of East Harlem, he witnessed long lines of downcast families and the despair of the immigrant poor and struggling working class. It changed Helffrich. On 104th Street, he first looked into the vacant eyes of Depression-weary men and women drained of hope.[17] Helffrich knew someone had to take action to help them, so he did what many sensitive intellectual liberals did during the early to mid-1930s: joined the Popular Front and became a "fellow traveler"—that is, a tag-along member of the Communist Party of the United States of America (CPUSA). Historian Michael Denning explains that these so-called fellow travelers *were*, in fact, the Popular Front; it was not a true political partnership of Communists and liberals, its base was really the labor movement. "The heart of the Popular Front," Denning describes, was "non-communist socialists and independent leftists, working with Communists and liberals, but marking out a culture that was neither a party nor a New Deal culture."[18] As banks collapsed and the shadow of Depression lengthened across the nation, the Union Settlement, a hot-bed of socialist, Popular Front, and CPUSA activities in 1934 and 1935, was abuzz with hope and fresh, progressive political ideas. The CPUSA was interested in primarily young, educated Americans on the party's ideological wavelength; they wanted true believers in the movement not Rooseveltian New Dealers, whom they considered political opportunists.

Things changed when fascism began to emerge across Europe in 1934 to 1935. That fascist threat was the catalyst that forged the CPUSA with liberals, progressives, independent socialists, New Dealers, labor unions, artists, singers, and other left-leaning groups, thus forming the Popular Front—a coalition that lasted about five years. Thanks to Popular Front membership, the CPUSA grew exponentially, claiming almost one million members by 1939. Historian M. J. Heale maintains, "The stoicism of the poor was turning to anger, and it was in the years following [Franklin D.] Roosevelt's election that CPUSA membership swelled most rapidly. This was the period when many intellectuals were captivated . . . by the Soviet Union which now displayed an economic and social system that at least worked."[19] Author Robert Morse Lovett observes that the Soviets had "a government acting directly for public ends and not for the protection of private interest," and muckraker journalist Lincoln Steffens states the Communists provided "a scientific cure for all our troubles."[20] Historian Ellen Schrecker explains, "With capitalism in disarray, Socialism no longer seemed threatening." It also must be pointed out some CPUSA members were *not* merely "fellow travelers" but clearly rabid, blindly unrepentant, and ideologically pure supporters of the party's mission.[21]

It is clear that thousands of sensitive young Americans in the 1930s—some immigrants, some intellectuals—found inspiring answers in Communism. In the 1970s, author Vivian Gornick conducted nearly four-dozen interviews with men and women who joined and took comfort in the CPUSA when they were coming of age forty years earlier.[22] These conversations with former party members paint a frightening world of ascending fascism and economic chaos. Gornick explains that to many early joiners, the party was not a political movement as much as a kind of secular religion. These young, liberal men and women read (and were duped by) Joseph Stalin's cleverly managed press reports of total Soviet employment and continually raising wages. In Greenwich Village coffee shops, they argued the democratic ideas of Karl Marx, Friedrich Engels, and Lenin, and most agreed with Earl Browder's declaration, "Communism is twentieth-century Americanism."[23] Maurice Isserman echoes this sentiment, noting that by the time the United States entered World War II, local party units were organizing blood drives, assisting in the sale of war bonds, and collecting scrap metal. He claims there was actually little difference between a Communist and a member of the Kiwanis Club![24] Although that may be true, there was were also ideological hard-liners and unwavering Stalinists in the CPUSA. Helffrich, however, would not be found in that group.

Caught up in the idealism of youthful "radical politics," the CPUSA grew from about forty thousand in 1924, mostly in New York City, to over twice that figure by early 1939 and the coming of the Popular Front. What was more seductive to young Helffrich and legions like him was that Communists were actually *doing* something to mitigate the widespread hopelessness of the Great Depression. Schrecker relates that the CPUSA "mobilized unemployed workers and marched them to local city halls to demand relief. They organized neighborhood groups to prevent homelessness by carrying the furniture of evicted tenants back into their apartments. They rallied college students to oppose compulsory military training. They formed militant unions of migrant workers, miners, longshoremen, and textile workers. They saved nine black teenagers in Scottsboro, Alabama, from execution on trumped-up charges of rape. They sent delegations of intellectuals to help striking miners. Communists, it seemed, were everywhere—or, at least, in the big social struggles of the early 1930s."[25] Moreover, by 1933, the Roosevelt administration was steering American politics decidedly to the left by its recognition of the Soviet Union and support of the labor movement—in fact, union organizing became a top priority for American Communists.

With the rise of Adolf Hitler's Third Reich—foe of the working class and menace to Soviet Russia—the notion of a Popular Front emerged from the Seventh Comintern in August 1935. The Front was seen as an official policy change in Moscow's effort to initiate the tactic of an international coalition among antifascists, left-wing socialists, and bourgeois democrats both in Europe and the United States. Appearing less doctrinaire and more revolutionary, Stalin convinced U.S. Communists that the USSR was abandoning its demands for a socialized American government. Such a shrewd gambit revived interest in the CPUSA and, says Schrecker, "made a strong appeal to what was to become its most important constituency: [the] urban, upwardly mobile."[26] Helffrich, as well as many college-educated Americans, exactly fit the demographic profile that the party was trolling.

It was during this socially chaotic time that Helffrich met Murray Berman, a Harvard Law School–educated, criminal-lawyer-turned-union organizer.[27] Berman, Philadelphia born, Jewish, and a lifelong socialist, was charismatic, idealistic, and acted as mentor, big brother, and role model to Helffrich—still shy and unsure on political issues. Berman's social convictions and his clear, democratic solutions to difficult economic questions resonated deeply with Helffrich. Under Berman's tutelage, Helffrich became a dedicated organizer, activist, and party member. Helffrich discreetly toiled like a double agent—by day a hard-working, loyal employee of RCA/NBC, an emblem of powerful, free-market capitalism, and by night an activist committed to subverting the same system he now saw as heartless and undemocratic. At Berman's urging, Helffrich joined the American Labor Party,[28] "the political manifestation of New York's Popular Front,"[29] and while at the Union Settlement, Helffrich organized a phalanx of "revolutionary" stripling groups: the militant Young Communists, the Young People's Socialist League, and the Negro Youth League. He also proudly marched in at least a half-dozen always-controversial New York May Day Parades.[30] Therefore, when Stalin signed a nonaggression pact with Hitler in the late summer of 1939 and redefined the war as an imperialist struggle against Hitler *and* the Western bourgeois democracies, Helffrich was stunned as were most American leftists. Several oral histories confirm such a jolt. The memoirs of Schrecker, Isserman, Gornick, and Peggy Dennis, for example, present evidence from former activists remarking that the Stalin-Hitler pact came as "'a complete shock,' 'a megaton shock,' 'a thunderclap,' 'an utter shock,' a 'shocking thing and quite hard to take. It threw the party 'into utter confusion,' 'left us limp and confused . . . [and] 'in conflict.'" Because of the Moscow initiative, many quit the organization, but Helffrich remained, despite his undermining doubts, because of Berman's continuing encouragement.[31] Thus began a slow erosion of trust and allegiance to the CPUSA for Helffrich. As a result of such an incomprehensible reverse in policy and news of Stalin's unremitting atrocities, Helffrich was convinced the moral authority of the CPUSA had evaporated.[32]

Stockton and Delores

In 1936, Murray Berman introduced Stockton Helffrich to Delores Alejandra Faeber Marreno, a Puerto Rican national, who would become Helffrich's first wife. They met at the Union Settlement, not far from her family's Lexington Avenue home. "He looked like a dream, dressed all in white," recalls Delores. "[Stockton] was the most glamorous, wonderful, and intelligent man I'd ever met." Three years later, Stockton and Delores were married in a simple Catholic ceremony and took up residence in New York City. Delores was a bright, bilingual, dark-haired beauty who eventually went to graduate school and enjoyed a long career teaching Spanish-language courses at New York's Hunter College; at age twenty-three, though, Delores saw marriage and children as most important in her life.[33] Delores was also a CPUSA member[34] and shared Helffrich's intellectual, ethical, and politically progressive values as well as his love of literature, poetry, music, and the arts. As the early 1940s began, surrounded by the turbulence of the expanding European war and persistence of great social and economic inequity in America, she and Stockton, sharing great optimism in the future, delivered their first baby, Clara Denis, in 1941. The infant died at birth of pulmonary complications, causing Delores to lapse into profound depression.[35]

America—and Helffrich—Go to War

Early on Sunday morning, December 7, 1941, 353 Japanese bombers attacked the U.S. Pacific Fleet at Pearl Harbor, Hawaii, killing twenty-four hundred American servicemen. This event galvanized the nation and more than five and one half million citizens joined civil-defense programs to fortify the home front.[36] Helffrich was drafted in 1941. Fervently antifascist, Helffrich saw Hitler, Benito Mussolini, and Hideki Tojo as madmen threatening the democratic socialism in which he believed. Helffrich chose to serve in the navy and was made a pharmacist's mate, third class. Learning he could make (and thus send home) more money as an officer, Helffrich tested out of the ranks, was accepted as a junior-grade lieutenant for officer's training school, and learned the techniques of secret coding and decoding during basic training in New Jersey. After a thirty-six-month tour in the Pacific, Helffrich was honorably discharged at the rank of lieutenant, senior grade. He had served three years as a naval communications lieutenant, coding and decoding classified messages on the Island of Samoa in the Philippines—"a strategic beachhead for allied troop advance into Asia."[37] Samoa was one of seven thousand tiny islands off the coast of the Philippines, and while stationed there, Helffrich never saw enemy combat. However, he and his unit played an important part in intercepting and decoding messages for the bloody three-day naval campaign in the Gulf of Leyte, one of the largest naval encounters in the history of the world and the last fleet battle of World War II.[38]

On December 6, 1942, almost a year to the day of America's entry into World War II, the Helffrichs had their second child, Richard. Nine months later, by mid-August 1943, Helffrich had completed his basic training and left New York to begin his naval tour. While he was away, Delores gave birth to Jackie, the Helffrichs' only daughter.[39] Fearing he might be killed in the war, Helffrich asked Murray and Lillian Berman to be godparents to his children. Helffrich also exhibited a growing concern that Delores would be unable to care for the kids. Both wanted to entrust their children to a couple in whom they found a commonality of values; the Bermans were that couple—Murray, a lifelong socialist, union organizer, and lawyer, and Lillian, a worker in the union movement and committed Communist Party member. They accepted his offer and became legal guardians of the Helffrich children. With his mind at rest, Helffrich settled in for the long, hot, and lonely days of duty in the South Pacific.[40]

Without Stockton around to help raise the kids and provide companionship, parenting was difficult for Delores, alone in Elmhurst, New York. As the months and years passed, she began relying more heavily on her mother-in-law, Clara, now living nearby, for child care, emotional support, and reassurance. Then, news of the American defeat at Corregidor, an island off the Philippines but thousands of miles away from where Helffrich was stationed, stunned young Delores. She was terrified by the disturbing media reports of the Bataan death march to

Japanese prison camps where thousands of Americans, Filipinos, and Australians were shot to death or died of disease.[41]

Despite Helffrich's string of reassuring letters and poems from the Pacific and even a few visits home during leave, arguments ensued between Delores and him, feelings were hurt, important things went unsaid, and the Helffrichs' marriage began to unravel. The long stretches of time away from each other, the unresolved psychological sadness of losing little Clara, the wild highs and manic lows tied to news of war fatalities, the paucity of money, and the copious needs of insistent infants were simply too much for Delores. Not long after her husband returned from the Pacific on March 1, 1946, the thirty-two-year-old mother and housewife experienced a "nervous breakdown" and was hospitalized for five months.[42] It is not known what treatments Delores Helffrich endured during her hospitalization. Modern psychotropic drugs were still being tested in the late 1940s, however some limited drug therapies (Sparine, Vesperin, and Thorazine) were being used as a treatment for psychological illnesses at the time. According to historian Carol Warren, Delores may have had to suffer any number of grisly treatments typical in state hospitals of the time, including electroconvulsive-shock therapy, although "insulin injections to induce seizures besides electricity were [also] used," and hydrotherapy, "the use of cold sedative tubs or [wrapping patients in] wet packs of sheets to control and calm" them. Warren explains shocking the patient into convulsions by sending electric current through temporal lobes (or using other chemical-convulsive therapies—a full schedule being twenty treatments) were thought effective to "erase" the memory of a patient.[43] Because of his experience with Delores's affliction, Helffrich's sensitivity on such issues was heightened, and from many NBC-TV programs, he personally cut or changed derogatory references, such as "you're nuts," "he's crazy," and "she's cuckoo," when a character's lines alluded to the mentally ill. More on that coming up.

Postwar America

Fraught with widespread economic depression, business and labor strife, deep racial hatred, social-class suspicion, and rampant financial inequity before the war, a new, dynamic, and uncertain America emerged after it. The sweeping social changes wrought by World War II might be characterized as the functional equivalent of a social and cultural A-bomb having dropped on the United States. The dramatic postwar economic transformation in every sector of American life was astonishing—what would not change as rapidly as the economy was the culture's inherent racism and segregation. Nonetheless, during this time, a new social course was set, and the coming civil rights struggle would affect legal change within the decade.

Between the end of the war and the dawn of the 1950s, consumer spending jumped 60 percent, and, as industry retooled from war to consumer production, a flood of more than six million cars and refrigerators saturated the U.S. marketplace.[44] Almost five million new housing starts were counted between 1945 and 1950.[45] By mid-decade, over forty-six thousand miles of federally subsidized roads were built, costing taxpayers $130 billion.[46] The American gross national product hit a staggering *$350 billion* by 1952—over three times what it was before the war. With savings accounts bulging, Americans went on a voracious, nonstop spending spree the likes of which had never been seen. "At the dawn of the atomic age," writes historian Mary F. Corey, "the . . . cornucopia was bursting with a vast array of futuristic goods: frozen foods, plastic toys, Styrofoam coolers, vinyl flooring, automatic transmissions, garbage disposals, long playing records, and, of course, television."[47]

During this time, Helffrich was gladly welcomed back to his former job, as were so many other American soldiers and sailors.[48] However, he did not report to his previous job, instead, Helffrich was named director of script adaptation for the newly established NBC Television Department. At first, the job only required Helffrich to determine whether or not performance rights were available for given theatrical properties, and because stage plays and other nontelevision works needed to be adapted for the time constraints of network television, Helffrich was also asked to edit or condense material. "I was not the adaptor or hired to write a script for TV use," Helffrich mused in a 1987 interview, "[but] in due course the position got me into rewriting, changing, or editing scripts for a family audience. It was a so-called gatekeeper job; what some people would call censorship—and it was a form of censorship, no non-sense about that."[49]

With television-set sales already booming and telecasting stations increasing, it was clear that more programming would be needed to feed television's voracious programming appetite.[50] Helffrich's new job was essential to that end, and while he enjoyed the work and was grateful to be given more network responsibilities, he was angered to be kept at the same rate of pay he earned *before* he left for military duty. Helffrich was also shocked at NBC management's capricious attitude toward worker complaints, its treatment of some returning veterans, and its general disregard for employee discontent with wages and benefits. The postwar boom was on, and RCA, like most American companies, was earning tremendous profits, while most NBC white-collar workers were being left behind. So, after consulting with his friend Murray Berman, Helffrich did what he had to do: he joined a union and led the fight for unionization at the network.

Helffrich Organizes NBC's White Collars

By the end of the summer of 1946, Helffrich publicly joined the Radio Guild of the United Office and Professional Workers of America (UOPWA), part of the Committee of Industrial Organizations (CIO).[51] Since his return to the network, he kept hearing the grumbling of other ex-service people that the jobs they had held at NBC before the war were being been given to others less qualified. Across town at the Columbia Broadcasting System (CBS) and New York City station WMCA, where union organizing had a foothold, UOPWA was already negotiating more than a dozen new employee benefits including salary and cost of living increases, better insurance coverage, and employee job security.[52]

Helffrich believed it was now the NBC "whitecollarites" turn. On the front page of *White Collar Mike*, the UOPWA–Radio Guild newspaper, a dramatic article by Helffrich declared he was joining the union and recommended others to do likewise: "I feel, and have increasingly felt since my return from overseas, that NBC executives are remiss in their handling of employee problems." Helffrich next detailed a list of other complaints: employee fear of being released to the now-glutted postwar labor market, comparatively low pay for NBC office workers, "turmoil beyond anything" he had ever seen after thirteen years with NBC, "a carefully unstated and arbitrary [personnel] policy," top management "sidestepping many current grievances by avoiding coming-to-grips with them," and "short-sighted [NBC] poli[cies for] the complex and difficult world now about us." He then challenged the NBC employees to "wake up to their own responsibilities" and "by democratic process . . . [to] pitch in and do their share." The unionization of white-collar workers "is now sweeping the industry," wrote Helffrich passionately, "with the UOPWA/CIO a union of decent people like ourselves, lending experience and guidance." He finally pledged to "do whatever I can openly and reasonably [do] to induce both NBC groups—Management and employees—systematically to help each other."[53] An adjacent front-page article's headline screamed, "Counting Noses—NBCers Agree With Helffrich."[54] Whether he intended to or not, Helffrich was in the thick of it and was now seen as the leader of the "NBC employee uprising." He was sharp, articulate, reasonable, and democratic in his approach, and although he openly claimed, "I have no trade union experience,"[55] his prewar years of covert Communist Party association and work with his union-organizing comrade and mentor Berman would serve Helffrich well in the tortuous times ahead.

Helffrich thought himself well liked by both the rank-and-file and his friends in NBC management. He claimed, "I am not at ease as a dissembler," and "I have never been mistreated as the result of conscious policy directed at me, personally, by NBC's management."[56] Yet when money and corporate control were at stake, as happened in the NBC employees push for unionization,[57] past relationships fell away, and the gloves came off. It was a particularly harsh fight for Helffrich, who, notes his FBI file, "made the speeches and carried the burden of the agitation."[58] For his efforts, Helffrich endured anonymous phone threats and letters suggesting possible bodily harm to him and his family.[59] On another occasion, an unknown anti-unionist broke into Helffrich's NBC office during the night and left a bowel movement in his trash can.[60] After several exhaustive months of Helffrich's continuous pro-UOPWA speeches, letters, and leaflet distribution at the Rockefeller Center picket lines, NBC employees voted and rejected unionization. "Oddly enough," Helffrich said later, "[of all the items we had demanded as a union,] every one of those things was a reform move taken by the company" after the vote.[61] Helffrich received what he and the union had asked for after all. Despite this moral victory, he was still disappointed with many issues in his life: the anti-union vote, his foundering marriage and mentally ill wife, the psychological changes he felt marked by his time in the Pacific, child care and finances, and his total disillusionment with Communism.

Before the outset of the Cold War and second Red scare, the CPUSA went underground lest it should be outlawed.[62] Internal security and repression were the order of the day as informers began to surface and cite names at the many political trials of the late 1940s. Also, for the sake of security, the CPUSA leadership unceremoniously expelled known homosexuals from their ranks, saying they would be easy targets of federal-government blackmail.[63] Banned for the same reason were any members who sought psychiatric treatment.[64] With Helffrich's faith ebbing in the movement, he saw an opportunity to sever a part of his past that had now become a liability. Having very real emotional problems to work through, anyway, Helffrich began "the expenditure of three years' effort in a thorough-going psychoanalysis."[65] He tendered a formal resignation to the party, even though he was automatically and unceremoniously dropped from membership for seeking medical treatment from a psychiatrist.[66]

Helffrich Recants Communism

Also, during this introspective period, Helffrich was summoned to the office of Niles Trammel, chairman of the board for NBC. Helffrich and the engaging, southern-born Trammel had a "heart to heart talk" in which Helffrich admitted he had been a member of the Communist Party.[67] Helffrich characterized Communism as a "totalistic religion"[68] much the way Will Herberg, a prolific author and ex-Communist, had in his review of *The God That Failed*.[69] Herberg explained Communism should be considered a kind of unshakable belief system, requiring a faith that could not be destroyed from without; only a deep soul-searching and personal decision could break true believers from its attraction.[70] Helffrich confessed he had an epiphany, "resigned" from the party, and was in the throes of a divorce from his wife, also a CPUSA member.[71] Trammel, who was said to have "the courtly mannerisms of a plantation aristocrat,"[72] appreciated Helffrich's candid forthrightness. Trammel said Helffrich was considered an "extremely smart young man prior to the war," and the network was now ready to place him "in a very important position." Trammel offered him the job managing the Continuity Acceptance Department not solely because NBC wanted him out of any more union organizing activity but because several high ranking company executives thought Helffrich would be proficient at it.[73]

Helffrich gladly took the position (and its concomitant pay raise), while his UOPWA comrades, loath to stop his rise through company ranks, reluctantly accepted his resignation. They reasoned it would be to their benefit to have a sympathetic ex–union member in upper management than none at all. However, during the recent NBC unionizing ordeal, feathers had been ruffled, and some on the management team did not trust Helffrich to put the best interests of the company first. Therefore, an accommodation was struck whereupon Helffrich promised to report every morning and evening, "like clockwork," to an overseer who would check his daily comings and goings and watch for any union fraternizing or political activity. The manager in charge of such unseemly duty was NBC programming executive Ken R. Dyke. Dyke, personally embarrassed by the arrangement, jokingly said to the likeable Helffrich, "Well, you've been a bad boy [with your political and union organizing and] as far as [NBC top management] is concerned.... You've got to be kept in line!" Helffrich later remarked, "It was all kind of crazy, but that's the way it was."[74] On August 16, 1946, Stockton Helffrich became manager of NBC's Continuity Acceptance Department. For nearly a year, the NBC organization kept an eye on Helffrich, watching for any signs of antimanagement activity. His rehabilitation proclaimed a success, Helffrich was eventually welcomed into the management fold.

Helffrich, the FBI, and the *Kraft Television Theatre*

The Kraft Television Theatre, early television's first and most prestigious dramatic anthology offering, began its eleven-year run on NBC on May 7, 1947. As manager of the radio *and* television Continuity Acceptance Department (the two would not be split into separate divisions until the 1960s), Helffrich oversaw that historic first broadcast, entitled "Double Door" and starring Broadway stage actor John Baragrey. Helffrich and his editors would supervise more than 650 teleplays for the Kraft Foods Company, a major supporter of live, network-television drama. None of these programs gave Helffrich as much trouble or revealed his ideological sympathies more than a show that aired the Wednesday before Christmas 1949 at nine o'clock in the evening. It was Kraft's 137th play, a translation of a drama by German-Russian playwright W. O. Somin, titled *The Glove.*[75]

The Glove takes place in a unnamed European country, and throughout the drama, characters Liesa and Gustav refer to "the secret police," "the movement," and a "country run by a tyrant . . . that . . . must be overthrown." The setting is "a dingy apartment in the slum outskirts of a large city." It is not a stretch to interpret this setting as prewar Stalinist Russia. Essentially, the story is about Gustav, a member of "the wretched Freedom Movement," who thinks himself framed for the homicide of a district political dignitary. It was his wife, Liesa, who with Gustav's gun and gloves killed the blackmailing politician, and buried the murder weapon and gauntlets near the victim's body—facts she does not reveal to Gustav. The play develops into a psychological drama of fear and growing paranoia as the central characters listen to news bulletins of the homicide on the radio. Convinced they are about to be discovered and tortured (or murdered) by the secret police, each commits suicide. The irony becomes apparent when we learn the police misinterpreted the clues and set off on a wild-goose chase, suggesting that Gustav and Liesa, now dead by their own hands, would have never been caught.[76]

The FBI agents wrote that they perceived this program as "derogatory to the bureau," and in a memo to Associate Director Clyde Tolson, J. Edgar Hoover's second in command, agent L. B. Nichols pointed to Helffrich as "responsible for clearing the Kraft Television program." It is uncertain in what way the program was seen as disparaging to the FBI, although the drama makes clear the inept "secret police" bungle the case by misreading the clues, thus keeping the killer at large. It is also possible the bureau was simply unhappy with the general theme of the show, that of "wretched freedom fighter" dying by his own hand in an unnamed country (but probably the Soviet Union). According to the same government memo, Trammel told the FBI that "he would have to take action against" Helffrich for clearing the "derogatory" program.[77]

It is also apparent that Hoover was keenly aware of the power of popular culture (movies, radio plays, pulp novels, comic books, and the like).[78] Throughout his forty-eight-year reign as FBI director, Hoover was always in some capacity involved with writers, actors, and producers in sustaining the myth of the machine-gun-toting, crime-busting G-man, a durable parable created during the Depression. With more TV sets purchased by the mid-to-late 1940s, television was quickly becoming an important national disseminator of American myth and culture and could not be ignored. It appears that Hoover's minions, charged with watching and interpreting media content, saw the Kraft program as a slight against law enforcement or as a victory for the Soviet enemy at the expense of the forces of freedom.

It is unknown what rejoinder if any was taken against Helffrich regarding this complaint. No records were found. Helffrich evidently escaped House Un-American Activities Committee (HUAC), U.S. Senator Joseph McCarthy, and the vicious Red purges of the era despite a detailed FBI file.

Postwar Communist Hysteria

To better appreciate the complexity of this "Helffrich–NBC management" riddle, one need examine the Zeitgeist of the immediate postwar era. By the late 1940s, in addition to the insidious "Red" specters conjured by President Harry S. Truman's U.S. government "loyalty review" program, other hard political realities could not be ignored— real events that served to reinforce the imagined fears of the time. In 1948, for example, Czechoslovakia fell to the Communists; the same year, the Soviets dropped an "Iron Curtain" on West Berlin, and Whittaker Chambers accused former State Department official Alger Hiss of revealing American secrets to the USSR. By 1949, the Russians had detonated their first atomic bomb, and Mao Tse-tung's communist coup had taken China. In the early 1950s, Ethel Rosenberg and Julius Rosenberg were found guilty and executed for being "atomic spies." The Korean War brought more anxiety, as did a fear of homosexuals in government, juvenile delinquency, and organized crime—each in some weird way considered part of the "communist plot." By June 23, 1950, the University of California fired 137 of its professors for refusing to sign an anti-Communist oath, and later that month, ten Hollywood writers, producers, and directors were convicted of contempt of Congress for refusing to tell the HUAC whether they had communist ties. Municipal clerks, local public-school teachers, even janitors could be fired for simply holding dissenting views; textbooks were banned, and libraries closed.[79]

Mass media also worked to buttress the belief that Communists were omnipresent. Respected national magazines ran stories titled, "How

Communists Take Over," "Communists Penetrate Wall Street," and "The Reds Are After Your Child." From 1947 to 1952, more than fifty anti-Communist Hollywood films were made—one quarter alone produced in 1952—including *I Was a Communist for the FBI, The Red Menace*, and *I Married a Communist*. Bookstores sold so-called anti-Communist titles, among them *The Red Plotters* by Hamilton Fish and *I Led Three Lives: Citizen, Communist, Counterspy* by Herbert A. Philbrick, a tome that was nationally serialized to five hundred newspapers and eventually made into a popular television program. From 1953 to 1956, 117 half-hour episodes of *I Led Three Lives* aired in national syndication. Other popular anti-Communist television shows include *Biff Baker, U.S.A., Foreign Intrigue* (a syndicated show, filmed in Europe, 1951 to 1955), *Passport to Danger*, and *Secret File U.S.A.*[80] These programs followed the same villains, which historians Douglas T. Miller and Marion Nowak describe: "The popular image of a communist conveyed by such massive propaganda was that of a nearly superhuman demon, a devious and highly skilled fiend, the master of techniques of hypnotic intellectual seduction who would be more than a match for ordinary mortals operating under the lawful ways of democracy."[81] George Gallup Poll and National Opinion Research Center surveys conducted during the mid-fifties concur with Miller and Nowak's assessment. Many Americans clearly imagined the United States locked in a cultural battle of good versus evil, of Christianity versus atheism and the "Godless communists." Such generalized apprehensions eventually spawned a popular following for McCarthy.[82] In a 1954 national poll attempting to gauge the reach of the Red Menace, one Massachusetts respondent said, "Communists get children into cellars, educating them in warfare." A housewife from Indiana declared, Reds "poison the minds of young people . . . with [ideas] that are contrary to the Bible." An Illinois man imagined "commies scattered all over our big factories and . . . working underground in all of them." When pollsters asked how one might identify Communists on sight, representative answers included: "I saw a map of Russia on a wall in his home" (Michigan man); "[She] would not attend church and talked against God" (Pennsylvania woman); "He was always talking about world peace" (Oregon woman); "He brought a lot of foreign looking people into his home" (Kansas woman); and "[She] distribute[d] literature about the United Nations" (Indiana woman).[83]

Blacklisting

NBC also seemed less concerned by government or independent Communist witch-hunters than did CBS. While it is true NBC was involved in one of the first blacklisting cases—that of actress Jean Muir, hired to play the role of mother on *The Aldrich Family* radio show (sponsored by Jell-O)—it appears the network bowed more to sponsor and advertising-agency insistence than to government pressures. General Mills' advertising agency, Young and Rubicam, placed no claims on Muir's disloyalty; instead, it underlined the need to avoid controversial actors on its sponsored programming. Putting advertising revenues ahead of politics, NBC simply accepted the decision. Historian John Cogley explains that to avoid a public-relations nightmare similar to that faced by General Foods, advertisers checked employee backgrounds "*before* they were hired, then the local groups of the American Legion, the Catholic War Veterans, or the readers of *Counterattack* would have no cause to write letters or phone in their protests. . . . And since there would be no firings, because controversial persons were not hired in the first place, the liberal groups would be frustrated. The inevitable result . . . was the institutionalizing of blacklisting."[84]

In 1947, three former FBI agents, Ken Bierly, Ted Kirkpatrick, and John Keenan founded *Counterattack, the Newsletter of Facts on Communism*. The trio called their New York–based publishing group American Business Consultants and acted as "informants" to the broadcasting industry with occasional special reports. One such report was *Red Channels: The Report of Communist Influence in Radio and Television*, published in 1950 and regarded as the "formal beginning of blacklisting in the radio-TV industry." In the report, the editors named 151 industry persons linked to "Communist causes." Cogley writes that the publication was "'the Bible of Madison Avenue'" and that "its underlying thesis— that Communists were infiltrating the radio-TV field and should be removed—became something of the doctrine of the industry."[85] Indeed, advertising agencies, sponsors, program packagers, and network executives used the information in *Red Channels*.

After the coming of McCarthy and the infamous blacklisting publications *Counterattack* and *Red Channels*, CBS hired Daniel T. O'Shea "as a corporate vice-president and general executive in a consultative and advisory capacity."[86] More plainly, O'Shea was a "security officer" for the network from 1950 until 1955, responsible for screening actors, writers, directors, and producers for any Communist involvement. NBC employed no such officer and used its existing legal department when similar questions arose. In addition, CBS implemented a so-called loyalty oath, as former CBS news executive Sig Mickelson relays, that "began with the usual 'Are you know or have you ever been a member?' and appended the attorney general's list of subversive organizations; the important questions concerned membership in the Communist party[,] . . . membership in fascist organizations[,] . . . and . . . membership in any . . . organization that threatened to overthrow the government of the United States."[87] NBC, on the other hand, had no "loyalty oath" for its employees but had required personal "loyalty statements" since the mid-1940s from all new hires.[88] One CBS executive, Robert Heller, vice president for radio programs, *was* listed in *Red Channels*, and during the Christmas holidays of 1950, he was suddenly and unceremoniously fired. Mickelson, Heller's colleague, "assumed his sudden departure was in some way connected with the citations in *Red Channels* or perhaps the CBS 'loyalty oath,' but no one [at the network] was talking."[89]

By contrast, Helffrich, a known, *admitted* Communist with documented ties to the American Labor Party, the union movement, the Popular Front, and the CIO was *not* listed in *Red Channels*, as were no NBC manager's names. Moreover, within the CPUSA, Helffrich had a reputation as a popular, competent organizer and certainly could identify many party members from the 1930s. Yet, I found no evidence that Helffrich was ever questioned or deposed by the U.S. government while at NBC-TV. How could this be? Speculation abounds but documentation goes begging. Clearly, this is an essential area for future scholarship.

Without question, Helffrich's broadminded beliefs informed his censorship duties at NBC. As early as 1949, he advocated the end of African American stereotypes in television portrayals. Helffrich also pushed for more-adult themes in drama and negotiated with writers to have mentally ill characters treated more sympathetically, a feat for which he received praise from the American Mental Health Association.[90] In addition, he was tireless in his advocacy of "truth in advertising," often using moral arguments against major sponsors and their agencies to enforce compliance with network guidelines. While his ideas and actions were clearly progressive for their time, also remember that

Helffrich did not act unilaterally; he simply did what he could to advance his agenda within the corporate structure at NBC. Correspondingly, Helffrich studiously avoided direct comment on specific politics in his CART reports. It is obvious. nevertheless, that his political beliefs, tempered by layers of corporatism though they were, still found expression in his continuity acceptance reports.

However, to understand Helffrich's notion of censorship for early network *television*, foundational NBC *radio* policy has to be carefully considered.

*N*BC began its radio broadcasting service in 1926, and by 1934, a codified set of programming polices were in place but never officially made public. Trade magazine *Sponsor* notes, "NBC made such a secret . . . of its Continuity Acceptance [CA] Division that when CBS published its own program standards in 1935 its executives got the credit for being such advanced thinkers." Notions of what constituted "acceptable" broadcast fare had quietly evolved through trial, error, and experience as NBC radio grew.[1]

Television was different. Here was a conundrum that enjoyed both overwhelming consumer acceptance and relentless criticism. Therefore, it became crucial for the budding industry and its leader, NBC, to have a set of well-considered censorship polices in full view, an authoritative mechanism that a viewer-citizen could count on to control the new medium. Equally important was to make television appear as a "public servant" of the American people—a tone set in the early days by Radio Corporation of America (RCA) president David Sarnoff. For RCA to project such an image, business, government opinion leaders, and the general audience had to be taught the vagaries of NBC-TV program censorship. That tutelage was accomplished, at least in part, by a public-relations flourish: an early, brief volume titled *Responsibility: A Working Manual of NBC Program Policies.* This essential policy guidebook for NBC was use as a template for the development of network-television censorship in general.

The booklet was divided into three broad classifications: program content, commercial content, and operating procedures.

Section 1—Program Content

The first category discussed in the program-content section of *Responsibility: A Working Manual of NBC Program Policies* is children's programs, which, instructs the booklet, "are designed to convey the commonly accepted moral, social and ethical ideals characteristic of

American life[,] . . . contain no material which jeopardizes sound character development [and] provide opportunities . . . for cultural growth." Such vague, nonspecific wording tells a great deal about the cautious business climate of the time. Also, by keeping the tenets of the guidebook reasonably acceptable, nebulous, and free of any dangerous liberal caveats, those who read it could project upon it their own personal biases and proclivities and, thereby, "understand" what it meant. Because it is impossible to codify every questionable word, image, or idea, vagueness becomes a fundamental part of any censorship document in order to allow for myriad situations and multiple interpretations. NBC could also have treated the publication as a preemptive gambit. On its face, talk of "commonly accepted" American ideals appears to demonstrate "responsibility" toward questions of moral and ethical children's television programs, it also worked as a pragmatic piece of public relations to blunt possible negative attacks by government or pressure groups on the subject. The document states, "Cruelty, greed, and selfishness are never presented as worthy motivations [for children and that u]nfair exploitation of others for personal gain is not made praiseworthy."[2]

Although the idea of "antiexploitation" figured prominently in Marxist theories, and ordinary political discourse frequently invoked it, the above wording is the only one to approach a true collectivist statement in the booklet. While it is unclear what portion of the censorship manual Helffrich wrote or influenced, there is no author given—however, "unfair exploitation" is distinctly part of an anticapitalist philosophy, founded on the concepts of antioppression and the ethical obligation of people to help each other reach their full potentials as human beings.[3] Based upon what is known of Helffrich's past communist political leanings, one cannot argue that this short burst of ideology reveals a conscious political agenda. Yet, this idea (and its exact wording) does make its way into the broadcast industry's TV censorship code published in 1952.

Other areas precluded in children's programs were references to or threats about kidnapping, profanity and vulgarity, and "morbid suspense." The policies booklet preaches, "Just as thoughtful parents refrain from putting mystery novels on their children's bookshelves, NBC radio and TV [choose] to restrict their crime and mystery dramas to 9:30 P.M., Eastern Time."[4] A policy that relegates "adult" programs to later time periods was presented as commonsensical, good for children, and in the public interest. The manual did not specifically blame the audience nor invite parents to share the responsibly of children's access to network shows, but it did subtly imply such was also their duty. The booklet was aimed primarily at vanguard opinion leaders in business, government, and media, and every child pictured in the booklet was that of a smiling, white youngster; apparently postwar children in this booklet were imagined as the offspring of a homogeneous and white, middle-class audience. But, for purposes of mass-communicated commercial commerce, *all* of early television's audience were so imagined: white and middle class. This is not to say the mass was not differentiated, for, indeed, it was. However, more valuable to NBC and its advertisers at this time were not targeted demographic cohorts but gender, race, and day-part considerations. Men, for example, were imagined to rule radio listening in the evening; thus, NBC broadcasts gave the impression of "inviting" women into the nighttime audience.[5] Women were *later* visualized to be the main consumers of TV, important because women were also seen as controlling the family's finances.[6] Both mediums took pains not to advertise certain "questionable" products—that is, deodorants, toiletry goods, laxatives, and the like—during evening hours (or other "sensitive times") or on shows with black entertainers for fear of stigmatizing these manufactured goods as "Negro products."[7] That notwithstanding, a network demonstrating a commitment to protect kids from contestable TV shows could perhaps generate enough public goodwill to pick up larger audiences and a more profitable bottom line. Clearly, this segment of the *Responsibility* manual was also written to keep Congress, the Federal Communications Commission (FCC), and special interest groups at bay and out of influencing (or regulating) broadcasting. It was intended to reflect NBC's desire to *share* with parents and guardians the responsibility of inappropriate TV watching by children. This "we're doing our part, now you do yours" attitude was voiced countless times in Helffrich's Continuity Acceptance Radio and Television (CART) reports, especially when questions arose of children's inappropriate exposure to sex, violence, vulgar language, or commercial messages.

Under the NBC programming manual's crime-and-mystery category, one may note a policy similar to the old Hays Commission motion-picture code: crime shows should not glamorize criminals or condone felony, and law enforcement should be depicted with deference.[8] This dictum underlies a transcendent "what you reap you sew" tautology; a karmic-like belief that said, in effect, if radio and TV sent out good to the culture, good would come back to it. Therefore, dramatizing suicide was banned, as was the use of "specific . . . poisons by name . . . in such detail as to invite imitation."[9] Such wording suggests Helffrich and his Continuity Acceptance Department acknowledged the then widely believed hypodermic-needle hypothesis, the first quasi-theory of mass communication, later called the "magic bullet" model.[10] A relic of the early decades of the twentieth century, this paradigm no longer represents productive scholarship since its thesis presumes that all media-transmitted messages inject powerful and subliminal stimuli that directly manipulate human behavior, with no agency on behalf of the viewer. Credence in this power of television presumption (in effect, the stimulus-response (S-R) theory), although not specifically mentioned, is inferred throughout the program-policies manual. If such inferences were not presumed, a policy booklet would not be required in the first place.

Television was considered an invited guest into the home—entertaining, exotic, and suspect—so without proper censorship, it was thought, TV had the power to seduce and deceive the great, weak-minded masses—a classic third-person-effect model. The third-person effect intertwines two hypotheses—perceptual and behavioral—strongly suggesting that media, while not powerful enough to affect you or me, can and will affect (and damage) others. Historian James L. Baughman also offered a paternalism rationale, linking an overestimation of media influence on others, with support for restrictions on "harmful" media content.[11] After reviewing the evidence, one might argue the entire NBC Continuity Acceptance Department, indeed all of TV censorship, was built upon classic third-person effect and now dubious S-R principles.

Like the early movie code, *Responsibility: A Working Manual of NBC Program Policies* overtly ensured all broadcasts evinced "respect for the sanctity of marriage and home,"[12] thus removing shows with adulterous or extramarital themes. Divorce could be used as a narrative theme in programs but could not be treated as a suitable alternative to solve marriage difficulties. Such was not really a controversial stance when one considers the profamily attitude during postwar America. Historian Stephanie Coontz notes annulment rates rose significantly right after the World War II.[13] But by the 1950s, writes Coontz, "Marriage was almost universally praised . . . [and] the family was everywhere hailed as the most basic institution in society." It was definitely beneficial in the early postwar era to be known as a public protector of the family unit, despite what Coontz terms "the 1950s marital facade;"[14] a facade because a little more than one in four marriages ended in divorce.[15] Language was also a major category in all the CARTs, yet in the NBC policies manual it was treated with a murky two-line charge: "Sacrilegious, blasphemous, profane, salacious, obscene, vulgar or indecent material is not broadcast."[16]

Then as now, words had power. Use of language taboos, writes historian John C. Burnham, was "part of the ritual of antisocial behavior. . . . [S]wearing conveyed symbolically and publicly . . . the lower order/underworld culture."[17] But more than a reflection of class, lewd language in the 1950s was seen as an aggressive attack on social and religious institutions. An errant "damn" or "hell" or even the *mention* of sex on a television show became an example of the ongoing annihilation of civilized, middle-class conventions. Suggestive, on-air expressions provided additional evidence for the breakdown of society argument, increasingly exposing "valueless" Americans as easy prey for the ubiquitous, infiltrating Communist.

The encouraged cultural consumption of alcohol and depicting adults afflicted with insobriety are other areas of concern in NBC's *Responsibility* manual. The policy suggests, "[E]xcessive drinking [is] not portrayed as [one of the] desirable or prevalent factors in American life and reference thereto is kept incidental to the development of plot or character," and "narcotic addition is never presented except as a vicious habit."[18] Yet, alcoholism soared in the 1950s, the decade in which the American Medical Association officially designated it a disease.[19] Conspicuous consumption of liquor was vital to class station during the 1950s as well. A poll of more than 80 percent of households that subscribed to the upscale *New Yorker* magazine responded that they frequently drank or served alcohol. Hard drinking was commonplace across classes, as historian Mary F. Corey observes: "Postwar liquor advertisers promoted their products as metaphorical keys to the kingdom of distinction . . . presenting [alcoholic] products in high status contexts."[20] Corey reveals that the status-conscious *New Yorker* audience was faithfully shown a "bibulous world" of alcoholic products in "swanky settings" where everybody drank.

During this time, Americans also began consuming tranquilizers by the handful. Usage of sedative drugs in the United States, almost non-existent in the late 1940s, increased to over 462,000 pounds ten years later. By 1958, that figure had more than tripled to 1.5 million pounds.[21] Regardless, substance abuses were not "portrayed as . . . prevalent factors in American life" on NBC-TV because to show such "truth" would expose America's break with orthodox, middle-class ideas of work, order, and temperance.[22] There was also a working-class, ethnic-stereotype component to drinking—the Irish with whiskey, Germans with beer, Italians with wine, and so on—whose references all but disappeared in TV shows when television production left gritty New York and became bleached and anglicized in Hollywood.[23] Besides, shows about people caught in the soporific spiral of drugs and alcoholism were too downbeat for most advertisers, who demanded happy programs that told universal stories with inoffensive homogenized families who *had* to be white.

The section "racial considerations" was another important CART category, yet *Responsibility: A Working Manual of NBC Program Policies* gave it short shrift. The manual, for example, includes this elastic bromide: "All program material presents with dignity and objectivity the varying aspects of race, creed, color and national origin."[24] Not what one might call a definitive statement of principle by NBC; it was, however, more than lip service. Helffrich and his department did take early steps to root out stereotyped images of African Americans, Jews, Italians, Germans, Cubans, and the Irish from the beginning of network television. It is also important to remember that postwar America in many ways was a simmering racial cauldron that would boil over in the 1950s and 1960s. When NBC published its *Responsibility* manual, the country was still years away from some of the bloodiest civil-rights clashes since the Civil War.[25] Lynchings and mutilations of blacks occurred throughout the 1950s, and a patchwork of Jim Crow and "separate but equal" laws was nearly impenetrable in the south.[26] From Indiana to Florida, the Ku Klux Klan continued to terrorize towns, small and large, in their efforts to eliminate "miscegenation,"[27] as so-called White Citizens Councils—often labeled as the KKK in suits—organized to prevent "race mixing" on TV; even President Harry S. Truman still privately spoke of "niggers as if that were the way one naturally referred to blacks."[28] This was also a time of distinct ethnic differences and "gentlemen's agreements" (i.e., invisible anti-Semitism collusion by business).[29] Helffrich and his censorship departments were highly sensitive to cries of all ethnic stereotyping and discrimination and frequently in his CART reports invoked the manual's "dignity" principle—programs were required to present all aspects of race, creed, color, and national origin with honor.

As the 1950s began, American population hovered near 151 million, nearly 87 million of whom claimed some kind of religious affiliation.[30] Nonsecular programming was a touchy subject in a republic built on the notion of the separation of church and state and where the state itself granted licenses for broadcasting. NBC's *Responsibility* manual noted more than 250 different denominations in the United States. In order to deal with this potential religious hornet's nest, Continuity Acceptance and the network decided *not* to sell airtime to any specific religion, "feeling that to do so would result in unequal representation of those who were better able to finance broadcasts."[31] Instead, NBC provided time, gratis to nonsecular groups but only permitted on the air what they termed the "three major religions"—Protestants, Catholics, and Jews. Islam and the many Eastern and Far Eastern religions were not even considered. For the privilege of being seen on network television, no solicitation of funds for any specific religion was permitted, a practice that was seen as unfair. It was, however, an opportunity for the chosen religions to spread their dogma within the confines of the network's dignity principle, so no creed bashing was allowed. NBC asked each recognized religion "to suggest speakers and prepare programs"[32] for these "public service" broadcasts. Catholic TV producer Mike Gallagher, skeptical of the network's generosity, remarked, "I have a rather cynical attitude. . . . They're just using religious shows to fulfill their FCC obligations."[33] Gallagher had made an arguable point, one that brings us to a discussion of government-mandated broadcast obligations.

On March 7, 1946, the FCC distributed its controversial report *Public Service Responsibility of Broadcast Licensees*, also known as the "Blue Book" (because its cover was blue). It cited four factors evaluated by the FCC in order to determine if a local broadcaster operated as a public servant during the station's license renewal, at that time occurring every three years.[34] One of the factors was the carriage of "programs which by their very nature may not be sponsored with propriety, such as . . . religious" shows.[35] The commission did not prescribe a set percentage of time for on-air religion (or any other category), saying only that the licensee was obligated to strive for a "balanced program schedule" that would serve the particular needs of a community. If a *local broadcaster* could use network-provided religious programs—shows that cost NBC almost nothing to produce—the affiliate, at least in theory, would have complied with FCC regulations and federal-government mandate.

Of the nineteen categories in the program-content section of NBC's *Responsibility* manual, the last one considered was "sex."[36] However, images of sex, sexual language or innuendo, and advertisements of products sold with sex and titillation constituted the largest single category on which Helffrich wrote in his nearly eleven-year run of NBC CART reports. Still, had the policies manual begun with a discussion of sex (rather than with the protection of children, as it had) or included too much expository sexual language, such could have created a public-relations problem the policy booklet intended to prevent. Historian J. Ronald Oakley relates that in the 1950s, "an unofficial Puritanical code . . . [still] existed in the midst of a society permeated with sexual hypocrisy. . . . [It] restricted sexual relations to married heterosexuals, treated homosexuality as dangerously abnormal . . . and frowned on . . . talk about sex (especially in mixed company or before the children), incest and other perversions, and abortion."[37] At that time, *anything* sexual or "perverted" was heavily policed, which, of course, only caused heightened morbid interest in the subject. Historian Benita Eisler explains, "Of all the secrets of coming of age in the fifties, sex was the darkest and dirtiest."[38] At that time, New England doctors would have committed a felony if they even talked about sex with their patients—a vestige of the Comstock Laws that were not struck down in the northeast until 1965.

Responsibility: A Working Manual of NBC Program Policies was published in 1948, the same year as Dr. Alfred C. Kinsey's bestseller *Sexual Behavior in the Human Male.* Kinsey studied thousands of American men and exposed "shocking" sexual proclivities: 92 percent had masturbated (at least once), about four in every ten had homosexual experiences, and half had committed adultery by the age of forty.[39] In 1953, Kinsey followed with another bestseller, *Sexual Behavior in the*

Human Female. More than six thousand case studies revealed half of all women admitted having premarital sex, about four in ten experienced nocturnal orgasms, and four percent said they had intercourse with animals.[40] Kinsey found both men and women participating in sexual behaviors that were considered unnatural, immoral, and in most cities illegal.[41] In any case, "Reference to sex," the NBC *Responsibility* manual instructed, "is kept within the limits of good taste and decency. Dramatic situations, dialogue or lyrics which are indecent, specifically or by indirection, are not used."[42] Here again one encounters another example of strikingly amorphous writing, startling in its slipperiness yet probably not intended as such. The author, most probably Helffrich, wrote as if no explanation of what constituted "good taste" was necessary—and, indeed, in the postwar era, it was not. Although now a bit puzzling to decode, those to whom such prose was directed in 1948, knowingly nodded, stroked their chins, and understood exactly what Helffrich and his crew was driving at. But how could they know? How did they understand such vague language concerning sex? The secret lies, in part, within the social culture of postwar America itself.

Alan Ehrenhalt, a social historian and journalist whose work explores civic values in 1950s culture, explains that mid-twentieth century is often considered "the golden age of community" because postwar citizens were much quicker to accept boundaries in their lives, and expected government (or some authority) to enforce them. "This was a *moral* culture, much further removed from our own than we have ever stopped to realize," writes Ehrenhalt. "They lived with good and evil, right and wrong . . . in a way that is incomprehensible to most of us." He calls it "a world for which Wonder Bread and Black and White TV are appropriate symbols. . . . Most people [of the time] believed, as many of us have ceased to believe, there were natural limits to life. They understood . . . that choice and privacy were restricted commodities, and that authority existed, in large part, to manage the job of restricting them. . . . And they believed in one other important idea that has been lost in decades since: they believed in the existence of sin."[43]

So the products of uncontrollable sex—what the *Responsibility* manual identified as "seductions, rapes, and sex anomalies"—were simply not considered "acceptable as subjects for broadcast."[44] This NBC statement does not mean such things were not happening in the culture, for, indeed, they were according to Kinsey's research, but those viewing television as well as those advertising on it did not wish to recognize or sponsor shows on or about sex or sex crimes. At the time existed a persistent, widespread public ethos of "let's not deal directly with social problems; let's call them something else, and they might go away." For example, cultural historians Stephen Mintz and Susan Kellogg reported that postwar psychiatrists labeled women abused by men as "masochists [that] provoked [their] husband[s] into beating [them]."[45] Linda Gordon, a historian who examined thousands of caseworker records on intrafamily sexual relations from 1880 to 1960, notes the issue of incest was recoded as feminine "fanaticizing" or female "sex delinquency." Also, despite incontrovertible evidence to the contrary, "experts" of the time simply dismissed the psychological anguish and profound shame of incest as a "one-in-a-million occurrence."[46] Since television "reflected reality," those controlling commercial TV logically inferred there was no reason to broadcast programs about incest, rape, or battered spouses when experts said such "morbid deviance" occurred in only a tiny percentage of the audience. Besides, during this early time in television's history, most (not all) decisions were still viewer, not advertiser, driven. Indeed, Helffrich often wrote of the network losing money for not accepting ads for toilet paper and female undergarments, among others, because the accepted opinion was that viewers would simply not tolerate them. Big tobacco was the exception. Since the days of network radio, tobacco ads held a privileged position at NBC and eventually at every major network. By the late 1940s, cigarette advertising accounted for almost 20 percent of *all* television revenue.[47]

Section 2—Commercial Content

The *Responsibility* manual lists a plethora of "business classifications [that were] unacceptable [for advertising] on NBC," such as doctors, lawyers, dentists, chiropractors, osteopaths, and the like; speculative selling of stocks and bonds; mortuaries, cemeteries, casket manufactures and other "services associated with burial"; and matrimonial agencies. Wines and liquors were also prohibited, but "beer [was] acceptable, subject to local and federal laws." Nonetheless, many CARTs discussed at length the public tension between beer ads (seen as okay) and states of insobriety shown or mentioned in TV programs (considered intolerable). Also nixed were advertisements for firearms and fireworks (although "sporting rifles [and] gun powder for industrial uses . . . [were] acceptable subject to local and federal laws)." The list continues: horse-racing organizations, racing publications, and schools that promise jobs at the conclusion of course work.[48]

This final category is a reminder of how deeply the Servicemen's Readjustment Act—the so-called GI Bill of Rights—was entrenched in postwar America. Nearly eight million returning war veterans took advantage of the U.S. government's entitlement program by attending college to earn a degree rather than just heading back to the farm or taking a hard-labor job. Historian John Patrick Diggins explains that the GI Bill "expanded the entire system of higher education, creating new community and state colleges" and more "proprietary schools" looking to get a piece of the nearly $15 billion in subsidies the government was ready to spend. With such big money on the line, abuses of the system were commonplace. Dozens of fly-by-night "schools" popped up like mushrooms, overpromising World War II veterans great jobs, big pay raises, and an "upsweep in status" upon graduation.[49] NBC, therefore, checked with state education boards and the Veterans Administration to make certain schools that advertised were legitimate and did not "imply promises of employment . . . to those who enroll for courses."[50]

Other areas of commerce in which NBC refused advertising were "fortune telling, astrology, phrenology and other forms of occultism." Why should the occult industries be singled out and prohibited from placing commercial messages on television? Because the early postwar audience held television itself culpable for the presentation of any kind of charlatanism, network public-relation problems could result if any of the dark arts were presented in a positive light.

Spiritualism and an irresistible interest in the occult were a hidden part of American middle-class culture for generations.[51] In 1948, just as in 1848, society demanded verifiable physical evidence of those who claimed the ability to commune with the dead, see into the future, or read minds. The moral and religious guardians of both eras saw occult beliefs as part and parcel of a "constellation of minor vices" found in the lower, superstitious, less-educated and immigrant classes.[52] Fortune telling and mind reading were simply mendacity, condemned by Jew,

Catholic, and Protestant alike.[53] In 1824 in English law, for example, the practice of astrology was declared a crime "against His Majesty's subjects," making it easier for the next hundred years for the government to assert that the practice was a devious perversity.[54] Such deception would not be tolerated in network broadcasting, either. It was the stuff of hocus-pocus and snake oil, and NBC, as a good public servant, stood as a buffer between charlatan and citizen. There was obviously a smug paternalism about this network policy, but with government and special interest groups breathing down the necks of postwar broadcasters, any chink that might allow for federal regulation had to be filled. Blocking the TV advertising straw man of fortune telling and occultism was one "outrage" upon which religious, business, and government opinion leaders could righteously agree.

That notwithstanding, a certain amount of hypocrisy was evident when, in 1948, Helffrich and his censors permitted Joseph Dunninger, a popular "mentalist" of the time, to costar on *The Bigelow Show* with ventriloquist Paul Winchell.[55] While on the air during his program in New York, Dunninger "read the mind" of a U.S. Congressman, shown live via split-screen, standing on the Capitol steps in Washington, D.C. The mentalist was frequently featured with NBC's most popular personalities, including Milton Berle and Perry Como, then later with Steve Allen and even Johnny Carson. Furthermore, Dunninger had been a very popular radio star on the NBC network system during World War II. Indeed, Joseph Atmore, an expert on Dunninger states, "A poll in the 1940's revealed [Dunninger's] voice was more recognizable than President Roosevelt's."[56] In the 1955–56 season, Dunninger starred in his own network TV show. On that program, he also "read minds" and posted a standing $10,000 reward to anyone who could document he used accomplices. It must be noted that Dunninger never claimed nor advertised any supernatural or psychic powers and referred to his ability as "telesthesia," or *thought reading*, not *mind* reading.[57] Apparently, such semantic hairsplitting was what separated Dunninger's act from the policy-banned, catchall category of "other forms of occultism." It appears Helffrich and CA did not see him as a sorcerer promoting necromancy on television; instead, Dunninger was considered a bankable entertainer with skills simply rooted in acceptable legerdemain, not the paranormal. Yet, in his presentation, Dunninger was not afraid to use stark lighting techniques, mysterious music, and odd camera angles to invoke a sense of the cryptic and preternatural. Despite his protestations to the contrary, Dunninger plainly promoted and engaged in a form of sortilege on national television that massaged a belief in the supernatural—he was not just doing card tricks. And the NBC-TV network, despite its strident rules against occultism, sanctioned him.

Also unacceptable to NBC, and so codified in its policies manual, were *references* to products or slogans considered unsuitable broadcast fare. Specifically, comic gags, routines, and sketches that might have included a toilet tissue's slogan or trade name may not have been permitted on the air "based on good taste, common sense and entertainment value." Again one sees the subjective, imprecise but necessary boilerplate language of moral guardianship. Clearly, what was most important to the network was *mentioning the right categories of censorship* in the NBC policies manual, not necessarily specifying tangible ways to deal with them. Specificity went begging when one had to divine the vagaries of "good taste, common sense and entertainment value." Nevertheless, by alluding to "problem areas" in the handbook—like a comedian's reference to a well-known but commercially unsuitable product—NBC could at least publicly declare to federal regulators and angry citizens alike that the dilemma was covered, and a mechanism, albeit imperfect, was in place to respond to it.

Through *Responsibility: A Working Manual of NBC Program Policies*, Helffrich also acted as a kind of de facto Federal Trade Commission for its broadcast audience. The CA office and its editors thoroughly examined sponsors' claims, commercials, and products before permitting any to be advertised on the network. The manual specifies that NBC would only accept ads for products and services "when [it was] satisfied [with] the integrity of the advertiser, the quality of product or value of service, the validity of claims made, and the good taste of the commercial presentation." Further, the network acknowledged its right to "carefully examine surveys, polls, and other consumer opinions to determine that [the prospective advertiser's] findings are supportable and to be certain that claims are confined to the data included." Why would NBC go to such lengths to "protect" its audience from unscrupulous advertising? Answers include the extraordinary pressure the industry felt from interest groups opposed to overcommercialization, threats of regulation by the government if television could not demonstrate control of itself, and the notion that airing inappropriate or tasteless advertising would bring moral discredit to NBC-TV, thereby tarnishing the mystique of the new medium itself.[58]

However, an organizational consideration overshadowed even those mentioned above: the presence of Brigadier General Sarnoff, chairman of RCA, NBC's parent company. The general passionately detested commercials on NBC. Business historian Thomas K. McCraw explains that Sarnoff always "hoped that broadcasting could be financed through payments from stations, usage taxes on radio sets, and percentage-of-sales taxes or contributions by set manufactures. He did not anticipate the endless commercials that became a hallmark of radio [and] . . . TV. He abhorred them and until the end of his life protested bitterly that excessive advertising had 'debased' the new medium."[59] Nonetheless, television's economic structure followed in lockstep with radio, and despite Sarnoff's reputed loathing of commercials, NBC amassed great corporate wealth through advertising. Still, Sarnoff insisted his company's ultimate objective was to serve some lofty (albeit unspecific) "public service" ideal while keeping the U.S. Congress and the FCC *out* of broadcast regulation.[60] The above discussion of Sarnoff and his affect on broadcasting's early economic history is foundational in understanding NBC's *Responsibility* policies manual.[61] The manual was one of the many early public-relations tools NBC and Sarnoff used in their mission to dominate American television broadcasting.

Section 3—Operating Procedures

The final portion of *Responsibility: A Working Manual of NBC Program Policies* dealt with "guidance of advertisers" as well as the major ad agencies that produce television for broadcast on NBC. The guidebook presented very specific details concerning the approvals and clearances for programs must go through before broadcast. Foremost, the CA department had to have enough lead time to review all material prior to air. The manual demanded that "all continuities, including the words of all songs or spoken lines as well as the wording of commercial copy, be submitted at least forty-eight hours in advance of the broadcast." Exceptions were made for news shows, advertisers' last-minute copy changes, or ad-libbed programs. These, too, however, were "subject to strict supervision and control" by the director and production person-nel on duty.[62]

The Policies Manual Reworked and Retitled

In the spring of 1951, Helffrich and NBC CA had reworked its policies manual to more specifically address the concerns of emerging TV broad-casting. The new guidebook was essentially the same as the publication discussed above, just reworded to place greater emphasis on televi-sion, and retitled *NBC Radio and Television Broadcast Standards*.[63] This "new" NBC Code, as it shall now be called for the purposes of clarity, was considered the freshest, "most comprehensive" collection of self-regulatory TV standards available. It was especially important to the development of the National Association of Radio and Televi-sion Broadcasters' (NARTB) Television Code, hereafter referred to as the TV Code. The NBC Code was one of three self-regulatory source documents used as a template for the TV Code, along with the Motion Picture Production Code, hereafter referred to as the Movie Code, and the 1948 National Association of Broadcasters (NAB) Standards of Good Practices, hereafter referred to as the Radio Code.[64]

By April 1951, as the infant commercial-television industry faced its greatest threat of regulation from Congress and the FCC, the NAB—broadcasting's influential trade association—decided immediate steps had to be taken. First, as is often the case with any business or orga-nization besieged by public-relations problems, the NAB changed its name to the National Association of Radio and Television Broadcasters (NARTB)[65] and established a Television Board of Directors "to transact business relevant only to television."[66] On July 30, 1951, the Television Program Standards Committee began drafting a code, and by October, a final draft was presented to NARTB delegates convening in Chicago. Thad Brown, NARTB's director of television, said later in a speech to the American Television Society: "I can tell you that if you are famil-iar with the [Radio Code], with the [Movie Code], and with standards and principles as enunciated from time to time by the networks, then you're already familiar with two-thirds of the language of the Television Code."[67] Mass-communication scholar Robert Shepherd Morgan points out that the finished TV Code "had not been a monument to original-ity." Nonetheless, sixty-one convention delegates, a representative from the DuMont Television Network, and Helffrich from NBC ratified the TV Code, and by early December, the NARTB TV Board approved the document, which became effective on March 1, 1952. "The major goal of the drafters of the Code," Morgan determined, "was to reduce or eliminate pressure on the industry from professional critics, reformers, and the government."[68] *Broadcasting-Telecasting* magazine confirms, "Uppermost in the minds of these men . . . [was] to block [Connecticut U.S. Senator William] Benton's and the blue-nosers who would saddle this new medium with . . . direct censorship."[69]

NBC's Contribution to NARTB's TV Code

The TV Code was split into a preamble and seventeen segments. Following the preamble, nine sections addressed program presentation and content. In the area of "Controversial Public Issues," the TV Code largely quoted the NBC Code and *Responsibility* manual verbatim, charging that telecasters had to "give fair representation to opposing sides of issues which materially affect the life or welfare of a substantial segment of the public." The TV Code went a step further, adding that the telecaster should take responsibility to "seek out and develop" content for such programs.[70]

Programming

Of the negative or prohibitive parts of the TV Code, almost half of the sanctions were quoted verbatim from the NBC Code or Movie Code— that is, circumscribing verbal attacks on religion; prohibiting profanity, smut, and the like; respecting the sanctity of marriage; not treating divorce casually; removing sex crimes, perversions, and abnormalities; not showing drunkenness or narcotics as desirable or prevalent; avoiding gambling and liquor; deemphasizing physical or mental afflictions and deformities, suicide, cruelty, greed, selfishness, crime techniques, and criminality; portraying law and law enforcement with respect and dignity; and not emphasizing "anatomical details" with costuming, movement of dancers, camera angles, and so on; not ridiculing race and nationality; and following the dictum that "locations closely associated with sexual life or with sexual sin must be governed by good taste and delicacy."[71] Separately, it must be noted the earlier-discussed (and apparently Helffrich-inspired) line, "Unfair exploitation of others for personal gain shall not be presented as praiseworthy," was a *new* caveat placed in the TV Code and lifted directly from the policies manual and NBC Code.[72] Other provisos in the TV Code concentrated on "Responsibility toward Children," specifying, "Violence and illicit sex shall not be presented in an attractive manner, not to an extent such as will lead a child to believe that they play a greater part in life than they do."[73] Again, this segment is copied word-for-word from the NBC Code and polices manual, including the verbiage in the sections on kidnapping, excessive violence and crime, and mystery shows.[74]

Advertising

The final eight segments of the TV Code fundamentally replicate both the NBC and Radio Codes. "Courtesy and good taste" were again foundational for presentation of TV commercials, requiring them to be "in harmony with the program in which they are contained, within program limits, and free from claims disparaging competitors of their products."[75] Such statements sustained the NBC Code's notion of "television as a guest in the home" and asserted the telecaster had to be vigilant in its supervision of commercials in both form and content.[76]

In the TV Code's next section, "Acceptability of Advertisers and Products: General," the Radio Code was reiterated, including the three benchmark criteria to accept commercials: advertiser integrity, commercial veracity, and legal compliance with applicable federal or state regulations.[77] Like the NBC Code, this section also claimed some products were unacceptable for commercial TV advertising, such as toilet tissue, products that mask bodily smells, women's undergarments, fortune telling and astrology, tip sheets or race-track publications, and hard-liquor advertisements (beer and wine being excepted from restrictions on alcohol advertising).[78] Finally, the notion of commercialized or "dramatized appeals" was banned from the TV Code. This meant no advertiser could have fictional TV characters buy the sponsor's product or service in a television commercial. Also, the dramatized use of "statements by doctors, dentists, nurses, or other professional people [was banned, or the commercial had to make apparent] the portrayal [was] dramatized."[79] Once again, these were concepts taken in whole or part from the NBC Code. Morgan sums it up, "The drafters [used] the previous codes . . . replete with clues as to what the more vocal portions of the public, as well as professional critics, reformers, and the government might object to in the content of mass media."[80]

With postwar hegemonic television censorship in place, next to regard is how Helffrich and his Continuity Acceptance Department dealt specifically with all manner of questionable images or language on the NBC-TV network. The discourse of sex on television was a major, if not *the* major, issue early network-television censors faced.

4. Sin, Sex, and TV Censorship

*T*elevision's arrival was part of a mutable cultural landscape after World War II, and many of the nation's anxieties about sex and deviance—especially what was considered "sexually normal"—were played out on the home screen. Many older Americans living in smaller cities and towns, as well as conservative rural Protestants and urban Catholics, hearkened to past notions of gender, class, and religion to guide them through these new and uncertain times. They were shocked by the looser moral codes exhibited in some early television shows, as were some newlyweds starting families. These young marrieds were stunned by television's frequent examples of less than virtuous behavior and fretted over how such representations would affect their baby-boom children. During the postwar era, foundational notions of what was proper and tasteful were continually being negotiated. An important area of those negotiations was the public space created by television.

Sex in the Decade following World War II

At the threshold of the 1950s, nearly every state in the nation lived under strict laws making it criminal to participate in unconventional sex and acts of homosexuality. An Indiana statute named masturbation a heinous offense punishable by fine and up to fourteen years in jail. Kansas convicted anyone practicing bestiality, calling it a "detestable and abominable crime against nature." Some states outlawed cuckoldry between consenting (but unmarried) *heterosexual* adults.[1] Historian J. Ronald Oakley argues that such postwar amatory codes "existed in the midst of a society permeated with sexual hypocrisy and titillation." Ubiquitous advertising sold a dizzying array of products, while movies, magazines, and television featured a procession of seductive male and female stars equipped to titillate. The dominant discourse concurrently promoted sex as attractive yet repulsive, at once permissible but unacceptable. Across the nation, citizens paid lip service to what Oakley calls "an unofficial Puritanical code . . . that [even] frowned upon . . . *talk* about sex (especially in mixed company or before the children)."[2] It is not surprising that Helffrich and his NBC-TV Continuity Acceptance (CA) Department worked determinedly—albeit capriciously—to enforce most of these questionable, amorphous social codes.

When commercial network television began its rise, few people would talk openly about sex. In polite conversation, even uttering "leg" or "breast" would be unacceptable. These and other words associated with the body bordered on the pornographic because of the mental associations they evoked. Clearly, such social prohibitions conflicted with natural urges, but mainstream 1950s society regarded sex as sinful, so following normal human desires would inevitably result in feelings of guilt and social opprobrium. To elude the unpleasant sense of shame and confusion, mannerly gentlefolk often simply avoided the dangerous subject of sex altogether.

For the post-Victorian generation, a sense of cultural dislocation settled in after the World War II. Mothers and fathers of returning GIs found themselves challenged by a confusing combination of social and market pressures. Historian Beth Bailey located a reason for this bewilderment in the remnants of past sexual convention: "What changed were not sexual acts so much as what those acts *meant*—how they were perceived, what symbolic freight they carried. . . . Individual sexual expression changed less [in the 1950s] than the *context* of that expression."[3] Moreover, Bailey explains, the war forced recognition of "different mores and customs, different definitions of respectability, and sexualized images of popular culture and advertising, produced on a national scale for a national audience."[4] With the postwar explosion of consumer goods and for most American's startling personal economic growth, many older citizens worried such affluence would engender moral flabbiness and sexual deviance. Cold War political tensions at home and abroad, the threat of nuclear annihilation, changing gender roles, a "baby boom," deep-rooted fear of "sexual deviants" and Communists, emerging civil-rights activism, and a general upheaval created by retooling for a peacetime economy each in its own way contributed to the climate of American apprehension. Within this period of profound social and economic metamorphosis, an undefined, free-floating anxiety coalesced around certain objects of concern, among them sex, gender identity, and television.[5]

Undoubtedly, media were sending mixed messages about sex, and on the first day of January 1950, eminent psychologist Dr. Albert Ellis set out to discover the character of those discourses. Shepherding a massive media survey scrutinizing all manner of American sexual beliefs and opinions, Ellis conducted a detailed and painstaking content analysis by collecting what he termed "a 100-percent sample of [U.S.] mass media extant," examining each for what he coded as "sex, love, and marriage content." He considered the *New York Times* bestselling fiction and nonfiction books, representative newspapers from all over the United States, popular magazines, journals, comic and joke books, movies and plays, radio and television shows and scripts, and the lyrics of popular songs.[6] Ellis wanted to learn what democratic media were telling citizens about sex and what could be inferred, implied, or deduced through them about American culture and behavior. His societal snapshot taken on New Year's Day 1950, found in part: "The average American—in fact, *virtually every living American*—is completely muddled-, mixed-, and messed-up in his sex views, feelings and acts. Much of the time he is quite consciously confused and knows that he does not know sex 'right' from 'wrong.' Or else he keeps changing his mind about what is sexually proper or improper."[7] This mercurial, jumbled sense of public and private sexuality might be seen as a blueprint for how the "erotic" would be portrayed on commercial television.

Should the coming of network television "reflect" comfortable old ways or unsettling new ones? That hand-wringing question caused tensions to run high. Still, it will become clear that NBC-TV's chief censor from 1948 to 1960, Stockton Helffrich, and his decisions on sex in television programming made certain the new medium would *not* become the destabilizing influence many feared. One example of the control Helffrich wielded over sexual discourse on NBC-TV can be seen in his handing of the Kinsey Report.

Television and the Kinsey Report

In the same year network television made its national debut so did zoologist Dr. Alfred C. Kinsey's book *Sexual Behavior in the Human Male*.[8] The 1948 report, a study grounded in over eighteen thousand case histories, stunned the nation and became canonized as a scien-tifically accurate survey of American's sexual proclivities. But many say Kinsey's faulty data gathering—what social scientists call "a sample of convenience"—did not permit generalization to the entire population. His conclusions were, nonetheless, perceived and reported as fact by mainstream media.[9] Kinsey's flawed work revealed a vast, covert world of sexual experience sharply at odds with publicly espoused standards of fidelity and heterosexuality. It is not surprising, then, that some of Helffrich's earliest Continuity Acceptance Radio/Television (CART) references to sex on NBC-TV mention the Kinsey Report.

One incident forced the network to address directly the use of Kinsey's findings in comedy-variety shows. In mid-December 1948, Helffrich wrote about a deleted joke from *The Arrow Show*, starring comedian Phil Silvers. The show, itself less than a month old, had already come under fire for making offensive remarks about actual places in Lakewood, New Jersey, and for caricaturizing homosexual behavior. The extirpated joke went as follows: A couple had been waiting for a table in a crowded restaurant. The impatient chap posed a rhetorical question to a waiter, "'What are a man and woman supposed to do?'" referring only to what steps might be taken to end the pair's frustratingly long delay in being seated. The joke—hence the problem—rested in the waiter's double-entendre sexual rejoinder: "'How should I know,'" he said, "my name's Ginsburg not Kinsey.'"[10] Network policy from that point forward prohibited "casual and jocular" references to Kinsey's findings on all NBC network shows.[11] Helffrich and CA extended this ban to advertising agencies that produced, sponsored radio and television programs for NBC. The memo reminded agencies of the network's "desire to keep references to the Kinsey Report on a serious and mature plain."[12] By 1951, the CA department deleted any breezy reference to Kinsey they found on all NBC-TV entertainment programs.[13]

The findings of the second Kinsey report, published in 1953, again unveiled a chasm between accepted and deviant behavior, this time focusing its research on the sexual proclivities of the American woman.[14] This report, Kinsey's *Sexual Behavior in the Human Female*, was again statistically unsound and, consonant with his earlier effort, an immediate public success.[15] Like his first book, its conclusions revealed an astounding number of women practiced sexual behaviors considered "shocking" or "transgressive," with Kinsey suggesting such activity should not be considered aberrant. "Opinion polls [also] indicated that [Kinsey's] research met with approval from the vast majority of Americans," writes historian John D'Emilio, "[the popular press] discovered that articles about sex did not provoke an outraged response from the majority of their readers."[16] In separate investigations, researchers Donald B. Hileman and Paul D. Brinkman discovered Kinsey's report, in fact, encouraged revisionist thought on earlier sexual beliefs and established the theme of sex and sexuality as a valid topic for mainstream magazines and newspapers.[17] That same attitude appears to be at least partially the case for the much more tentative broadcast media.

Television and radio commercials trumpeting magazine articles on Kinsey's latest findings in popular periodicals like *Ladies Home Journal, Saturday Evening Post, Time, Look,* and *Colliers* were accepted for broadcast by NBC but with some qualifications. Helffrich noted the ads were "in excellent taste and show good judgment in the main. We did chuck from one of those [commercial spots] a statement—'I wish I'd known this when I got married, it would have saved me months of uncertainty and stupid embarrassment'—as being cheap and more like something you'd find in a pulp magazine." The CA Department's policy was only to accept Kinsey commercials that were "soberly handled and free of details which might create unnecessary antagonism among family audiences in varying sections of the country." *Variety* commented that censors at all the networks were against having the book "gagged up," and *Radio and Television Daily* reported Kinsey's findings on the NBC networks would be "confined to straight news announcements with caution prevailing to prevent radio and television comics from treating the subject lightly." In the same story, NBC's press department commented that "essentially no directives went out and good taste [was] the order of the day where comedian's material is concerned." The inherent message was that sex was neither fun nor funny. Rather, it was a sober topic that broadcast media may talk about but only in the most circumscribed technical and scientific of terms. As long as its presentation was treated seriously within news broadcasts, discussion programs, occasionally in television drama, and in commercials, NBC had no problem with airing allusions to Kinsey's conclusions. However, when as somber a subject as sex was used in comedy routines or as punch line to a comic's joke, the CA department deleted it.[18]

In postwar America, using humor as a social discourse on sex might call into question intrinsic values linked to traditional moral beliefs. If those social values were destabilized, perhaps formal legal codes would next be interrogated or the authority of the government to enforce such codes. Moreover, any exposé of Kinsey's findings on the hidden sexual habits of Americans by a television comic or in a program's comedy sketch might anger, undermine, and further unbalance the heretofore confused erotic notions of an already anxious public. D. H. Monro, a philosophy professor who has written extensively on theories of humor, explains "Humor is more penetrating when it brings to light a real connection between two things normally regarded with quite different attitudes, or when it forces on us a complete reversal of values. . . . Humor, according to incongruity theories, may be said to consist in the finding of 'the inappropriate within the appropriate.' It is not merely that unexpected connections are found between apparently dissimilar things: our notions of propriety are also involved. In any community certain attitudes are felt to be appropriate to some things but not to others; and there develop 'stereotypes.' . . . The humorist drags into light the inconvenient facts which (sic) shatter these attitudes and puncture these stereotypes."[19] But Helffrich would not permit such discourse to prevail on NBC-TV. He had angry older viewers with whom to contend, some of whom had powerful enough voices to produce significant public-relations problems. Even a relatively few complaints strategically positioned could affect network revenues or stoke the regulatory fires of government.

Still, as an open-minded eastern liberal, Helffrich and many like him found value in "serious" presentations of certain sexual themes. Therefore, the Kinsey discourse was not completely muzzled. It did, however, have to find different ways to communicate and be popularly heard. News and discussion programs, as mentioned, were two of its sanctioned outlets. But challenging perspectives on sex and sexual attitudes often spoke louder, albeit somewhat more disingenuously, through television drama.

Sex in Television Drama

Like many anthology dramas of television's golden age, *The Armstrong Circle Theatre* occasionally explored significant U.S. social problems, among them racial tensions, mental illness, nuclear war, and existential loneliness.[20] One emotional offering of that series, describes Helffrich, "concerned itself with [the story] of a straying wife apprehended by her indignant son. The boy's father steps in [and] in due course . . . counsel[s] understanding and forgiveness with resultant rehabilitation of the family unit." Harriet Van Horne, television critic for the *New York World Telegram and Sun*, gave the program high marks for presenting a play "so wise [and] so grown-up in its approach to a touchy problem."[21] *Variety* commended the show for its courage "to tackle 'adult subjects,' credit[ed its] sponsor, Armstrong, with a willingness to go to bat on this Kinsey involvement, and [praised] the production force for a worthy experiment in serious, grown-up drama," remarks Helffrich. Such acclaim notwithstanding, Kinsey's research estimated that only about a quarter of American women had extramarital affairs but *half* of men did.[22] So despite its slanted perspective, extant sexism, and *Father Knows Best* ending, the Armstrong drama was significant (and shocking) because it challenged the long-standing double standards applied to men and women. Kinsey's work, as interpreted by this teleplay, suggested women could no longer be seen as traditional and virtuous paragons of family morality. Like men, they, too, were sexual beings, capable of straying and breaking conventional mores. Helffrich reports he received "violent objections" from New York City viewers, one calling the material "depraved and immoral." Helffrich shrugs, "I guess . . . dramatic fare pointing up . . . facts about ourselves is going to disturb viewers concentrating [only] on the illusion."[23]

But even plays with "classic" sexual themes were heavily circumscribed. *Masterpiece Playhouse*, a summer replacement for NBC-TV's *Philco Television Playhouse*, presented truncated versions of dramas by Henrik Ibsen, William Shakespeare, Anton Chekhov, and Luigi Pirandello. Of the four productions broadcast, the single show in the *Masterpiece* series about which most is known in terms of Helffrich's influence is Pirandello's *Six Characters in Search of an Author*, adapted for television by NBC-TV producer Caroline Burke.

Nobel laureate Pirandello's 1921 play *Six Characters* was considered a dangerous, controversial work and proved a difficult transition for television. Earlier, Hollywood censors had rejected the legendary Irving G. Thalberg's proposal to turn it into a major motion picture—a fact not lost on Burke, a young TV producer. Even Helffrich remarked to Burke, "If you can't work this out we'll be limited in the classics we can do in the future." Could Helffrich approve this controversial play dealing with the then taboo-subjects of incest, prostitution, pathologic guilt, suicide, and aberrant sex? Just how was the play altered to fit the audience imagined to be watching Sundays from 9 to 10 P.M., "without," as Burke opines, "emasculating Pirandello's intent"? Helffrich changed words as well as whole scenes—the bordello became a dance hall; the stepfather paid his stepdaughter/prostitute not with money but with the "gift" of a dress. The striptease and suicide scenes were cut entirely, even the proscenium stage setting was replaced with a television studio and a behind-the-scenes backdrop of lights, cameras, and boom microphones. "Once we had captured the inner script," Burke relates, "we said what Pirandello wanted to say, although we may have had to say it more politely." She characterizes the way Helffrich, CA, and she conspired to change the story as "helpful censorship," writing that the experience had placed her "entirely on the side of NBC's Continuity Acceptance Department."[24]

Whether NBC-TV was true to Pirandello's "inner script" or not, Helffrich and company definitely eviscerated the original wrenching psychological story, its seamy, shocking social commentary, and angry, impolite words. Moreover, by changing the setting from theatrical stage to television studio, lost were Pirandello's innovative critiques of theater convention and his exploration of the peculiar understanding of reality itself by both character and audience. Burke comments, "It is regrettable that we had to [make these changes] . . . but you'll admit it was necessary."[25] And it *was* necessary because network public-relations requirements during this sexually confusing era demanded such script redaction. One, therefore, may be dismayed but not surprised at how Pirandello's classic work was handled by Helffrich and NBC-TV.

Postwar television, after all, was not a comfortable venue for agitprop or controversial theater, nor was it established as a genuine forum for political discourse. To the advertisers who used it, television was looked upon as an electronic marketing tool. Therefore, producers, writers, actors, and censors existed only to the extent of how each contributed to a positive environment in which to entice consumers. Any television story considered uncomplimentary or threatening to the commercial/cultural power system that underwrote it, would, in some way, be modified or not used at all. To the ad agency, sponsor, and network, it made little sense to be associated with a show that could possibly damage business no matter how important the writer's "message." As the postwar columnist and author Marya Mannes remarks, "[Advertisers] are not here to elevate taste, to inform, to enlighten, to stimulate. [Television's] business is to move goods. Period."[26] To "elevate taste," "inform," "enlighten," and "stimulate" are provinces of art, drama, and theater; although television used the symbolic forms of drama, the palette of the artist, and many techniques of theater, television programming in the strictest sense was (and is) not art. It might be considered an illusion of art because its prime purpose uses artful expression for the ongoing commodification of culture. In 1960, CBS President Frank Stanton said, "Since [television is] advertiser-supported [our programs] must take into account the general objectives and desires as advertisers as a whole. An advertiser has very specific and practical objectives in mind. He is spending a very large sum of money—often many millions of dollars—to increase his sales, to strengthen his distribution and to win public favor. . . . [I]t seems perfectly obvious that advertisers cannot and should not be forced into programs incompatible with their objectives."[27]

Christine Jorgensen

Then—during this complex postwar negotiation among notions of art, commerce, and the place of sex and gender on television—came Christine Jorgensen. Christine, formerly "George," Jorgensen was an erstwhile GI who traveled to Denmark and underwent a sex-change operation in late 1952.[28] Within months, Jorgensen had become a stunning blonde and, according to *Publisher's Weekly*, the most written-about person in the popular press during 1953.[29] News of her sex change was sensational and brought with it another layer of widespread sexual uneasiness. Historian D'Emilio explains that postwar America viewed any eroticism, other than heterosexual lovemaking, as a perversion: "The matrix of religious beliefs, laws, medical theories and popular attitudes that devalued and punished lesbians and homosexuals remained in tact."[30] There was also a pervasive public anxiety about homosexuality, especially when it involved, in Jorgensen's case, government or military personnel. Jorgensen was not a homosexual and regarded homosexuality as a perversion. In her memoir, Jorgensen writes of the "horror" she felt over her earlier gay inclinations and drew careful distinctions between her transexism and the homosexual lifestyle.[31] For the mass media, Jorgensen was an object of morbid curiosity and ridicule. A number of reasons undoubtedly contributed to her notoriety, one of which was the perception that transsexual surgery could be a "cure" for sexual deviates—a paean most probably rooted in the nation's newfound reverence for medical and scientific capabilities at the dawn of the atomic and computer age. Arguably, another explanation for Jorgensen's popularity was the social tension about gender roles within the culture at the time. Recall that women were encouraged to relinquish their good-paying factory jobs to returning servicemen and drift back to domestic life.

Helffrich and CA removed all references to Jorgensen on the NBC network just as they had removed references to the Kinsey Report during roughly the same period.[32] NBC-TV forbade jokes or humorous adlibs about Jorgensen. "Kidding about Christine is being chucked from script[s]," reveals Helffrich, "and all of us working with talent are making every effort to caution them against adlibs along the lines which have [already] reached the American public."[33] Eventually, Jorgensen mentions were even embargoed from all NBC-TV news and public-affairs shows, and pressure from advertisers could not change the policy. Distinguished NBC-TV host and announcer Ben Grauer "received a request from the publicity department of one of our sponsors to interview Christine Jorgensen," writes Helffrich, "The idea was vetoed."[34]

Despite CA's caution, Jorgensen references and jokes still made it onto NBC-TV, and some viewers were not happy about it. Helffrich reported an "open-minded" New York City couple were quite upset over "witticisms at the expense of Christine Jorgensen" and demanded restraint by NBC-TV. "'We do not like jokes dealing with sexual misfortunes,'" the pair wrote, adding, "'What do we tell our young children?'" In the same CART report, Helffrich includes a quote from a *Tide* magazine article that expressed a similar position in its "One Adman's Opinion" column. The anonymous columnist worried that any explanation of Jorgensen to his children would make the wrong impression: "We parents are faced with a conflict between providing emotional security and supplying information."[35] Conflicted is an apt way to describe how many parents felt as they navigated the tricky waters of 1950s sexuality. They were not only trying to explain a brave new sexual world to their children but also were attempting to make sense of it themselves. And of the many new sexual questions being asked, few prompted as much concern as depictions of homosexuals on television.

Homosexuals on Postwar Television

Based upon his CART reports from 1948 to 1952, Helffrich's writings exhibit an awareness of the general homophobic attitude consistent with the tenor of the times. Found in his CARTs are the words "swish," "swisher," or "swishy " to describe perceived homosexual actions or attitudes—each is pre–Stonewall riot and a derogatory closet-culture epitaph (used synonymously with "nelly").[36] *Swish* has its genesis in the 1930s café society. Referring to a man as a swish or swishy in the 1950s would insinuate dark homosexual tendencies, weakness, or other negative character traits, according to psychiatrist George W. Henry.[37] A swishy character would have exaggerated gestures, an overplayed or mincing gait, and speech "made more conspicuous by placing undue or erroneous emphasis on certain syllables and intonations which leave little doubt of the effeminacy of the speaker."[38] According to cultural historian D'Emilio, many "liberals" of the era exhibited a range of homophobic attitudes during this period.[39]

As early as 1948, Helffrich wrote of deleting a "swish portraiture" on the *Arrow Show*.[40] Helffrich was also dismayed about a segment on *Stop Me If You've Heard This One*, a game show where well-known comedians offered punch lines to jokes sent in by viewers. Helffrich notes one comic "included a swish routine and other adlibbed jokes in such bad taste the trade press took us to task on them."[41] He was also concerned that "an interior decorator [character] would be given . . . the swish treatment" in a *Kraft Television Theatre* broadcast.[42] Helffrich worried that a sketch by comedians John Siguard "Ole" Olsen and Harold Ogden "Chic" Johnson in which they were to walk "with mincing steps" would play "in a swishy manner"[43] and had trepidation over

Eddie Cantor's routine of dressing like a woman doing laundry, fearing it, too, "bordered on a swishy interpretation."[44] Gender categories had to remain intact and unquestioned on early TV and clearly reflective of the popular prejudice of the time.

Throughout the 1951–52 television season, Helffrich continued his policy of "careful avoidance" of homoerotic themes. In one offering of *The Clock*, a suspense anthology program, he made certain the following scripted speech of a "young man" was deleted: "No woman's going to tie me down. No strings or marriage license for me. When I get my degree I'm going to a hotel for men."[45] On *The Colgate Comedy Hour*, guest hosts Dean Martin and Jerry Lewis were doing a scene set in a gymnasium wherein Martin says, "Take off your things. . . . you're with men," to which Lewis replies, "How do I know?"[46] In both instances, Helffrich cut entire sequences, proscribing any overt sexual impropriety or underlying gay motif. The same went for a caricature of a Frenchman engaged in "cheek kissing,"[47] "two [European] men kissing each other on the lips,"[48] even homoerotic mentions in a usually benign audience warm-up activity. Before each network telecast, it was customary to have a studio announcer or comedian do a few jokes to break the ice with those in attendance. Word got back to Helffrich that some chatter performed during the warm-up "bordered on so-called swish inferences."[49] He writes, "This didn't go on the air but we should remind everyone that NBC policy flatly states that 'before a program attended by an audience at the point of NBC origination is on the air, material presented to the program's guests must conform to the same standards applied to the actual broadcast.'"[50]

Homosexuals had long been considered a morally weak and degenerate lot. From Biblical condemnation of same-sex love[51] through church-inspired sodomy statutes in the American colonies,[52] to "scientific" medical literature of the late nineteenth century coupling gayness with mental illness, to the "sexual psychopath" laws of the 1940s, Americans would simply not abide homosexuality, and by the 1950s, political conditions and federal statutes clearly encouraged homophobia.[53] During the Cold War, a U.S. Senate committee proclaimed, "Those who engage in acts of perversion lack the emotional ability of normal persons," adding the oft-quoted, "One homosexual can pollute a Government office."[54] The same committee recommended a government purge of all gay and lesbian employees. Homosexual Americans were by definition "sexual deviants," "subversives," and "national security risks," ready to betray their country in a heartbeat if blackmailed by a Communist spy.[55] A visiting European anthropologist in 1950 remarked, "'The overriding fear of every American parent' . . . was that a son would become a 'sissie.'"[56] During the same year, U.S. Senator Joseph McCarthy began his paranoid crusade to rid the American government of "sex perverts," rarely missing a chance to yoke Communism to homosexuality.[57] In 1953, President Dwight D. Eisenhower issued Executive Order 10450, which prohibited homosexuals from government employ (amending the earlier Truman administration's federal loyalty program), while the FBI and U.S. Post Office Department covertly surveilled anyone considered sexually suspicious.[58] Across the nation, in both small and large metropolitan areas, tens of thousands of homosexuals were entrapped, arrested, and jailed without due process.[59] Historian Lawrence M. Goldwyn's research found that a number of New York City magistrates aimed mordant ridicule and caviling language at homosexuals brought before them.[60] Even the traditionally liberal American Civil Liberties Union (ACLU) did little to help. The ACLU conceived of homosexuals as "a socially heretical . . . deviant group," viewed gayness as a moral rather than legal issue, and agreed with the government that the same-sex lifestyle posed a national security risk.[61] Considering the historiography of this unfortunate time, it seems Helffrich's CART writings unmistakably mirrored the period's intolerant attitude. Homosexuality was simply not mass-media fare and was to be scrupulously avoided. Permit it no discourse was the unspoken plan; ignore it, and it might go away.

But such was not the case, and in 1954, homosexuality came out of the closet and on to a local television talk show. An unprecedented series of programs was broadcast on WNBT-TV, NBC's owned-and-operated-station in New York City. The fifteen-minute shows ran at midnight for five consecutive nights February 8–12, 1954. Discussed was Nobel Prize–winner Andre Gide's landmark work *The Immoralist*, a controversial novel that had just been reissued. Its story regards one young man's moral and sexual awakenings and the abandonment of his oppressive notions of Christian duty, choosing instead hedonism, freedom, and homoerotic satisfaction. Gide's book made an uncompromising defense of homosexuality while it challenged accepted ideas of religious and personal ethics. Originally published in the 1921 and reprinted in 1948, the 1954 iteration of Gide's work created a whole new sensation for the avant-garde literati. In the wake of an exploding post-war economy, the baby boom, Kinsey's research, Jorgensen's revelations, growing sexual freedom in movies, the coming of *Playboy* magazine, the Beats and Bebop, and the infant stirrings of rock music, *The Immoralist*, a thirty-three-year-old work, deeply resonated with changing American social and cultural mores.[62] The local television program was called *About 'The Immoralist'* and hosted by NBC staff announcer/emcee Ben Grauer. It featured marriage counselor Dr. Abraham Stone, celebrities Ilka Chase and Charles Boyer, writer Abe Burrows, and Broadway tunesmith Richard Rogers—and that was just the first night! The show was presented "in adult good taste," and any same sex references were limited to the book's plot. Helffrich comments, "The full week of broadcasting did include a couple uses of the word 'homosexual;' and to the best of my current knowledge no material criticism has developed."[63] It remains curious how a famous literary work, of which a central theme is homosexuality, can be discussed *without* using the word *homosexual*. However, such concern tells much about the taboo. Homosexuality was a subject whispered about, hinted at, laughed over, and talked around, but until this 1954 Gide discussion, it had never seriously been broached on television. Such realization gave Helffrich pause to wax literary and prescient, noting how W. Somerset Maugham's work *Cakes and Ale* when first released was also condemned by critics and labeled obscene and offensive.[64] Helffrich, quoting Maugham, writes that the novel would not even "'bring a blush to the cheek of the most guileless'" and concluded that "such anxiety as was felt [by] *About 'The Immoralist'* will in retrospect and with the passage of time seem dated indeed."[65] By that statement, the reader may have glimpsed Helffrich's true colors on questions of homosexual themes on television—he believed eventually anything would be acceptable in "come of age" broadcasting. When one also considers the program was not a network offering but broadcast on only one local (albeit New York) television station at midnight, and its touchy subject was discussed indirectly through belletristic critique, one would assume interest in the show was light, its impact minimal, if at all. Still, *About 'The Immoralist'* set itself apart from other early shows on the subject because it gathered together a slate of diverse guests and used erudite literary criticism rather than pathology or legalism as a catalyst for discussion of homosexuality. In the meantime, Helffrich apparently set aside whatever personal, progressive beliefs he may have had on the subject and reflected the will of mainstream America by his consistent censorship of homosexuality or even its hint thereof on NBC-TV.

But apart from the anomaly of *About 'The Immoralist'*, homosexuality, if discussed at all on early television, was usually treated suspiciously. Historian Stephen Tropiano states that homosexual behavior was usually equated "with other 'social ills' (like alcoholism and drug abuse)."[66] The typical talk show panel, Tropiano explains, was usually made up of traditional experts—doctors, lawyers, and theologians—whose discussions were framed around sensational or exploitive show titles like "Homosexuals and the Problems They Present,"[67] "Homosexuals Who Assault and Molest Children,"[68] and "Are Homosexuals Criminal?"[69] Moreover, by Helffrich's removal of all television depictions of the homosexual presence—even its unfair, stereotyped presence—a space for public validation and potential discourse was also removed. Homosexuals were either nonexistent or in most cases when shown or talked about at all on television were depicted as "deviant" and "predatory."[70]

Queers in Control?

The irony about this entire homosexual hush-up was that gays and lesbians found more creative work in early television than in the movie industry, and there were real opportunities for gays on the small screen in the 1950 and 1960s. Gay actors, writers, and production designers found acceptance of their work in TV. One homosexual screenwriter—Jack Lloyd—wrote for *77 Sunset Strip*, *The Red Skelton Show* (for more than a dozen years), *Love American Style*, and *The Brady Bunch*. CBS-TV vice president Hunt Stromberg Jr. also gay, was the longtime network supervisor of *Green Acres*, *Lost in Space*, and *The Beverly Hillbillies*. Social journalist William J. Mann revealed that even technical fields, which were "implicitly off limits to gays in the movie studios," saw major gains for homosexuals. By 1964, gay industry involvement could no longer be hidden, and one tabloid, *Inside Story*, ran this headline: "How the Homos Are Ruining TV."[71] A particular portion of the article dripped venom, to wit: "Nobody knows for sure how many pansies there are in TV. But things have gotten so out of hand in this new Sodom on the

Coaxial Circuit that you can't tell the he-men from the she-men without a scorecard. . . . Right now the twisted twerps not only are in a position to tell you what you can see as entertainment, they are recruiting others of the lavender set to give it to you! Their numbers are legion. The shocking fact about homosexuality in TV is this: the queers make no effort to hide their twisted tendencies."[72] Because of such moral panic, the deliberate suppression of gay discourse remained intact. Even a passing mention of homosexuality on American primetime 1950s television would be unceremoniously cut, not only by Helffrich and NBC but by censors at the other networks, too. Period. No appeal.

Blooming Bosoms

Just about the time American television made its commercial debut, so did the return of clothing that overemphasized the female bust. Evangelist Billy Graham remarked that Americans had become "absorbed and obsessed with sex, especially the female bosom."[73] It was, indeed, the age of "mammary madness," a time of cone-shaped brassieres—dubbed "torpedo bras" or "bullet bras"—that caused each breast to appear perpendicular and somewhat pointed like the head of a missile.[74] During the Second World War and throughout the postwar period, "breasts and bombs remained culturally entangled," observes scholars Maura Spiegel and Lithe Sebesta, pointing to persistent references to buxom women as "bombshells" in the press and movies, advertising, and on television.[75] Helffrich, in fact, wrote of the "devastation" wrought by Sophia Loren's cleavage on Dean Martin when she and Martin appeared on a 1959 Academy Award telecast as Oscar presenters.[76] It was a time when such breast exhibition sent dual messages: "make them big, but don't show them in the flesh."[77] Hollywood films responded with a new (and larger) iteration of the 1940s "sweater girl," while television tried to mask any revealing décolletage with tulle. New restrictive, rubberized foundation garments pinched female waists and pushed pulchritude upward with the help of underwire bras and padding.

Some historians pinpoint the fashion emphasis on breasts to early 1947 with the introduction of Parisian fashion-designer Christian Dior's première collection.[78] Dior intended to turn women "into flowers with soft shoulders" and provide them "waists slim as winestems . . . [and]

blooming bosoms."[79] Cultural scholar Karal Ann Marling writes that Dior's fashions actually made women appear synthetic and fabricated by exaggerating female anatomy to conform to pre- and postwar "sexual dimorphism."[80] Women's studies scholar Carolyn Latteier suggests that it was just a nostalgic yearning for safety, security, and familiarity that spurred acceptance of Dior. His fashions, she argues, were but updated restatements of the earlier "hourglass figure" en vogue during the Victorian era, which also featured a cinched waist and voluptuous bust. "It took the shock of World War II and the horror of the bombing of Hiroshima and Nagasaki," Latteier declares, "to frighten the western world into a conservative retrenchment that brought back the breast[s . . . which may be seen as] emblems of plenty during this era of greatly expanding prosperity."[81]

However, eroticized breasts were not "brought back" by postwar "conservative retrenchment" at all because their sexualized usage never really went away.[82] Throughout history and even before written records, female breasts, at one time or another, have been sacralized, domesticized, politicized, psychoanalyzed, and, of course, commercialized.[83] Womanly breasts also played significant sexual and cultural roles in "low class" burlesque strip shows, and "high class" Ziegfeld-produced Broadway extravaganzas. Precode Hollywood allowed actresses Dorothy MacKaill, Renee Adoree, Norma Shearer, and others to show their naked chests though thin and flimsy costuming.[84] World War II GIs were not discouraged from pinning up leggy or busty images of female sex icons—movie stars mostly but some fantasy drawings, too—and chesty, dishabille female totems were painted on airplane fuselages for good luck. So, it is not as if interest in the female breast had faded away and was jarringly rediscovered on television during the postwar era. What had again shifted by the 1950s was the social meaning of the breast and the fact that its cleavage was frequently and for some too prominently featured on the new democratic medium of television. The specific social obsession with the female bust shown (or implied) on the nation's home screens quickly made bosoms the hypersexualized locus of negotiation for postwar network censorship. It was at this point of political, commercial, and technological convergence that serious problems arose for Helffrich and his NBC-TV CA Department.

Dagmar

Virginia Ruth Egnor's original stage name was Jennie Lewis, but she is best remembered from 1950s television as "Dagmar."[85] She was one of the first television-created icons, a "star" not so much for what she *did* on television, but simply because she *was* on television.[86] Dagmar was a tall, buxom woman of twenty-three, a former sweater model, hired to play the "dumb blonde" foil to host/comedian Jerry Lester on *Broadway Open House*—America's incipient late-night talk offering, precursor (by four years) to NBC-TV's *Tonight Show*. The televised image of Dagmar's empty-headed, full-bosomed character prompted viewer comments like: "Her dress was practically down to her waistline. She really is a disgrace . . . Send her back to burlesque."[87] Television historians Harry Castleman and Walter Podrazik write that other "sensitive viewers described Dagmar as 'nothing more than a walking pin-up picture,' apparently even more dangerous than [NBC-TV's other cleavage queens] Faye Emerson and Ilka Chase."[88] Helffrich once cautioned Dagmar on "what passes for a neckline" and shrugged, "*Radio Daily* . . . once raised an eyebrow on the girl, but otherwise [there] have [been] absolutely no clamorous protests. Bosoms would appear here to stay."[89] That may have been so, but a certain frightened NBC-TV affiliate in New England reacted differently.

Bill Swartley, general manager of WHDH-TV, Boston, expressed his concern over Dagmar's ample bosom and the unrestricted burlesque-like sexiness of *Broadway Open House*, which reflected similar objections from other Bostonians. Swartley noted the city's Catholic Archbishop, Richard J. Cushing, had blasted WHDH-TV for being morally lax in broadcasting the voluptuous Dagmar. Cushing further criticized television comics like Lester and Milton Berle for having "perverted sense[s] of humor,"[90] and, during the 1951–52 television season, an often-vehement public discussion on appropriate broadcast fare ensued in local newspapers, public schools, and churches throughout the city. U.S. Congressman Thomas Lane told the Boston press he had received "hundreds of complaints" from citizens in his district upset over seeing Dagmar and other "immodestly clothed" women on television. Lane later recommended a federal censorship board to control, what he termed, the "primitive state of nudism" being telecast. As it turns out, *Broadway Open House* was a short-lived phenomenon, with Lester quitting the show after his continuing feud with Dagmar could not be resolved.[91] Subsequent to 1952, there are no further references to the opulent Dagmar in the CART reports, although she was seen on network television for several more years.[92] Nonetheless, the controversy continued over what Helffrich described as "the under costuming of female performers"[93] on television.

NBC-TV's Cleavage Control

The viewers who complained the loudest simply did not want to see female cleavage on television, period. In an early CART, Helffrich notes that about 150 post cards, all from Brooklyn, New York, and addressed to then NBC President Joseph H. McConnell, included the same message: "'In the name of decency, I ask you to bar from your network all so-called modern styles which leave our women only half clothed. Please remember your programs come into homes where our young children and adolescents should be safe from improper displays. . . . Television should be a boon to humanity—not a curse.'"[94] Most letters, however, were not as literate. Enraged over the low-cut dresses on *Cameo Theater*, Helffrich quoted an anonymous viewer who blamed television for contributing to what he or she saw as the world's moral decay. This unnamed person, catalogued as reprehensible: "low neckline[s] revealing too much cleavage, violence, filth and murder everywhere, more filth on [the] next channel, dirty kissing[,] bending women down half way, dirty women drinking and kissing. Why isnt [sic] the people advertise [sic] good things such as . . . go to church [and] be a good Christian."[95] Helffrich comments, "A definite segment of the viewing audience of average articulation feels resistance to plunging necklines and cliff dweller sophistication in general [and] . . . included petitions totaling three or four dozen signatures, all of which support a call for greater decorum."[96] The "problem" of cleavage and "good taste" was perceived as so acute that McConnell sent personal letters to every female actor or singer featured on any NBC-TV program to address the pervasive dilemma. Plainly, NBC-TV was willing to go to extraordinary lengths to prevent broadcasting a shot of female cleavage or any other sexual images.[97]

Helffrich and NBC-TV management instituted a "good taste" cleavage-control policy the next year. After a particularly naughty image of a low-cut dress was broadcast and later deemed "in extremely bad taste on the plunging neckline front," NBC-TV's CA Department decreed it standard procedure to always place a censor in the control room during live broadcasts. The CA representative could then make split-second decisions on décolletage acceptability under code requirements. "If there is anything in dubious taste which requires Management action to enforce its deletion," Helffrich warns, "the Management is ready, willing and able."[98] Indeed, he was not bluffing, and as a battery of CA censors masked and deleted allusions to the female breast in likeness or reference, Helffrich resolutely supervised. Removed, for example, was a shot of a nude department-store mannequin because such an image played "too blue" for NBC-TV content examiners;[99] expunged were all references to the word *falsie*[100]—a kind of bra padding that appeared to make a woman's breasts larger; even jokes about udders or milking cows were eliminated because such humor was seen as "too graphic."[101] The taboo even extended to drawings and animated cartoons. The only animated cartoon cows cleared for television during this period were ones drawn wearing *skirts*,[102] otherwise, certain vocal portions of the neo-Victorian audience would be reminded that cows, too, were warm-blooded vertebrates burdened with the mammalian necessity of suckling their young. Actually, cow and udder jokes briefly became a humor substitute for breast jokes. On *The Hank McCune Show*, an early filmed sit-com and the first to use a laugh-track,[103] Helffrich and CA removed a gag that suggested one could "make a milkshake by getting a cow to jump rope, [as well as one] on the subject of a cow packing her bag . . . raw references to cow accessories . . . and a discussion of a cow's frozen faucets."[104] Helffrich muses, "It is a toss up whether getting rid of cleavage and [jokes] related thereto is any advantage if the substitute is going to be a concentration on bovine anatomy." Also, *any* natural image of or relating to the birthing of animals—even if done in a serious documentary style—was touchy. Helffrich passed a Disney film, *The Vanishing Prairie*, in which a buffalo calf was born. Outspoken viewers found the show "morbid and depressing." One thought it better suited to "a specialized audience such as medical students," another lectured that it "was the wrong thing for expectant mothers" to witness.[105]

Sexual Containment and Censorship

How is one to understand and place in perspective the ethos that spawned such censorious attitudes about female breasts and sexual content on television? Historian Elaine Tyler May submits that rigidly applied postwar notions of domesticity and strict gender roles within the home and family were social by-products of the American policy of foreign and domestic Communist containment. Her argument suggests such cultural constraint—primarily of female sexuality but any sex deviance was suspect—fit the concrete objectives of the Cold War. "The nation," May wrote, "had to be on moral alert," and domestic sexual restriction was part of such vigilance.[106] Literary scholar Alan Nadel asserts, "This containment of sexuality permeated the full spectrum of American culture in the decade following the war and contributes to explanations of such varied cultural phenomena as strictly censored television programming . . . [and] the constrictive and restrictive structure of female undergarments."[107]

That might be the case, but women on early television were not the only objects of sexual containment. Indeed, men's sexuality was just as proscribed as the udders of those cartoon cows mentioned earlier. That said, this work does not fail to recognize or seek to diminish the disparate social burden placed upon women in the culture during the war years and after. The 1940s and 1950s were difficult for women on many fronts. The government encouraged conflation of housewifery with stay-at-home patriotism; the stress of verbal mother-bashing emanating from ideas like "Momism"; the "Rosie the Riveter" fabrication of an expanding job market and pay structure for women in industry when, in truth, limited work options greeted the female labor force, and pay scales never reached parity with men. Culturally, lesbianism was linked to prostitution and degeneracy; pregnancy out of wedlock created a new iteration of the "fallen woman" or, worse, a completely invisible woman, a shunned outcast. After the war, little changed; the government, employers, and even unions blocked further industrial opportunities for women.[108] And on early national television, there was a clear and significant overemphasis on women's breasts and undergarments. But, based upon Helffrich's CART reports, *all* overt sexuality was circumscribed on the medium. Scholars of postwar culture, like T. J. Jackson Lears, George Lipsitz, and Joanne Meyerowitz, no longer try to identify monolithic, singular movements or specific events as clear indicators of significant historic shift.[109] Besides, writes Meyerowitz, "an unrelenting focus on women's subordination erases much of the history of the postwar years . . . [and] tend[s] to downplay women's agency[,] portray[ing them] as victims." This book views popular culture similar to Meyerowitz, who sees it as "rife with contradiction, ambivalence and competing voices."[110]

As noted, postwar America can be accurately characterized as a time of anxiety. May, for instance, documents in her writings how "fears of sexual chaos tend to surface during times of crisis and rapid social change."[111] This era surely exemplifies her point. Conventional wisdom instructed that if America fell, it would fall from within. It would topple from sexual upheaval, relaxed moral standards, and increased promiscuity; it would collapse from homosexual "perverts" in government, easy pickings for the wily, ubiquitous Communist; it would tumble from the breakdown of the independent, nuclear-family structure—working male as family provider, stay-at-home female as wife, mother, and exclusive sex partner—all other familial configurations were rejected as un-American. Some also believed such a breakdown could happen through the Huxleyan whammy of commercial television. Like communists, TV, too, was found everywhere. The brave new medium had to be monitored and when necessary coldly censored. Any program broadcast that was not seen as "American," family friendly or a recognized reflection of past religious, social, political, legal, and cultural norms was suspect. Historian Walter Kendrick writes that this uneasy attitude toward sexual representation in word or image reflects an American obsession "yoked to a passionate fear of images."[112]

While censorship of female breasts was clearly magnified in early television, subsequent chapters will show that bosoms were not the only objects of concern for finicky home viewers. For example, sexed-laced language, sex-tinged violence, and sexual expression through modern dance were highly suspect. It is this area of expressive contemporary dance to which this work now briefly turns. Its tight costuming and free, aggressive sexual expression through austere body movements made modern dance another point of heated discourse and negotiation for Helffrich and NBC-TV's CA Department.

Dirty Dancing on Early Television

"[It was]," wrote the shaken viewer, "one of the most sensuous and sensual programs I have ever seen. . . . As a teenager, it got me all stirred up with desires I know I shouldn't have as a Christian." The reference was to segment on *Frontiers of Faith*, a religious show, featuring a "dance interpretation of pagan rites" used to express the sweep of religious history through the millennia. "I am amazed that a religious group would present it," continued the agitated teen, "and that *you* did not tame it."[113] Helffrich made no further comment after this CART entry; the passage supposedly left to speak for itself. Postmodernists would surely argue it as an excellent example of how meaning is made not by the intentions of television producers but at the intersection of text (program) and reader (viewer). If nothing else, the story shows how watching human bodies engaged in dance on any NBC-TV offering was subject to calls for censorship and introduces the question of how to negotiate what some saw as "dirty dancing" on early television.

Ruth Mata and Eugene Hari were a highly skilled, athletic, and imaginative modern-dance team seen frequently on *Your Show of Shows*, among other NBC-TV programs.[114] Their interpretive dances, choreographed in the Isadora Duncan–Martha Graham tradition, revealed an interior passion by severe, angular body movements and close contact with the ground. Professionally known as "Mata and Hari," they were celebrated for their muscular, lithe dance routines, which frequently involved, among other things, leaping, tumbling, and sliding on the knees. While some viewers witnessed in their ballet the artful expression of "inner emotion," others just saw dance movements far too lewd and suggestive for television.[115] In his report to Helffrich, nighttime CA manager Burke Miller described the duo's first dance number on *Your Show of Shows* in May 1951: "The female dancer, in a sinuous routine, fell back on the stage with her legs spread apart and the pursuing male dancer fell upon her."[116] Helffrich replied, "With TV for the first time bringing ballet to many who have never seen it before it is just possible that some of these more free expressions will be misunderstood. . . . I don't think banning them is necessary but watching just how they are used certainly is."[117] Mata and Hari stayed on the air, but after any appearance by the pair, CA braced itself for messages of shock and outrage from the home audience. Viewers considered their dancing "too lurid," [118] unfit for the eyes of children,[119] "dirty filth," and "pornographic and revolting."[120] Likewise, their apache dance —a Parisian pas du deux cabaret that represents an apache, or Paris thug, slapping and mistreating his female partner—was criticized for being "lewd and disgusting,"[121] and persistent straddling moves in ballet sequences broadcast in early March 1953 brought heightened complaints.[122]

Ballet appears to be a favorite target of criticism not only for its sensuous movement but also its costuming. A mother's complaint was registered on behalf of an unnamed male ballet dancer's tights, seen on the *Ford Star Review*, as being "too revealing," causing Helffrich's droll reply, "in terms of contours [what the tights] revealed was strictly average."[123] The same parent added that seeing exposed male thighs was shocking to her daughters. To that, Helffrich blithely quipped, "The mother must be in need of a good anatomy lesson."[124] Helffrich dismissed most "dirty dancing" complaints with a didactic East Coast sniff: "Outside of the big cities, we still get scattered mail finding excess sophistication in material which the majority of our audience seems to find acceptable."[125]

Helffrich clearly drew specific distinctions in performance genres. In a comedy sketch for the short-lived, Chicago-based *Jack Carter Show*,[126] the twenty-five-year-old host made an appearance in too-tight long johns causing the home audience to clearly see the contours of his penis. Complaints came in as far away from New York as Memphis. An angry Helffrich wrote, "Stage business around this [was] in no way anticipated by the script. . . . [It] was . . . a pornographic bit . . . unbelievably out of line," adding he did not think it was the job of CA to tell performers to wear "appropriate undergarments . . . where costuming indicates."[127] Why would Helffrich label one viewer "provincial" for her consternation over seeing an obvious bulge in tights worn by a male ballet dancer and find Jack Carter's bulge a bit more "pornographic"? The answer may lie in how Helffrich beheld the nature of culture itself.

Television's Role in Summoning Culture

The postwar notion of television's purpose as cultural missionary is a regular Helffrichian theme. A similar leitmotif was heard at the outset of radio broadcasting. Here, proclaimed its boosters, was an aural medium "sent from the gods" to lift up the people exposing them to finer music, more sophisticated drawing-room humor, and subtle drama. Television—despite its tavern-based beginnings—was also seen as a site for potential cultural enrichment, witness NBC-TV programming boss Sylvester "Pat" Weaver's idea "Operation Frontal Lobes." Weaver dreamed of inserting operatic arias, symphonic music, and scenes from ballet into "high-quality variety series."[128] Like Weaver, Helffrich also saw the medium as not only a conduit for professional wrestling and roller derby but also for bringing, at least occasionally, tasteful refinement to television viewers. It is this fusion of highbrow and lowbrow impulses that tells much about how Helffrich and others at NBC-TV viewed the medium's role. Until about mid-nineteenth century, American-performed ballet, opera, Shakespeare, and to lesser degree symphonic music were as much the domain of the working-class poor as the Brahmin rich. But historian Lawrence W. Levine locates a clear break with past behavior as the twentieth century approached and finds a decided dichotomy of culture. From the mid-to-late 1800s, romantic notions had the artist's vocation treated as a "religion"—what Levine termed "the sacralization of culture"[129]—which, in turn, prompted highbrow and lowbrow distinctions. Refinement was seen as a serious business that could only be understood and appreciated by the studied literati. These suffocating distinctions had currency in postwar television as well. It might be argued that Helffrich was not as concerned with audience complaints over ballet costuming because in it he saw a long and worthy European dance tradition. Ballet was simply perceived as "nobler" art than Jack Carter's comedy burlesque. Carter's actions were taken as vulgar, descending from a democratic and decidedly lowbrow, vaudeville-minstrel heritage. One was not intrinsically "better" than the other, which many postmodernists would argue, but ballet held sway because it was seen as an "important," "artistic," and abiding form of expression—one with which early television wished to associate itself. Classical dance was held as a sacralized "high culture" (i.e., class-based) illustration of human artistry, closer to God than vulgar vaudeville. Helffrich's attitude, on its face, was the standard neo-Victorian model of snootiness. If home viewers questioned or found themselves embarrassed by ballet, to Helffrich it signaled their parochial tastes were far too bucolic, suggesting it was they, not television that had to change.

Nonetheless, the NBC CART reports make clear that postwar viewers expected the "protection" of network-imposed censorship from a variety of secular evils they saw on television. And based upon Helffrich's notes, in most cases they got it. While there were seminal moments—Kinsey's work, among others—that loosened the strictures of sexual repression in media, ancient amatory codes were not easily severed. More open sexuality developed slowly on television, and its transformation took place in fits and starts. Sexualized images on television were clearly a major discursive area in early network-television censorship but so were sexualized speech and cultural and religious taboos.

5. Gagging the Gags

*O*n the 1950s, television was one of America's favorite objects of ridicule. An orthodontist in California claimed television was the source of crooked teeth in youngsters, caused by hand cradling the jaw while watching—he called it "Television Malocclusion."[1] The American Osteopathic Association cautioned, "TV can make children more susceptible to diseases . . . [and contribute to] 'bad body mechanics.'"[2] A group of dermatologists warned that excessive viewing of television Westerns brought about dandruff due to increased emotional stress.[3] In Chicago, a prison chaplain hyperbolized that television shows "cause a fever of the mind, tuberculosis of the heart and soul, [and] are more dangerous to youth than the atomic bomb."[4] Doubtlessly, the questionable images that television brought into American homes—some thought too often and with little restraint—provoked these wild accusations and overstatements. But aberrant TV images were just half the story. Offensive language in the postwar era was also cause for alarm. Deleting or substituting utterances considered invidious was central to the NBC-TV Continuity Acceptance (CA) Department's mission led by chief censor Stockton Helffrich.

Profanity

Profanity—the use of words or oaths that show contempt, irreverence, or disrespect to ideas or things considered sacred—was a productive area for nascent television censorship. As early as 1948, Helffrich wrote, "We continue to delete . . . quite regularly, expletive[s] such as 'My God' and 'God' from assorted . . . scripts. . . . Television writers seem to think violently of God a lot more than the radio writers do. . . . [since] we seem to be getting a rash of expressive uses of the word . . . and are quite consistently working against the same."[5] As a basis for his actions, Helffrich was quick to quote the section in *Responsibility*, the NBC-TV censorship handbook: "'Reverence marks any mention of God, His attributes or powers.'"[6]

The Continuity Acceptance Radio/Television (CART) reports also show that words and phrases like "jeez," "God," "in God's name," "my God," "by God," "good God," "thank God," "she's God's gift," and the like were consistently deleted from NBC-TV programming and replaced with "by golly," "gosh," and "gee whiz" or variations thereof.[7] Also, expressions of "what/where the hell" were changed to "what/where the Hades" or "what/where the heck," "I'll be damned" was bowdlerized to "I'll be darned," and "I'll be Goddamned" purified to "I'll be doggoned."[8] Such concessions left the religious taboo intact while permitting the rhythm of a profane oath.[9] Helffrich explains these cuts were "in accord with past and continuing audience resentment against a too-easy use of the word 'God.'"[10]

Yet, the historian John Burnham argues that during the twentieth century, profane speech became nearly "inoperative among most population groups," suggesting that swearing came more to encompass words dealing with sexual and bodily functions.[11] While this observation is accurate and seems certainly the case in television, profane oaths clearly did not become "inoperative." While one can find fewer examples of profane deletions than sexual and scatological ones in the CART memos, irreverent cursing still had currency in common parlance and was consistently removed from scripts of programs airing on the network. Why the apparent discrepancy, then? It appears Burnham may have not allowed for the phenomenal religious revival that informed social behavior at mid-twentieth century.

The postwar religious renaissance somewhat fueled concerns about television moral effrontery. A poll conducted in 1948 found that 95 percent of respondents said they believed in God, and as many said they prayed to Him.[12] In 1950, church membership expanded to nearly 115 million people, an increase of 63 percent from a decade earlier.[13] (However, those numbers may also indicate that many young people took up church going in part because they were starting new families; they were not necessarily more religious than their parents.) Both *Time* and *Life* magazines labeled America's "return to religion" as a significant phenomenon of the postwar.[14] Also, the notion of an "American way of life [as] the antithesis of godless communism," writes religious historian Robert S. Ellwood, "was to be preserved at all cost."[15] But NBC-TV's censorship was not prompted because the novice churchgoer constituted a majority or even a new majority. Helffrich and NBC-TV may have been responding to a smaller, more vocal, probably older but not necessarily representative body of Americans who were simply offended by profane speech. Television was one front on which such speech could be censored or contained thus keeping the facade of God-fearing Americanism preserved. Still, sensitivity ran so high in this area that in one instance the word "'Christ,' was going to be delivered in a poem in a most reverent fashion," Helffrich says, but was deleted from an early *Swift Show* in September 1948.[16] NBC-TV CA saw nothing wrong with the verse; nonetheless, the television-programming department said it wished to be chary even beyond the censor's recommendation, and the word was cut.[17]

Such was not the case in 1954, when Frank Sinatra ad-libbed the word *madone* (pronounced "ma-DOHn") on the *Colgate Comedy Hour*, a word considered by some Roman Catholics a profanity of the first order. Sinatra later tried to explain away the word as a sort of "exclamation some of the young and old male set tend to use when a pretty girl goes by or some other event occurs which calls for comment."[18] *Madone* is actually an Italian slang for the word *Madonna* or *Blessed Mother*, and quite a profanity to devout Catholics, who wasted no time in complaining to Helffrich about it.

On a later occasion, Helffrich opines that viewer mail "suggest[ed] the word 'damn' [as] unthinkable in [television] material no matter what the circumstances[,] . . . context . . . [or] hour of broadcast."[19] For the sake of "realism"—a dominant concern since the early twentieth century in American literature—many television playwrights were deliberately adding "damns" and "hells" in their scripts for NBC-TV. Realism is a literary technique that also denotes a particular kind of subject matter, especially the representation of middle-class life. It is a reaction to romanticism, therefore dialogue is spoken in the vernacular, not heightened or poetic; its tone may be comic, satiric, or matter-of-fact.[20] New York theater since the 1920s had used looser language on stage, and most if not all TV dramatists took their cues from Broadway, which in turn was influenced by modernist American literature. In modernist realism, characters are often more important than action or plot; complex ethical choices are often the subject. Characters appear complicated in temperament and motive; they are explicable in relation to nature, to each other, to their social class, and to their own past, and the events portrayed will usually be plausible as will the dialogue.[21] The use of *damn* and *hell* was peppered in showcase programs like *Goodyear* and *Alcoa Theatre, The Kaiser Aluminum Hour, Armstrong Circle Theatre, Kraft Television Theatre*, and *Lux Video Theatre*, among others. It was, reports Helffrich, only during these adult, dramatic programs—scheduled on NBC-TV after 9 P.M., eastern time—"in highly selective instances, and very scattered places" did CA allow the use of tough language. Despite that, Helffrich complained that parents charged NBC-TV with "exposing their children to realities of a corruptive nature."[22]

Throughout the 1950s and beyond, the use of profane oaths continued to be sensitive for the NBC-TV censors. "Don't . . . get the idea the bars are down in this always-delicate area of public relations," Helffrich cautions.[23] Historian Frederick Lewis Allen traces the new social value of literary frankness to the turn of the twentieth century, with "honesty" being a major thread in printed media.[24] After the "inversion of manners" following World War I, swearing and cursing steadily gained ground because now the "best people"—women as well as men, both wealthy and poor—used language that, before this time, marked the speaker as common or of lower social status. World War II sped the acceptance of the use of profane and vulgar language in the popular culture.[25]

Vulgarity

The Adventures of Hopalong Cassidy became one of early television's hit programs and an exercise in postwar logic regarding the vulgar treatment of American role models. First seen in June 1949, the Hoppy show became a staple on WNBT-TV, New York, and eventually across the NBC television network. Historians Tim Brooks and Earle Marsh claim Hoppy broadcasts, either in their original theatrical release or in edited half-hour offerings, date back to as early as 1945 when first broadcast in New York City.[26]

The character, originally created by Western writer Clarence Edward Mulford, was named Hopalong because he literally hopped along due to a bum leg; moreover, the grisly, whiskey-guzzling reprobate rarely washed, and he uttered streams of profanities.[27] Actor William Boyd quickly rehabilitated that image in his star turn as Hopalong, making the cowpoke an easy-striding, clean-shaven, silver-coifed paragon of virtue; a man who gleamed with range-riding justice, prudence, and temperance. Clearly Hoppy, a postwar television role model for many younger viewers, could do no wrong. So, when on the *Chevrolet Tele-Theatre*, an early NBC-TV dramatic anthology program, the "cranky grandfather had the line, 'Bah—Hopalong Cassidy is a fool,'" Helffrich wrote, "We suggested deletion of the last three words as being a little too iconoclastic for the small fry."[28] Because the beloved character embodied adult notions of justice and fair play, the script erasure presupposes that disrespectful comments could make a negative impact on children's still-forming ideas of moral uprightness and somehow lead to behavior that defied authority. Which is not as hyperbolic as it sounds. Clearly, Helffrich was concerned that heroes like Hoppy possessed an intrinsic moral value for children, a value that could be diminished if Hoppy's character was disrespected on other shows. Hopalong, therefore, had to be protected from the corrosion of adult cynicism. Boyd's Cassidy persona was not only a hero and exemplar for children, some cultural historians argue, it also stood as a metaphor during the Cold War. Like the United States on the world stage, Hoppy was portrayed as a gentle giant but when riled, woe befell the villain. The era's ideological confrontation with the Soviets soon turned into a military and economic projection of American power, and the morally upright, peace-loving but solitary gunslinger figure of 1950s television and film—a crude allegory for that power—seemed to resonate with the nation. That said, Hopalong Cassidy was not the most morally self-conscious of television's first Western stars. That honor goes to Gene Autry, who in the early 1950s authored the Cowboy Code:

1. The Cowboy must never shoot first, hit a smaller man, or take unfair advantage.
2. He must never go back on his word, or a trust confided in him.
3. He must always tell the truth.
4. He must be gentle with children, the elderly, and animals.
5. He must not advocate or possess racially or religiously intolerant ideas.
6. He must help people in distress.
7. He must be a good worker.
8. He must keep himself clean in thought, speech, action, and personal habits.

9. He must respect women, parents, and his nation's laws.

10. The Cowboy is a patriot.

With its emphasis on the work ethic and patriotism, the Cowboy Code adequately captures the benign values animating Westerns on television during the Cold War. "Thou shall not kill," one will note, is missing from Autry's ten commandments.[29]

Nonetheless, critical adult viewers and parent-teacher groups frequently bombarded CA with complaints about Western programs for their many boorish vulgarities. Disapproval ranged from the site of the show's main action to the incorrect syntax of its bronco-busting hero. A Morristown, New Jersey, gentleman wrote in part. "I am not suggesting that your actors and actresses all become Johnsonian soliloquists; nor am I suggesting that your writers surrender even a single iota of realism by avoiding regional dialect, colloquialisms, or the vulgate. But for heaven's sake stop using 'ain't' as the hallmark of rural heritage and 'ain't got no' as the identifying symbol of villainy. If you must identify the characters as bumpkins . . . let them go barefoot [or] chew straw."[30] Another complaint beseeching less vulgar diction in Westerns wrote, "Please ask your personnel to pronounce (I don't mean *pernounce*) common words correctly. There are no such words as: . . . kinvention . . . peticular, pergress, sitiation, [and] yerself. Children notice such mistakes on . . . TV. . . . Let's all stop murdering the English-American language."[31] Sensitive to such criticism, Helffrich sent a message to producers of horse operas on the West Coast recommending what he called NBC-TV's "1, 2, 3 formula" and asking it be "applied as often as reasonably possible."[32] He outlined: "Point One: Have the good guy with whom young viewers identify fight clean, talk clean, and [speak] grammatically. Point Two: Wing or nip the bad guys and lead [them] off to formal justice; don't be so casual about . . . plugging [the villains] and leaving [them] to die. . . . Point Three: Try to avoid too much of the action [happening] in a booze palace. . . . Recommended in place of barrooms are general stores, the post office, the [train] depot, a hotel lobby, etc."[33] The specifications apparently worked, at least on the oater *Tales of Wells Fargo*. Helffrich noted that two-thirds of the plots "have been able to eschew bar sequences," with justice achieved without the "'automatic' death of the bad guys."[34]

Westerns, however, were not the only concern. Below is a truncated listing of what Helffrich characterizes as "an unbelievable assortment of crudities and obscenities [that] cropped up for our Continuity Acceptance gentry" in Los Angeles, Chicago, and New York.[35] One line cut from the *Ford Theatre* program was, "You can take that mural and stick it . . . up your own wall." A few samples deleted from *the Kraft Television Theatre* include the following utterances: "the big, conceited Mick," "I'll belly blast ya," and "I'll personally gut ya and burn ya tripes before ya eyes."[36] Reported excised from the drama on *Robert Montgomery Presents*,[37] among others, were "Gladys, that witch;" and, "Am I out on my fanny?"[38] An agitated Helffrich comments, "A few of these astonished me chiefly because they are so obviously unacceptable for a family viewing audience that you wonder at the temerity of the writer[s] . . . submitting 'em to us. But submitted [they] were and, by jiminy (you'll pardon the vehemence) chucked out were they pronto."[39] Other examples of what rose to the level of "crude and vulgar language" in 1955 included the following deletions: "You crazy?" "Oh, you dumb idiot!" "That lousy louse!" "You little snotnose!" "Creeps! Idiots!" "Take your stinkin' yokel face away from me." Helffrich here again invoked the family-viewing principle that guided nearly all CA decisions, adding, his censors removed all of the coarseness from the script and "left what was necessary for adequate character delineation."[40]

Another circumscribed vulgarity was not a word but a gesture—nose thumbing, whereby the thumb tip is placed at the base of the nose followed by a quick flicking action. This gesture was cut from the *Texaco Star Theatre* as early as 1948.[41] In a portion of the ventriloquist *Paul Winchell and Jerry Mahoney Show*, Helffrich noted that the "dummy is scripted to thumb his nose. . . . We do not take nose thumbing on television so this one was chucked from the script."[42] Also cut as tasteless was a portion from one of Charlie Chaplain's classic silent films. The edited scene involved Chaplain nose thumbing a police officer.[43] The impulse for deleting the gesture may have its roots in nineteenth-century notions of social deviation. Character, personal restraint, and respect for figures of authority were highly prized and seen as central to the governance of a civilized society. Any breach of restraint or decorum was considered a defiant threat that, if not controlled, could overturn order and propriety.[44] A clear class issue is also at play. Coarse argot, swearing, and ill-mannered gestures each delineated social boundaries and categorized the user as part of a common or lower-order group, possibly associated with destructiveness.[45]

Network television's concern about reflecting consensus to a conceptualized "family audience" as well as keeping sponsors happy and government regulators at arms length drove Helffrich and Continuity Acceptance to cut any word or action seen as destabilizing. But perhaps NBC-TV censors overconcerned themselves with the nose-thumbing issue. On *the Kraft Television Theater* in early November 1951, Helffrich wrote of a sequence in which an "inmate in a penitentiary scene thumbs his nose at the warden." The gesture was ad-libbed, unscripted, and "in no way approved by NBC." Not one protest was registered over the incident. A bit puzzled, Helffrich concludes, "It is somewhat surprising . . . that no compliant came in on the point, possibly because the production was so excellent in all other respects."[46] It may also be that the home audience viewed the gesture as something expected of "those people," typical for a lower-order, jailed (i.e., controlled) social miscreant.

A "vulgarity" that had political overtones was depictions of the American or Confederate flags on television. Helffrich reported that NBC-TV viewers in Chicago found "subversive intent" in the televised Southern Methodist University (SMU) versus Notre Dame football game.[47] A panning television camera caught sight of a few SMU students waving a Confederate flag in the stadium bleachers. Helffrich explained that the nub of the criticism was the sense that preoccupation with Confederate flag-waving would encourage renewed "adulation of those who rebel against the constituted authorities," and he assured, "There is no trend within NBC to play up this business."[48] Moreover, flying the Confederate flag, particularly from the radio antenna, grill, or radiator of one's car, was quite a fad in the early 1950s and one that did not sit well with older, more vocal Americans. Motorists visiting Washington, D.C., while displaying the symbol of Dixie on their auto were told by police to remove the emblem, or they would not be permitted entrance to the U.S. Capitol.[49] *Life* did a feature article on the craze, including a photo of a group of young college men, students from the University of Maryland, displaying actual battle flags from 1864. Another photo depicted a man saying he bought his Confederate flag because he was "against Truman."[50] The idea of displaying the Southern banner in any context clearly appeared unpatriotic to the senior moral guardians of the time. It apparently was thought that this symbol could open old wounds or contribute to further American divisiveness during a time of exposed emotion from growing concerns over infiltrating Communism and African Americans' demands for civil rights. Raising high an emblem from the Civil War recalled an unstable and disunited time, and sent the wrong message.

A charge of inappropriateness was also leveled against the popular Chicago-based children's show *Kukla, Fran, and Ollie*, when it displayed the Bars and Stars in a sketch. The outcry caused its producer, Beulah Zachary, to inquire if NBC-TV had a policy against showing the Southern flag. Helffrich responded that there was no "flat ban" on it, but "a good deal of controversial talk surround[s] the matter not excluding outright concern in Washington." He mused, "I guess we would all be naïve to say there are no political overtones." Ultimately, Helffrich could not envision a way to stop broadcasting pictures or references to the flag but thought it "wise not to pass that which favors sentiments historically out of date."[51] In the scheme of things, the Confederate flag did not cause Helffrich near the trouble that "vulgar" depictions of the *American* flag did. "Almost every state and the District of Columbia provide," Helffrich writes, "that it shall be unlawful to use the flag for purposes of advertising or to place or cause to be placed any word, figure, design or picture upon the flag."[52] Even the NBC legal department weighed in saying that American flags were verboten in patriotic variety-show sketches, dramas, or for use in any "other action" including advertising.[53] "So don't go superimposing . . . Old Glory [over] some sponsor's pack of cigarettes or things like that there, see?" wrote Helffrich, tongue firmly in cheek.[54] But the flag issue was no laughing matter. On the *Tex and Jinx Show*,[55] one of television's earliest talk offerings, program sponsor Presto Cake Flour felt the sting of what might be called "pastry censorship." For Dwight D. Eisenhower's inaugural, Presto wanted a "cake . . . topped with a frosted replica of the American flag." NBC legal quashed the attempt calling it "exploitation" of the national banner.[56] The "vulgar indiscretion," caught in time, caused no further problem.

To better understand 1950s television's behavior on symbolic flag issues, one might also employ some productive notions provided by sociologist Robert Bellah. Throughout his career, Bellah studied the secular symbols by which Americans understood themselves and their world. He observed that many of these symbols grow primarily out of religious traditions and change by their interaction with alternative religions and philosophies as well as with social, economic, military, and political forces.[57] If one views America's postwar belief in government as a secular or "civil religion" whose ideals (freedom, democracy, and so on) are ones for which its followers would fight and die (as they did in World War II), then it becomes easier to see how symbols of that religion—its prayer (the Pledge of Allegiance), its hymn (the *Star-Spangled Banner*), and its flag (the Christ or emblematic embodiment of the belief)—could be treated with such blind reverence. Bellah's notions seem particularly appropriate in describing what animated the pro-flag American Legion and other patriotic, middle-class groups. Like their sensitivity to profaning religion, this may be another example of NBC-TV adjusting its censorship to appease an older, more outspoken, and most likely white minority of viewers. It was, therefore, important for television to show appropriate veneration for the flag of the United States and act as a deferential example of propriety. NBC-TV could not risk offending a small but vocal group for political, economic, and patriotic reasons. Television, after all, was a neoteric, significant, and growing part of an emerging postwar power structure, and consistently proscribed all vulgar, nondignified, or competing symbolic images.

The Pregnant Taboo

Saying the word *pregnant* or *pregnancy* was forbidden on postwar television. The word was rarely used in polite conversation as well. Even many married folks were loath to utter it. Take Miles and Betty Trimpey, for example. The couple was married in April 1943; Miles was shipped off to basic training and later saw World War II combat after Betty became pregnant with their first child. Although Miles wrote to his wife nearly every day, even his most intimate letters *never* used the word *pregnant*, nor did his bride in her return missives to him. Betty explained she would instead substitute "'my condition' . . . as proper young women were taught to do sixty years ago."[58] The story is exemplary of how deeply rooted spoken sexual taboos were in pre- and postwar America. If a *married* couple felt uneasy about using the *p*-word to discuss their own pregnancy in personal conversation, one can only imagine the social strictures in place that prevented such talk in polite company. After all, public use of the word implied erstwhile—and probably sordid—sexual engagements. And one could simply not find a more invasive medium than television to turn such private matters public. American homes and living rooms, said Television Broadcasters Association President J. R. Poppele, are "where standards of purity and decency are still anything but extinct."[59]

Still, innocent, sexual TV references were sometimes taken to an extreme. For example, a mother complained about a word used on *Ding Dong School*, a children's show that won a Peabody Award in 1952. It seems Miss Frances, the show's host, had mentioned something totally shocking and inappropriate for children to hear—that her gold fish was pregnant.[60] Postwar sensibilities being what they were, it is easier to understand why the manufacturer of Phillip Morris cigarettes behaved as it did when TV actress and comedienne Lucille Ball became pregnant in 1952. The ad agency for the cigarette brand, sponsor of *I Love Lucy*, hinted that she be written out of the show or wear baggy clothing to conceal her condition. Another suggestion was that Ball be filmed standing behind chairs and potted plants.[61] A minister, rabbi, and priest were on hand during the production of the birthing episode to lend a note of dignity—it was a comedy, after all—and, by the end of the show, the taboo remained unbroken; the words *sex* and *pregnant* were never mentioned.[62]

Yet, according to Helffrich's CART reports, CBS-TV's *I Love Lucy* was not the first sitcom to use pregnancy as a story line. The questionable honor goes to NBC-TV and what has been termed "one of the first domestic comedies," a show entitled *Mary Kay and Johnny*. The program was seen on NBC network during the 1948–49 season.[63] Helffrich revealed that the program "had as its leading lady an actual pregnant woman with her pending confinement a part of the script. . . . References are kept within bounds and camera treatment has so far been acceptable with no squawks from anybody."[64] It is unclear if the word *pregnant* was spoken, but Mary Kay was clearly seen in her parturient state. After the birth, her new son made his acting debut on the show, playing himself, of course.

Ten years later, in 1958, Helffrich displayed a more mature and decisively liberal bearing toward saying *pregnancy* and showing it on television: "Our puritan tradition looks suspect because it was dishonest. . . . Pregnancy . . . is not in bad taste." He spoke of children's natural interest in conception because they hear discussion of it and frequently "see . . . the contour of that discussion's current object. . . . Sex and what appears to be one of its more obvious correlatives, pregnancy, seems to be here to stay . . . and our relationships to it are changing."[65] And it is arguable that Helffrich and his cadre of censors were social contributors to that change and what became acceptable for talking about on television.

Taboo Language and the Television Writer

Self-censorship on television was commonplace in the 1950s, or so goes the collective wisdom. Television writers understood certain sexual, racial, or political references were taboo and would probably be scissored from their scripts; consequently, before sending their creations to the network's moral guardians, writers would censor their own words and ideas. Celebrated writers of the era, Rod Serling, Paddy Chayefsky, Horton Foote, Robert Alan Aurthur, Irve Tunik, Gore Vidal, Reginald Rose, and others, have admitted to engaging in such self-censorship practices.[66] These prominent writers believed that by editing themselves, they retained at least some integrity and control over their projects and avoided protracted arguments with sponsors or network censors. Yet, based upon Helffrich's CART reports, it seems that only television's top-tier playwrights imposed such censorship upon themselves or, at the very least, were the only ones who talked about it. Most of the hundreds of unnamed dramatists and comedy writers, about whom Helffrich regularly commented, clearly and overtly expressed themselves with outrageous verbiage, offensive notions, and double entendres. Early television writer Tad Mosel wrote that in the "golden age," as many as three hundred original dramatic anthology shows were telecast per year—at least seven shows a week running from thirty to ninety minutes each. Mosel explained these "plays were written fast, tumbling over each other to get on the air . . . half of them [were just] routine."[67] For the most part it appears middling writers, often for low-brow comedy shows, had little time to be cautious in what they said or how they said it. Nor were Helffrich and company timid in expunging their work.

In a 1949 Thanksgiving show starring George Jessel, Helffrich "deleted in its entirety" a thoroughly ribald comedy sketch. The writers had Jessel portraying a biology professor who was to make all manner of sexual and "anatomical references [to the female body using] German words [which,] when translated[,] turned out to be obscenities."[68] Also, writers of the popular Bickersons sketches, which had recently moved from radio to television's *Four Star Review*, were chastised for conjuring suggestive language dealing with the male sex organ. Before an Helffrichian overhaul, actors Don Ameche and Frances Langford, playing the incessantly quarrelsome husband and wife John and Blanche Bickerson, were to remark:

BLANCHE: Dr. Hershey says you snore because you have a long uvula and it flutters against your palette. Why don't you let him fix it?

JOHN: Okay, I'll do it in the morning.

BLANCHE: Do it now, go on. Get up and let Dr. Hershey pull out your uvula.

JOHN: I'm not gonna let that medical thief hack on my uvula.

BLANCHE: He doesn't hack. He snares.

JOHN: I don't care if he knocks it off with a hockey stick, nobody's gonna pull out my uvula.[69]

Along the same lines, comedy writers presented English music-hall performer Bea Lillie and comic Bob Hope a sketch in which Lillie portrayed a Polynesian maiden. She was to walk up to Hope and, in alleged Polynesian lingo, comment upon his "Donga . . . Longa." Producer Max Liebman "assured [Helffrich] the words would not be used by Miss Lillie."[70] They were not.

Dramatic scribes of time-honored works were also subject to cuts if their work got on television. In the classic Ruggero Leoncavallo opera *Pagliacci*, Helffrich changed "the verb in Tonio's line to Nedda from 'have' to 'kiss.'" The actual script had it: "I swear I will have you," a line that when translated to English, Helffrich said, "tends to over-emphasize and shock the hinterland."[71] Writers in the early dramatic anthology program *The Clock* wished to use the phrase "all bollixed up" to refer to a bungled situation. After consulting a slang dictionary, Helffrich, still concerned that the word *bollix* "had taken on special significance in connection with the male anatomy" (the testicles), had the phrase changed to "all messed up."[72] Moreover, a reworking of William Faulkner's *Sound and the Fury* had to be toned down—the line "you damn little slut" needed a "a milder synonym;" in an adaptation of an Oscar Wilde play, the word *bloody* caused a problem.[73]

Literally dozens of other descriptive examples of deleted language are in the CART reports that, without dispute, could fill a hundred or more pages. Which returns us to the question: was writer self-censorship as prevalent in postwar television as we have been taught? A reasonable conclusion might be that for at least those legions of obscure littérateurs who ground out daily material or low-brow humor for now long-forgotten television programs, self-censorship did not happen as frequently as past accounts suggest. But Helffrich and company were there to monitor the network's input and output and were a constant presence in the lives of television-program creators, producers, and writers.

The Infamous "Water Closet" Incident

Jack Paar became host of NBC-TV's revamped *The Tonight Show* on July 29, 1957; three years later, Paar angrily walked away from the immensely popular show because a joke he performed in his monologue was censored by the network. The gag was based on a double entendre, a misinterpretation of the initials W.C.—the woman in the story thought the letters meant "water closet" (or toilet), but the man in the jape intended the initials to stand for "wayside chapel."[74] The story's juxtaposition of bathroom imagery vis à vis a place of religious worship caused reservations for Lee Jahncke, an aide to James Stabile, NBC-TV's "top cop" in legal standards and practices. Stabile was unavailable, so Jahncke passed his concern onto senior vice president David Adams.[75] It was Adams who made the unilateral decision to "replace" the four-minute story with a not-so-important NBC-TV news bulletin.[76] Through it all, Paar was never notified and only learned of the censorship when he watched a playback of his live-on-tape program later that night.[77] The next evening, February 11, 1960, nine minutes into his monologue, a shaken Paar said, "I believe I was let down by this network," and walked away from his job.[78] In a comedy of management finger-pointing, the show's (unnamed) unit manager "strictly in the line of duty" informed Helffrich of the joke after both *Tonight Show* producers, Bill Anderson and Paul Orr, had okayed it. According to a *Variety* inquiry, Helffrich also "saw nothing remiss, recalling material far more off base," but still suggested it be checked through legal in Washington, D.C., where Stabile was based.[79] Such a "good taste" call, in the past, would have simply stopped with Helffrich's decision, so why not this time?

Apparently, the answer was connected with the network quiz-show scandals of two years earlier. *Variety* reporter George Rosen called the Paar incident "symptomatic . . . of what's been happening on the networks since the webs inaugurated their post-quiz reforms."[80] Big-money TV quiz shows on CBS and NBC—*The $64,000 Question/Challenge, The Big Surprise, Dotto, Tic Tac Dough*, and *Twenty-One*—first fascinated, then betrayed the hearts of Americans in the 1950s.[81] In 1958, disgruntled former contestants of NBC-TV's *Twenty-One* went public with allegations that the show's questions were rigged and contestants coached.[82] Such a public-relations nightmare prompted NBC-TV management to unofficially separate the Continuity Acceptance Department from Standards and Practices, the latter taking on more-formal legal responsibilities. Stabile was seen as NBC-TV's highest authority on any question of law; Helffrich and Continuity Acceptance were still considered specialists in questions of "taste." The Paar incident, reported *Variety*, left Helffrich "somewhat miffed" because it was unclear to him where "continuity acceptance begins and the where the 'cops' take over."[83] NBC-TV management said they would work to better clarify each department's boundaries, but Helffrich was not around to see that happen. After twenty-seven years at the network, the chief censor resigned from NBC later that quarter to become director of the National Association of Broadcasters' code-authority office in New York City.

Mental Illness on Early Television

Stockton Helffrich spent more than half his life working for NBC and, according to his daughter Jackie Austin, Helffrich's commitment to TV programming that dealt humanely with those suffering from mental illness was one of his most important contributions to nascent television.[84] Helffrich's insistence on fairness in TV portrayals of the mentally ill was no easy matter in the postwar era. His greatest opponents were indifference and ignorance to the nation's mind sick. Fearful public attitudes about those mentally afflicted were a common and long-held American tradition. In colonial times, "lunatics" were pilloried, shackled, and bled of their mental demons. By the mid-1800s, insane asylums were the vogue, along with moral management therapies (i.e., neuropathologic treatment by opium, laxatives, and ice baths). Then came Sigmund Freud's psychoanalytic techniques in the 1920s and electroconvulsive shock therapy about ten years later. Threads of tension and anxiety have always attended talk of mental illness in the United States.[85] A so-called nervous (or mental) breakdown, although treated medically, was still widely viewed as a character flaw, a feared personal defect about which mainstream America anxiously joked. And such jokes or rejoinders were made too frequently in the common parlance to *not* be reflected in television scripts. Because of Helffrich's familial and personal experiences with neuroses—his first wife, Delores, suffered a "nervous breakdown," her extended family was riddled with depression and suicide, and Helffrich himself engaged in three years of intensive psychoanalysis after the war—the censor was sensitive to jokes or hurtful epitaphs directed toward the mentally sick. His ongoing commitment to humane handling of mental and emotional illnesses on television was really quite startling and earned him numerous humanitarian awards from groups like the American Mental Health Association.[86]

Helffrich was a tireless advocate against any negative portrayals of mental illness on television. In one instance, NBC-TV programmers suggested a wacky new sitcom à la the antics of John Siguard "Ole" Olsen and Harold Ogden "Chic" Johnson, the zany vaudeville duo whose previous television efforts included the use of busty showgirls, pratfalls, and pies in the face. "[T]he setting of the shenanigans [would be] an insane asylum," writes a restrained Helffrich. "We feel this sort of thing very ill-advised." He suggests the locale of the piece be changed to a zoo or circus if the programming department was actually serious about the show, citing NBC-TV always sustained bad reviews from newspaper critics and angry viewer response if the network exhibited glibness at the expense of the mentally ill. Helffrich next cites statistics, as he did habitually throughout the CARTs when he discussed mental illness: "[O]ne out of ten will need psychiatric help before his life is over . . . and one out of eighteen will be hospitalized for psychiatric help." Helffrich also argues a comedy show set in a home for the mentally ill was just "bad business." He reasoned why alienate with vulgar, insensitive humor "large numbers of our audience whose relatives and friends have received, are receiving, or will receive psychiatric help?" The censor maintains that these ill people were not "'nuts' or 'insane' and they [did] not find amusing out-moded attitudes toward . . . mental sickness problems."[87] The opprobrious sketch never got off the ground and was never mentioned again in any CART report.

Helffrich clearly went to great lengths to avoid any negative representation of mental illness on TV. Even a harmless utterance expressed in the argot of the era—like, "you're nuts"—was forbidden. Variations on the phrases "you're crazy," "he's/she's/it's crazy," "you idiot," "you imbecile," "you moron," "he's off his rocker," "he's got loose marbles," "put her in the nut house/nut hospital," "to the loony hatch," "get the butterfly net," and "he's a crackpot," among many others, were routinely deleted from scripts by Helffrich and his CA teams in New York, Chicago, and Los Angeles.[88] An entire *My Little Margie* episode set in a mental hospital—the story treatment suggested the opening shot would show "'nuts' running around rampant" [89]—was disallowed, as were explicit shock-treatment scenes in the never-broadcast production script of *Your Jeweler's Showcase*.[90] Attempting to stem the tide of using the word *crazy* to designate "absurd behavior," Helffrich began micromanaging scripts. He explicitly clarifies that the word *crazy may* be used in a script but *only* when the scene "actually refers to mental illness . . . *and where no substitute is either realistic, logical or possible*" (his italics).[91] He prods television writers and producers to use instead the words "zany, silly, or foolish."[92] "Very few plots are . . . damaged," Helffrich chides, "if [the] line 'you're crazy' or 'you're insane' is changed to 'you're a fool.'"[93]

But what should be done with the word *crazy* when it is used in a different context and parlance? Sam Sharkey, an NBC-TV news editor, sent an interesting memo to Helffrich posing just that question: "Re your continuing controversy over 'crazy,' what would you do with that word as used by Steve Allen and assorted other bopsters and cool jazz men?" Sharkey said he could not envision jazz artists like John Birks "Dizzy" Gillespie, Louis "Sachmo" Armstrong, "or any denizens of Birdland . . . reacting with your suggested synonyms, 'Zany, man!' or 'Silly, man!' or even 'Foolish, man!'" Helffrich, sensing the humor, agreed with Sharkey on the specific exemption for jazz slang but insisted, "A part from that qualification . . . we'll continue to eliminate those misuses of the word 'crazy' which have no justification in general plot situations."[94]

Such careful regulation of script minutia kept things under control to be sure, but occasionally slips occurred. For example, during a monologue on the *Texaco Star Theatre*, comic Jan Murray ad-libbed a joke on "an asylum inmate who spent all his time painting the grass green."[95] Welfare workers called in to complain, pointing out "that television sets are installed in hospitals for the . . . unbalanced and that it constituted a cruel piece of unkindness to make fun of the mentally ill."[96] Helffrich demanded such off-script jokes be eliminated: "Let's not [put] NBC in a position of bearing a stigma that we don't know anything about the prevalent problem of mental illness in our country."[97]

Helffrich and his CA department had to be proactive as well as reactive in their censorship activities. As he writes numerous times in the CARTs, "Tain't enough to be against something patently malicious for a part or whole of one's audience; you have to be for something as well."[98] For example, before permitting the broadcast drama *Uncle Sam's Story*, a film about therapy provided to a GI suffering from schizophrenia, Helffrich discussed the project with Veterans Administration doctors and awaited their recommendation—it is unknown in this case what was decided, the CARTs make no further reference.[99] Helffrich and his colleagues also consulted with the American Mental Health Association to story edit a *Matinee Theatre*[100] script, "Rain in the Morning." The CA chief said that the show's specific purpose was "to help decrease the still too prevalent public fear of mental illness" held by relatives and business associates of those suffering from the disease.[101] He pushed NBC-TV to partner with the National Institute of Mental Health to present public-service announcements for Mental Health Week,[102] and made certain mentally retarded children portrayed in television programs were not referred to as "morons," "idiots," or "imbeciles," explaining changes were required out of "common sense" and "human kindness."[103] It is unclear how many serious television programs or public-service announcements dealing with the severely neurotic were broadcast on the network, but there were apparently enough in number to have *New York Times* television critic Jack Gould comment that both NBC and CBS had a "preoccupation [with] morbid psychiatric themes. . . . [T]here is more to art than muck, misery and mayhem. If characters from . . . insane asylums were as numerous as TV suggested most viewers would be either trustees or hospital orderlies. With all the time and effort that goes into TV shows, it cannot be asking too much of sponsors and networks to try another tack more frequently. Just for shear novelty there could be additional programs about persons of intelligence, wit and substance. Why do so many TV programs apparently hold a grudge against interesting people?"[104] Contrary to Gould's protest, it was not that Helffrich held enmity toward dramas whose characters possessed "intelligence, wit and substance." Nor obviously was it that he refused scripts that dealt honestly with mental illness. Instead, it was Helffrich's interest to assure sympathetic television discourse in shows that dealt with this or any disease. To those who groused about NBC-TV's policy of programs sensitive to mental illness, Helffrich reminded them that "one billion dollars of taxpayer's money" was used to care for three-quarter million patients in mental clinics—more than the combined number of all other hospitals. He notes, "17-million Americans of all ages . . . suffer . . . from mental and emotional disturbances; one in every ten school children." Helffrich concludes, in no uncertain terms to Gould or anyone who complained about the network's prerogative in this area, "[T]he folks who throw . . . stones [at NBC for this] are buck passers more often than not."[105]

"Sweet Violets": WWJ-TV, Detroit

NBC affiliate WWJ-TV, Detroit, gave Helffrich and CA big headaches in November 1951. The local station opted to delete one song, "Sweet Violets," from *The Wayne King Show*, originating live from Chicago and seen only on the NBC Midwest network.[106] WWJ-TV claimed the song was in bad taste even though Wayne King, a swing-era big-band leader, was known for his noncontroversial, sedate dance music. The station insisted this case was different. The popular novelty tune (known as a "teaser") included harmless, double-entendre lyrics that were apparently a bit too edgy for the Detroit of that era. Several renditions of "Sweet Violets" were available by 1950s singers Doris Drew, Jane Turzy, Tony Martin, and Dinah Shore (Shore's version even made it to number three on the popular-music charts).[107] WWJ-TV also deleted "Sweet Violets" from the TV version of *Lights Out* program—an anthology of thriller and mystery dramas. When Helffrich heard about the deletions, he wrote, "I have no idea what this is about. Are the songs dirty?"[108] The song was heard frequently on TV and radio programs but was obviously considered vulgar by the WWJ-TV management.

WWJ-TV carried the program but banned the song by fading out the audio. Viewers at home watched in puzzled silence as people danced without music, and musicians played soundless instruments. Following the local station's "musical excision," Helffrich's office was in a quandary over "Sweet Violets," and the situation was about to get worse because the local newspapers got into the act.

Press coverage alerted local Michigan moral guardians to WWJ-TV's steely resolve, and hundreds of letters of both praise and condemnation were forwarded to New York. Neither Helffrich nor the network needed a new cause celebre over "tasteless" programming during this time of heavy criticism aimed at the young television industry. Charges that all TV genres were violating good taste arrived daily via phone, letter, and telegram at NBC headquarters, New York. Irritated, morally upright viewers incessantly groused about evening gowns exposing too much cleavage, comedians' "vile" comedy material, explicit dance numbers, and, yes, "dirty" song lyrics. Helffrich, therefore, thought it best to let this WWJ-TV incident pass with little comment for fear of exacerbating an already tense situation. Moreover, the complaints came in not only to the network but also to Federal Communications Commission (FCC) commissioners and to dozens of U.S. Congressmen and Senators. Massachusetts Representative Thomas Lane claimed television was "abusing the hospitality of American homes with lewd [lyrics and] images . . . [to] excite those who are underage and distress every adult and suggested a TV censorship board be set up to "scrutinize every telecast in advance, and to cut out all words and actions that arouse . . . passions."[109] Earlier in the year, Connecticut U.S. Senator William Benton actually introduced a bill that called for a TV advisory board appointed by and responsible to the United States Senate that would file a yearly programming report to the government.[110]

Such pointed revulsion with television's product prompted Joseph H. McConnell, then president of the NBC Television Network, to "clean up his own backyard" and send a furious memo to all production personnel, declaring in part: "I am sick and tired of receiving justified criticisms of NBC television programs where bad taste is concerned. . . . It is not acceptable to me that material in bad taste where the American family audience is concerned has in one way or another got on NBC. . . . I don't care one bit who flags it just so somebody does. . . . If something

you think you wouldn't want in your home or the homes of your relatives is going on before your eyes in studio rehearsal or in script, raise
a question whenever you think it will be effective. . . . Any borderline
material not questioned from here on in, and subsequently the target
for public censure, will be the cause of considerably more than censure
from your company's Management for the personnel responsible."[111]
This ultimatum may have had teeth at the network level, but what *local*
stations did was still up to them, and the Detroit affiliate was at it again.

Next, WWJ-TV decided "I Get Ideas," a song made popular by Louis
Armstrong and Peggy Lee (with their respective renditions recorded in
spring and summer of 1951), was also in bad taste. The station banned it
from NBC's popular show *Your Hit Parade*, sponsored by Lucky Strike
cigarettes.[112] WWJ-TV master-control engineers were directed to delete
the audio portion of the broadcast whenever the song was played. Again
in its place, Detroit viewers experienced silence for two minutes but
this time saw a slide on their TV screens reading: "This portion of the
program omitted in the interest of good taste."[113] Helffrich complains,
"Regardless of [WWJ's] autonomy . . . refusal of the station to [carry this
song] raises complicated problems for broadcasters."[114] That may have
been true, but some viewers favored the censorship. A letter of gratitude
from the League of Catholic Women of Detroit reads in part, "My hat
is off to WWJ-TV for the action they have taken . . . to refuse to allow
into decent houses the suggestive songs which have been TV'd in the
past."[115] This particular "suggestive" song, "I Get Ideas," was a remake
of a 1932 work by Dorcas Cochran and Julio Cesar A. Sanders, based
on an Argentine tango.

A viewer in Lapeer, Michigan, who saw nothing wrong with either
song, mailed a letter of support to NBC. Helffrich included it in his CA
report of December 17, 1951, as "a little Christmas present since so few
. . . take the time to praise an action which has caused other[s] . . . to
complain." A portion of it reads: "There is nothing wrong with 'Sweet
Violets' or 'I Get Ideas' and I can't understand why they should be allowed to be played for months then all of a sudden be stopped. These
songs have been on 'Hit Parade' for well over 12 weeks and I don't think
the public could be wrong. . . . Probably some . . . had their minds in
the gutter, and decided that millions of people were wrong and they
and only they should have the say. I myself do not have such a low mind

and I don't think the majority of the public has either."[116] In Jack Gould's *New York Times* column of November 26, 1951, the television critic "took violent exception to [WWJ-TV's] censorship of the original *Hit Parade* rendition of 'I Get Ideas'" and called for network action.[117] NBC's legal department shrugged, "We cannot require the broadcaster to transmit material which it reasonably believes to be against the public interest."[118] In Detroit, just a week earlier, Harry Bannister, beleaguered WWJ-TV general manager defended his decision and called for acceptance of an industry-developed censorship code: "This television business is NOT radio. It's too powerful, too vivid, too compelling to be allowed to run loose."[119] Songs like "I Get Ideas" and "Sweet Violets" were issues of major controversy when the Cold War raged. Both the patriotic and pious exhorted that simply being exposed to such songs (jokes, comic books, movies, TV, and the like) would corrode proper values and work to tear apart the nuclear family—America's secret weapon against an advancing fifth column.

Such strident condemnation against sensual themes may also have been a reaction to the increased sexually playful musical styles that were being embraced by white, mainstream adolescents, a harbinger of the soon-to-arrive rock 'n' roll era. As the so-called youth culture took root, the social and market parameters of what was acceptable in popular music changed, and that shift was obviously felt in broadcasting. For example, Shore, Ethel Merman, and Tony Bennett each had hits with a "naughty" novelty song, "Doing What Comes Natur'lly," from Irving Berlin's 1946 smash musical *Annie Get Your Gun*.

Newly popular was the sensuous singing style of Lee, as was Rosemary Clooney's sexy and joyously raucous first big hit, "Come on-a My House."[120] Folks could now see and hear TV production numbers of these popular songs—songs whose sheet music or recordings they would have never actively sought out. Some were shocked by what they had "invited into their homes," and others, of course, delighted.

So just how did Helffrich and the network brass resolve the problem of WWJ-TV's "audio cancellation" of "I Get Ideas" on *Your Hit Parade*? To atone for the interruption, NBC-TV awarded the advertising agency that produced the show for the American Tobacco Company, Batton, Barton, Durstine, and Osborn, two extra minutes of commercial time on the network, while the amount of compensation shared with the

Detroit affiliate was deducted pro rata.[121] Because the two main sources of station income were local commercial sales and network revenue sharing—where affiliate compensation in populous urban centers like Detroit could exceed $1 million a year—how to deal with future problems of this type became clear: trust NBC and its policies to handle all questions of "good taste." Besides, as Barry R. Litman, a broadcast economist, explains, "Having a network affiliation [meant] the difference between profits and losses, life and death."[122] Affiliated stations earned so much of their money from the network that NBC had tremendous bargaining power over them, as was surely the case with WWJ-TV.[123] When the NBC Detroit affiliate realized that interrupting or modifying network programming would lose them money, the "high-minded" practice appears to have ceased and stood as a warning to other affiliates. Helffrich never again writes about such problems in any CA report.

While sexual, profane, vulgar, or insensitive language were points of negotiation for Helffrich and American postwar television, another pivotal area of concern was violent programming, an area about which viewers incessantly grumbled.

6. TV Violence

*O*n the heels of World War II, a national survey asked, "Do you know what television is?" and "Have you ever seen a television set in operation?" Some respondents claimed to have had "heard talk" of television, but in 1945, most Americans had never seen a TV picture.[1] Four years later, about 2 percent, or approximately twelve million, American homes had television sets. By 1954, this number increased threefold to over thirty-two million.[2] In the stretch of just a few years, an astonishing seventy-eight million Americans—more than half the population of the country—were watching television. Children spent more time with it than radio, comic books, friends, and family combined.[3] Concern grew over what effect this ubiquitous new commercial medium might have on children, especially in the area of violence, as television became a staple of American culture.

Portrayals of violence in American mass media have historically caused anxiety among the nation's moral guardians. During the nineteenth century, numerous vice societies cautioned that crime stories in newspapers and dime novels would eventually sweep impressionable young readers down the river of wanton misdeed.[4] In the 1920s, righteous conservators were horrified at what they considered sin and mayhem in the cinema. Their concerns informed early movie censorship codes and the Payne Fund studies of the late 1920s.[5] Radio crime dramas and popular detective magazines were next accused of continuing and reinforcing the chaos. In 1948, comic-book gore and violence were cited as contributing to adolescent delinquency, forcing the Association of Comic Magazine Publishers to draft a code banning torture, sadomasochism, and detailed accounts of criminal acts.[6] Then along came network television.

The First Congressional Probe

In the spring of 1952, Arkansas Representative Ezekial Candler Gathings introduced a congressional resolution—HR 278—sanctioning the first investigation of "television programs [that] . . . place improper empha-sis upon crime, violence, and corruption." The congressman had seen what he termed a "hootchy-kootchy dance" on the television show *You Asked For It*, declaring the program "obscene and lewd." Gathings also attributed to the influence of television a wave of college "panty raids" and other "violent" crime, causing trade magazine *Sponsor* to write, "Whether consciously or not, the medium is engaged in a battle for respectability."[7] After more than five hundred pages of testimony that spanned nearly two weeks of hearings, the Committee on Interstate and Foreign Commerce was unable to come to "any conclusive judgment."[8] However, writes mass-communication historian Keisha L. Hoerrner, thus set a familiar cycle—what she calls the "establishment of the 'game' played between the broadcasting industry . . . and Congress. . . . The accepted activity of discussing the problem [of media violence] seems useful to all the players of the game, as the public is assured that both Congress and the industry are concerned about children. No further action is attempted by either side, however. The rules established in 1952 remained in place for decades to follow, so the game could be played over and over again to everyone's benefit."[9] Hoerrner maintains her observation is an example of "symbolic politics," a theory developed by political scientist Murray Edelman.[10] The Edelman hypothesis suggests that Congress and industry, in this case the broadcast industry, regu-larly engage in metaphorical rather than essential public discussion in an effort to assuage and beguile public opinion. By using this "all talk and no action" gambit, both sides appear concerned and "working for change," but, in the end, no substantive legislation is passed to alter the status quo.

But this does not mean such government/industry efforts bore no fruit. While threatened government-legislated structural change of commercial broadcasting did not happen, early congressional inquiries did have the effect of prompting network television to reexamine pro-gramming and bolster its self-censorship codes. NBC-TV's chief censor Stockton Helffrich made certain that substantive change *did* occur in early programs, as did his counterparts at CBS-TV, Herb Carlborg, and at ABC-TV, Grace Johnson.[11] For that reason, any direct govern-ment intervention—which would have undoubtedly infringed upon the First Amendment—was unnecessary. Helffrich's Continuity Acceptance

Department took seriously its obligation by timely and conspicuous response to public criticism or by working proactively so that opprobrium toward network television by citizen and government alike was avoided or at least diminished.

Violence on Chicago Television—A Case Study

On the Monday after Christmas 1952, television columnist Jack Mabley's report stretched eight columns across the front page of the *Chicago Daily News*. Just beneath the masthead, a banner headline screamed "TV's Holiday Fare for Kids: It's Murder," and four photos of bloody television mayhem spread from margin to margin. One of the disturbing pictures, poached from a television screen during its broadcast, was a tableau of a man shot and bleeding, crawling on hands and knees up the steps of a church.[12] "That had impact," Mabley writes. "Anyway, it helped. For a while."[13] The columnist reports that during the final week of 1952, a group of thirty "concerned parents" monitored Chicago television stations for depictions of violence. By the end of the first four days of viewing, the group had counted seventy-seven murders, over fifty shootings, nearly sixty fistfights, and varying totals of kidnappings, robberies, and knifings.[14] In another front-page story the next day, Mabley reported as fact some questionable conclusions he extrapolated from the still incomplete and clearly unscientific content analysis. He wrote that the survey revealed more than twenty-five hundred violent crimes and nearly a thousand murders were broadcast each year to Chicago area viewers, many of them children. Youngsters from four to ten years of age, watching as little as two hours of television a day, "see every conceivable method of killing by gunfire, strangulation, stabbing, poisoning, drowning, suffocating and beating," Mabley declares.[15] However, it was not until New Year's Eve 1952, in yet another front-page story, that Mabley disclosed it was he and the *Daily News* that instigated the "survey [of] juvenile TV fare."[16]

Mabley had contacted Mrs. Leighton Cooney, a PTA officer at a local school who had "taken a lively interest in children's [TV] programming,"[17] to organize the "study." Cooney masterminded a schedule and contacted likeminded parents in Winnetka, Glenview, West Chicago, and Wilmette, Illinois, to monitor all children's programs from December 25 through 9 P.M. December 31, on WENR-TV, WGN-TV, WBKB-

TV, and WNBQ-TV, Chicago's four commercial broadcasting stations. Wilmette, by the way, was overrepresented in the survey and, not so coincidentally, was the suburb in which Mabley lived at the time.[18] In all cases, mothers were assigned to watch one station a day, with fathers and some teenagers pitching in, too.[19]

Mabley, a concerned parent as well as a television columnist and critic, had long been an advocate of toning down violent and offensive TV fare. As early as 1951, he recommended Chicago broadcasters categorize and label their television offerings. "They could have three kinds of programs," Mabley advises, specifying shows "for children, for the family, and [for] adult entertainment."[20] Also, his column once instructed all parents to teach their kids that TV cowboy mayhem and fisticuffs were not acceptable ways to handle disagreements.[21] But it was Mabley's series of articles on excessive television violence that shocked the moral guardians of Chicago, prompting a hotly contested debate—most of it played out on the pages of the *Daily News.* The monitors watched 134 shows during the week from Christmas to New Year's Eve 1952, Mabley reported, counting a final total of 295 violent crimes, 93 of which were murders.[22]

Outraged parents and community leaders flooded the newspaper with angry letters, wires, and telephone calls over what they perceived as dangerous television content. The storm of protests included a Chicago woman who maintained, "We as parents are trying to fight juvenile delinquency. . . . Why then must such [television] slop be thrown at them?" Another, identifying herself only as "a frustrated mother," asked, "Are these programs aimed to undermine the youth of America by subversive agents? They could hardly be more damaging had they been planned by the communists." Pastor Reuben T. Nyren's sent a righteous missive that was fully reproduced on page 3 of the January 2, 1953, edition of the *Daily News*, in which he notes that the Christmas Day "Chicago television bloodbath" would "give occasion to atheistic communist peoples to point with ridicule to America's observance of Christmas."[23]

By the second week of January 1953, Chicago Police Commissioner Timothy J. O'Connor weighed in: "I'm certain there must be a relation between these television programs and the rise in crime."[24] The same day, Alderman John J. Hoellen introduced a resolution asking the City

Council of Chicago to "investigate . . . crime and violence on children's TV programs . . . and correct the situation."[25] Earlier, Hoellen said he believed there was a clear "connection between the showing of [TV] crime films and the increase of teenage crime in Chicago."[26]

Chicago City Council Judicial Subcommittee hearings on the volatile subject would begin in mid-January culminating in a full report and hearing two months later. If the local Chicago stations did not "give clear evidence of their good intentions" during the city-council probe, Mabley predicted "extreme embarrassment" for broadcasters "that could lead to federal action to prevent renewal of their licenses." The crusading reporter vowed he would continue the pressure on the stations "until the present situation no longer exists. . . . Anyone who thinks that the current exposure of crime in children's shows is merely a circulation stunt which will soon blow over seriously underestimates the deep sincerity behind this campaign." That statement notwithstanding, interest generated in the controversy accrued favorably for the *Daily News* and Mabley. The reporter next contacted the management of each Chicago station for reaction to the controversy. WGN-TV, WBKB-TV, and WNBQ-TV (the NBC owned and operated) had "no comment," but WENR-TV's general manager, John H. Norton Jr., responded. Norton said that while the *Daily News*'s criticism was not unfounded, Mabley and the others had ignored other key factors. Norton reminded that in America, a viewer was free to change the channel or turn the set off if unhappy with programming, and he lectured parents not to use television as a babysitter for their children—providing essentially the Helffrichian argument. He also chided Mabley and the monitors for ignoring many "splendid" nonviolent shows, citing as examples, among others, *Ozzie and Harriet* and *Beulah*. "Of one thing we are certain," concluded Norton jingoistically, "our American system of telecasting is the best in the world and enables us to produce more good programs than are available in any other country."[27]

By the time the judicial-subcommittee report was ready for a public hearing, other significant events had transpired. At least one local advertiser, Mages Stores for Sports, switched its advertising from Sunday afternoon movies to soccer games. Owner Morris Mages said that until Mabley and the *Daily News* had provided what he termed "documentary proof," he had not "realized the adverse effect some of these movies on

TV might have." Mages pledged to carefully screen any future movie he sponsored to assure only "clean entertainment [went] into homes where children are watching."[28]

By early March 1953, Mabley was taking credit for the significant ratings drop in televised afternoon cowboy and action shows. During December 1952 and January 1953, the American Research Bureau surveyed ten of Chicago's most popular adventure or cowboy films and discovered a near 40 percent drop in aggregate audience after Mabley's crime series ran. Some of the significant losers were *Hopalong Cassidy* sliding from a rating of 19.6 to 13.3, *Gene Autry* going from 13.8 to 7.2, and *Adventure Time Theatre* losing more than half its audience, plunging to 7.5 from 14.7.[29]

Harry Ward, NBC's Continuity Acceptance director in Chicago, represented WNBQ-TV at the council committee hearings on March 20, 1953. Ward characterized the testimony as "a cooperative effort of all stations in meeting the intemperate criticisms resulting from Jack Mabley's series in the *Daily News*," continuing with a flourish, "Here for the first time in the history of man, the television industry of Chicago has put up a united front." That was factual to a point, but Mabley later pointed out *only* WNBQ-TV—a station he characterized as having "the highest standards in Chicago for children's shows"—had dispatched a top executive as their representative to the council proceedings. The other broadcast outlets sent low-level managers, suggesting to Mabley that top management considered the issue of television violence unimportant: "If other station's had WNBQ's standards there'd be no need for council investigations."[30] Such a statement suggests Ward performed an invaluable public-relations service for the O&O by attending that city-council meeting.

Each station representative and supporting witnesses hammered away at two key points: there is no link between television and juvenile delinquency; and censorship is aberrantly un-American. Thus also began a protelevision public-relations barrage including a doctor from the Psychiatric Institute of Chicago who testified, "Not one of over 2,000 juvenile offenders questioned . . . attributed his downfall directly or indirectly to television." (The only exception: a marijuana user who said he smoked the substance after viewing a public-service announcement that advised against recreational drugs use). Similar testimony came from a representative of the Chicago Bar Association, who declared that TV had not motivated juvenile criminals to misconduct, in fact "just the opposite." A Chicago Crime Commission delegate took issue with Alderman Hoellen's resolution that first prompted the city council's inquiry, testifying there had been no rise in juvenile crime as assumed, certifying that the peak year for such delinquency was 1945—well before the arrival of television in Chicago. The only real opposition came from one Chicago parent and grandparent who agreed with Police Commissioner O'Connor's ungrounded statement that the deleterious effects of television crime shows on children "may not be apparent for six months to a year." Finally, in an unprecedented joint statement by the four Chicago television stations—coordinated by Howard Bell of the National Association of Radio and Television Broadcasters (NARTB)— the broadcasters declared "their devotion to the best interests of the City . . . and the people of Chicago." Their unified statement again insisted that yoking actual crime to television crime would be like calling the classic plays of Shakespeare "crime plays" or labeling "the daily newspapers of Chicago . . . crime papers," concluding, "Even the Bible would be suspect on this theory."[31]

After all testimony was in, the Chicago City Council's Judicial Subcommittee passed a toothless "recommendation" that urged the local television industry to "improve its product by strict self-policing." It should set up "an effective self-regulating organization similar" to the movies' Hays Commission, preached the council. The irascible Mabley in his follow-up column remarked, "Such [self-]policing [had better] be tougher than the ineffective [NARTB] Code of Good Practice which allegedly governs the nation's TV stations," wryly adding, "In Chicago it's a joke."[32] But a scolding was about all the Chicago City Council could muster since the question of television censorship is and will always be a federal issue and does not fall under local government jurisdiction. It was, however, good politics.

The disposition of this contentious event takes us back to the argument by historian Hoerrner. She observes that when a given public perceives a threat to children—specifically television violence imagined as promoting antisocial behavior—a symbolic game begins among the governed, the government and, in this case, the broadcasting industry.[33] By openly "discussing" the problem, the public is assured that both government and offending enterprise are sufficiently interested in the welfare of children. But because of America's deep anxiety over government-imposed or legislated censorship, no further action is usually taken or even necessary in the short run. The industry is reprimanded and told to police itself, which it does for a period until it is again necessary for another public outcry and new rounds of government scrutiny. Such tautology is part and parcel of the Edelman hypothesis of metaphorical rather than essential public discussion.[34]

But, even before the government got involved with public hearings on violence, NBC-TV's chief censor Stockton Helffrich was at work toning down excessive mayhem with a particular eye toward an abiding social taboo: suicide.

Personal Violence: Suicide

As early as 1948, five years before initial congressional hearings, Helffrich wrote of his concern over violence in the first telecast of the *Chevrolet on Broadway* dramatic anthology series.[35] Its inaugural offering was entitled "Home Life of a Buffalo," a tale of a depressed vaudevillian who decides to kill himself and his family by turning on a kitchen gas jet. Thinking better of it, the show ends with the melancholy character shutting off the gas, rejecting suicide, and embracing new hope. The program ran, despite Helffrich's protest, with no deletions. He writes, "The production detail of showing the gas being turned on [was] entirely too suggestive," and advised the programming department that NBC-TV could be held responsible for any copycat suicide attempts.[36] In a rare *reperformance* of the show a week later, Helffrich again noted his "grave concern because of the overly graphic and realistic treatment of [the] attempted suicide sequence," concluding it was "highly suggestive to any vulnerable viewer." Until Helffrich's significant objection, programming managers seemed oblivious to the public-relations damage such shows could cause the network. The program department later agreed future plays with similar themes "should avoid any detailing of suicide methods."[37]

But similar plays *were* produced, and Helffrich was always on hand to remove anything that could potentially "harm" viewers or the network. For example, on the *Philco TV Playhouse*, he substituted the phrase *sleeping pill* for the brand-name depressant "Seconal" because the *Responsibility: A Working Manual of NBC Program Policies* states,

"The specification of poisons by name are not [to be] presented in such detail as to invite imitation." Helffrich comments, "We endeavor to give out as little specific information as possible to potential suicides, killers, etc."[38] Although Helffrich explicitly rejected the brand name, the phrase *sleeping pill* was still used—how that might not invite imitation remains unclear.

Frequently, the Continuity Acceptance Radio/Television (CART) reports made certain that programs eschewed specific techniques of suicide or homicide. For example, in the show "Ladies in Retirement," seen on the *Kraft Television Theatre*, Helffrich passed a "strangulation scene" that he considered essential to the plot but required the strangling sequence to be "handled more by suggestion than . . . detail."[39] In a *Lights Out* episode, Helffrich recommended that one of two suicides be changed "to an accidental rather than intentional death"[40] and let stand a self-murder of drinking deadly cleaning fluid in a *Robert Montgomery Presents* program. Helffrich actually passed the death-by-poison period piece over objections from the Lysol Company, makers of a household disinfectant, writing mordantly, "Historically speaking, I don't think Lysol existed at the time of the drama."[41] Occasionally, as Helffrich found out, uneditable violent events occurred in the midst of an on-the-spot, unrehearsed program. During the live broadcast of an interview show, *We, The People*, a police rescue squad was to simulate negotiations with an actor playing a suicidal man threatening to jump from the ledge of a New York City building.[42] While the simulation was in progress, a gathering crowd watching from the street below spontaneously began to yell "sadistic encouragement" to the jumper. Network timing considerations meant the live segment could not be cut, but by carefully selecting less-offensive video images from the multiple camera shoot, censors on hand reported it was considerably "toned down." While noting the crowds actions as disturbing, the actual "broadcast brought us in no criticisms," writes a relieved Helffrich.[43] Helffrich did not shrink from minor changes to full deletions of suicide-themed programs, nor did he establish an outright ban of them. Instead, he argued that suicide happens regularly in life and saw such realism as indispensable to television drama.[44] Early-television writer Tad Mosel recalls his first teleplay, a story of suicide and adultery, was passed by NBC.[45] However, Helffrich frequently insists that taking one's life should not be "presented as a satisfactory solution for any human problem"—a line taken directly from the NBC-TV *Responsibility* manual. Here is a clear and fundamental tension in Helffrich's tacit policy. He believes realism indispensable, yet he diluted teleplays depicting explicit or gratuitous violence. Those scripts, Helffrich says, gave "the morbid in our audience someone with whom to identify and . . . emulate." As for suicide, he states, "The mentally sick need encouragement to get well and keep living rather than too many examples . . . [of] people throwing in the sponge."[46] Apparently, Helffrich wanted the possible events of real life but without the specificity of gore. Although ultimately a puzzling and difficult balancing act, Helffrich's approach fits his activist attitude against encouraging television presentations that depicted the mentally ill in a less-than-favorable light.

The Effects of Television

Obviously, Helffrich and others imagined television as an irresistible force with powers that could alter a viewer's perception and behavior. By television's overwhelming adoption and rapid diffusion throughout the nation, early gatekeepers knew they were unleashing a medium unprecedented on the American culture. Abundant anecdotal evidence also suggests that television stimulated interest and sales in a variety of products from lipstick to aluminum foil.[47] However, whether or not witnessing feigned television violence in entertainment programming—like specific techniques of suicide or homicide—actually prompted copycat behavior remained unclear. During the medium's formative days, no one could predict viewer reaction, but Helffrich and others were aware that television's power for good or evil remained unplumbed in the first decades after World War II.

In 1949, Helffrich reported that WTMJ-TV, NBC's always-cautious Milwaukee affiliate, carried *The Clock*, a violent mystery drama, "on a delayed basis as a result of local audience pressures" Perhaps by seeing a dramatized shooting, stabbing, or bludgeoning on television, Helffrich muses, a viewer's response "might be similar to how movie patrons reacted when they first saw kissing or the shooting of a gun . . . in early cinema."[48] Could a home television viewer be similarly affected?

Helffrich's observation was very similar to a phenomenon attributed to nascent motion pictures called "the train effect."[49] Historian Stephen

Bottomore explains, "In the early years [of movies 1894 to 1913], there were instances of audience members flinching and feeling nervous while watching films of approaching trains or other vehicles; on occasion there was a stronger reaction and it is just possible that in some rare cases there was some audience panic."[50] An 1896 Thomas Edison short, *The Kiss*, in which actors John Rice and May Irwin smooch in a close-up, prompted early and violent indignation from the procensorship set. Film historian Robert C. Toll cites a Chicago newspaper critic as saying after the movie premier, "Magnified to gargantuan proportions, [the kiss] is absolutely disgusting. . . . Such things call for police intervention."[51] Linda Williams, a cultural historian, claims that moral guardians actually found violent pornography in a filmed sneeze. *The Sneeze*, produced sometime between 1894 and 1896 and considered Edison's earliest film, was the first movie to use an actor and employ a cinematic close-up. The eighty-one-frame short ostensibly shows an attractive young woman sneezing. In her discussion, Williams relates that Barnet Phillips, a reporter for *Harper's Weekly* (who suggested using a woman rather than Edison's mustachioed technician, Fred Ott), printed and analyzed several frames of the film by parsing them into such elements as "nascent sensation" and "expectancy," culminating in "beatitude . . . oblivion . . . explosion . . . and ecstasy." Williams's point is that a "pretty young woman lent prurient interest to the [violent albeit] involuntary comic action of a sneeze[, and the film] stands as a marker in the trajectory of the prehistoric . . . motion studies of [Eadweard] Muybridge . . . [to] the more advanced stages of primitive [hard core] cinema."[52] Could viewer reactions to violent depictions in early television be similar? On this point, no one knew for sure.

As the forms and effects of television programming were literally in the process of invention and discovery, references on what to cut were scarce. Video censors relied upon standards and practices fashioned from movie and radio codes as well as their personal reading of audience taste and sense of decorum. Moreover, only a few "scientific" theories of the "effects" of mass media, not yet tested in television, were floating about the culture. One of those theories, circulating since the mid-1930s, was the "direct-effects model" or hypodermic-needle model. This now-discredited hypothesis suggested that media inject powerful messages into the culture, and the helpless, hypnotized mass respond in ways prescribed by those messages. As movies and radio began their rise in the 1920s and 1930s, the direct-effects model or "cause and effect model" was introduced by German academics, among them Theodor W. Adorno and Max Horkheimer, from the Institute of Social Research, also known as the Frankfurt School.[53]

Considering Helffrich's strong negative reaction to the portrayal of suicides or other violent behavior on television, he appeared to embrace the direct-effects model. However, in cases of television violence being watched by children, his evaluation relied heavily on the responsibility of parents. For example, when a column by Walter Winchell of the *New York Daily Mirror* linked the mass media to easily copied violent acts, Helffrich's reaction was different. The item in Winchell's column reads: "It happened in mid-town last week. . . . A five-year-old tot, after being thrilled by so wholesome a story as *Peter Pan*, was caught just in time as she gleefully cried, 'I'm going to fly like a fairy!' and was almost out the window." Helffrich grumbled, "It's a bit annoying . . . to have to combat some of the pretty preposterous charges of irresponsibility hurled at broadcasters." He railed that "everybody" blamed television "continually" from "extremists like Dr. Fredric Wertham to the most well intentioned housewife for the anti-social eruptions of children." While allowing that television had "a very definite responsibility" to children, Helffrich insists parents could not escape culpability in the matter.[54]

Helffrich quickly cites others in censorship reports whose opinions matched his on parental responsibility. He delights in "tweaking the oversimplification set"[55] and excerpted press accounts of author and culture critic Max Wylie's public feud with Fredric Wertham, the psychologist who led a crusade against violent comic books. Wertham's 1954 book, *Seduction of the Innocent*, "exposed" the industry by using what most experts agree were hysterical sophistry and exaggerated polemics.[56] "Every time [Wertham] gets into a twitch," said Wylie to *Variety*, "he blames juvenile delinquency on the Ford Foundation, *Dragnet* and the like. . . . To what would he have attributed a comparable outburst of sexual violence forty years ago? Chautauqua?"[57] Helffrich next quotes Dr. Paul G. Edgar of the New York State Guidance Clinic who confirms that television *without supervision* can be "abused . . . [and] destructive."[58] The implicit argument is that television, comic books, or other mass media do not plague society with social problems, but far too lenient or uncaring parents do. On one occasion, a viewer complained that an electrocution scene in a *Ford Theatre* drama was "unsuitable for little children who had stayed up late to see it."[59] Helffrich lectures this parent not on the appropriateness of exhibiting death by electric chair on television but on permitting his child to stay up so late: "The program is featured from 9:30–10 P.M.," notes Helffrich, "[and] we submit in all sincerity our view that little children ought certainly be denied TV viewing rights by that time of day."[60] While always recognizing NBC-TV shared "a very definite responsibility"[61] toward younger viewers, he labels as "unfair" any liability parents placed upon the network for their children's bad "reaction . . . to television fare offered from roughly nine o'clock in the evening to sign off time."[62] Similarly, when New York television critic John Crosby chided NBC-TV's "house built"[63] show *Lights Out* as being too morbid for featuring "a plague of rodents," Helffrich again deigns the show "appropriate" since it played after 9:30 P.M. reiterating, "Parents have got to take responsibly for what their children watch."[64]

This frequent theme of parental accountably weaves itself throughout the CART reports. It suggests Helffrich may have theorized that television was simply *not* puissant enough to cause most viewers to change their existing behaviors. By this notion, television only *confirmed* certain social values and cultural attitudes extant in the 1950s, but it did not influence or affect them. Also, as early as 1951, Helffrich comments, "Conclusions on the behavior patterns of children cannot be solely confined to media influences since . . . other factors exist."[65] Communication-effects researcher Wilbur Schramm dubbed a similar concept "the minimal-effects model" and after conducting numerous tests, surveys, and inquiries throughout the late 1950s, released his findings in 1961. Although well before Schramm's findings, Helffrich's ideas are compatible with Schramm's explanation of the minimal-effects model, which the latter describes: "For *some* children, under *some* conditions, *some* television is harmful. For *other* children under the same conditions, or for some of the same children under *other* conditions, it may be beneficial. For *most* children, under *most* conditions, *most* television is neither particularly harmful nor particularly beneficial."[66] Schramm also explains that the term *media effect* is misleading and that the term suggests television "acts" upon viewers who are inert:

"Nothing could be further from the fact. . . . It is the children . . . who use television, rather than television that uses them."[67] This "uses and gratifications model" suggests agency on behalf of the viewer and acts as a middle way between the direct and minimal-effects archetypes. The "uses" model in mass-media research addresses the *function* and *meaning* rather than cultural *impact* of the television medium. Nonetheless, notions of how meaning is made by and through television texts remain a central area of investigation for postmodern cultural studies scholars.[68]

Helffrich's actions demonstrate that he wanted to appease viewers calling for less violence while also upholding his notions of quality television. Recall his decision on one program concerning the use of a brand-name sleeping pill in a suicidal overdose scene. Helffrich says that allowing names of actual poisons sanctioned imitation. He cut the brand name of sleeping pill that prompted the death but permitted broadcast of the suicide. Why was not watching a demonstrated suicide technique also considered an act that sanctioned imitation? Plainly, Helffrich imagined the medium with very specific direct-effects on its viewers, but his association of "quality television" with "realism" prompted a capricious middle-ground decision. Yet, in comments noted during the *Peter Pan* illustration above, Helffrich also appears to embrace the minimal-effects model. It appears that Helffrich made his decisions according to a changeable combination of sometimes one theory, sometimes both, sometimes neither, or perhaps some quiescent unnamed notion of the moment. Having little to chart his course, Helffrich called upon any reasonable idea that fit a given censorial situation. From 1948 to 1951, he appeared to rely what he called "common sense." In addition, Helffrich regularly studied thousands of critical letters, telegrams, and phone calls that poured into NBC-TV and used them to intuit viewer trends or hot spots in language and violence to be avoided. In the main, however, he looked at each question of taste separately, determining his censorship of controversial images and words by the context of the script and time slot of the program or commercial in question.

Helffrich also acted as a tireless booster of television, traveling around the northeast, giving speeches to concerned professional, civic, and parents groups and solidifying his position as one of NBC-TV's premier public-relations voices. He called attacks on television violence "hog wash" and "lies" and was quick to shift liability away from the network while still encouraging program suppliers to insert conflict into their shows. For instance, just before the 1955 Kefauver juvenile-delinquency investigation commenced, Helffrich suggests to crime-story *Dragnet* producers some of their programs "seemed a little too brutal in light of current senatorial subcommittee interest in *so-called* violence on television." Still, in the next breath, he states, "We are quite aware that producers have to establish conflict by the use of violence . . . [but should] not [go] beyond that point." Harnessing the excesses in the creative urge is what censorship is all about, Helffrich lectures, for by not cutting "the length and degree of mayhem[,] . . . sadism [and] sensationalism" result in a scenario, he says, that can cause "audience criticism hurt[ing] the company's, the talent's, and the client's public relations." His spin on the effect violent television had on children was a fairly common response within the broadcast industry. When organized collections of teachers and parents (or other "special-interest groups") complained, citing negative television studies on broadcast violence, Helffrich frequently countered with his own *positive* studies. Quoting, among others, a Yale Divinity School survey, 69 percent of parents who own television sets [in the New Haven, Connecticut, market] "generally favored children's programming as they are. . . . Only one quarter of the objections were directed at 'excessive violence' in a non-humorous context on children's TV."[69]

General Violence

The ways in which television conjured graphic violence in the 1950s were numerous but mostly pretty tame. For example, the postwar television audience might hear the sound of a weapon discharging and see the intended victim clutch his chest and fall to the ground, but the audience would witness little if any bloodshed in a scene portraying a gun murder. That said, there were still many cruel and unusual ways postwar TV writers called for sadomasochism in their teleplays *before* script vetting and actual production.

Helffrich's early CART reports document many gruesome death or torture sequences modified or censored outright by NBC-TV. Deleted from one 1949 script was what Helffrich termed a "juicy sequence" whereby a sadistic criminal illustrates his "murderous proclivities by squeezing a guinea pig's neck accompanied by appropriate sound effects." On a *Dragnet* episode, the scenario called for a small elderly woman to be repeatedly stabbed with an ice pick that was then used to crucify "her to the floor . . . through hands, legs and feet." It was quickly removed and, in a masterpiece of understatement, Helffrich changed this action to having the criminal "slug the old lady and escape . . . with her life savings." In another sadistic scene, the action called for "hanging somebody from the rafters [by] his feet and 'caressing' him with a hot poker." Needless to say, it, too, was removed. In *Hey Mulligan*, a short-lived sitcom starring Mickey Rooney, a script had Rooney "hitting a man in the mouth . . . feeling his [teeth] cave in and his skull crackling like cellophane." This gore was also excised. In the same series, and with Helffrich's blessing, the NBC-TV Los Angeles Continuity Acceptance Department demanded that another *Hey Mulligan* script be completely rewritten "because of excess brutality . . . [by a] sadistic character using brass knuckles, broken beer bottles, etc., [and for making] morons out of police." Rejected completely was a fifteen-minute "educational" film on the tribes of Africa featuring "natives plastering the hair of their [forefathers] . . . to their heads with blood and cow dung [followed by] poachers killing all [of them] . . . and smoking opium to boot."[70] Each of these examples notwithstanding, Helffrich, clearly, permitted more forms of violence and morbidity on television than he allowed sex. While it is true he "toned down" some aspects of video violence by script deletion or rewrite, Helffrich did not—indeed, he could not for fear of losing audience—ban violence outright.

Violence, death, and mayhem are central and important storytelling devices, used throughout history in powerful drama. Their use simply could not escape television programming. In an NBC-TV *Hallmark Hall of Fame* presentation of *Macbeth*, some newspaper critics were captious of Duncan's murder scene, commenting it could have been done a little less bloody. Helffrich strongly disagrees, "How do you establish . . . a basis in reality . . . for Lady Macbeth if you have no indication that actual blood did indeed irrevocably soil her hands?"[71] Realism in literature, theater, and early television *meant* violence more than it meant the use of sex or strong language—although the occasional "damn" or "hell" was permitted for the sake of realism. But just because he refused to expurgate Shakespeare does not mean Helffrich was shy about editing the great masters of literature for television.

Helffrich was unafraid to tame Luigi Pirandello and mercilessly expurgated *The Letter*, based upon W. Somerset Maugham's 1927 play. The program was to run as the first installment in yet another NBC-TV dramatic anthology series, this one sponsored by Lucky Strike cigarettes. In the opening sequence, a woman kills her paramour and later admits the death and adulterous affair to her "trusting spouse." Here Helffrich had to deal with the double whammy of murder *and* fornication: "Both points can be adequately handled without [removing] them at the expense of the plot."[72] First, Helffrich refused to permit the initial scene of the woman shooting six bullets into her estranged lover, as originally written. Instead, the opening television action picks up immediately *after* the shooting, with the character of murderess Leslie Crosbie standing atop the veranda, her smoking gun still pointed and her eyes on her victim. Secondly, Crosbie's husband's involvement in covering up her homicide is emphasized rather than the issue of adultery. Finally, since no crime can go unpunished on television, the dead lover's husband, using only shadows to suggest the plunging of a dagger through the heart, "tastefully" kills the murderess herself.[73]

This theme of evildoer never escaping punishment is a carryover from the old movie pandect and was reiterated in the NBC *Responsibility* manual and NARTB code, both of which Helffrich held as exemplars.[74] For example, the original scene of a 1949 *Chevrolet on Broadway* script called for a child murder at a bus terminal. As the story ends, a character mentions the perpetrator was not caught. Helffrich shot back very specific instructions to the producer regarding this unacceptable conclusion: "The final arrangement will not feature the girl being murdered before camera and there will be inserted at the close a shot of a gendarme running down the street blowing a whistle to make it obvious that the crime will not go unpunished."[75] The stated reason for such censorship was to prevent copycat crimes by the socially derelict. It was believed that without respect for state authority and law, there would occur a rip in the discursive cultural fabric and the very foundations of civilized society might be threatened. And in the 1950s, civilized society had much to worry about, both from television and juvenile crime.

Television Violence, Juvenile Delinquency, and the Kefauver Committee

A 1954 George Gallup poll asked Americans if the mass media were contributing to juvenile wrongdoing. More than 70 percent of respondents said yes, citing television and comic books as major players in the so-called delinquency problem.[76] So why the sudden interest in connecting mass-media portrayals of violence to what was perceived as a growing national issue?

Media researchers Ellen Wartella and Sharon Mazzarella suggest there was nothing at all "sudden" about it. Wartella and Mazzarella trace back to the 1920s a nascent, peer-driven "youth culture" that was "independent of adults, outside the home, unsupervised, and increasingly commercialized."[77] By the 1940s, a bona fide, high-school–targeted teen market was in place and increasingly took its cues from the mass media. Moreover, anecdotally, postwar adolescents seemed to change. Parents had to endure and make sense of the different haircuts, music, dances, fashions, and the vernacular used by their offspring when addressing their elders—not to mention what was seen as their shameless, overtly sexual conduct. Grown-ups became alarmed by the high visibility of these strange-talking, odd-dressing, and, to many parents, hostile or sex-obsessed teens. Adults demanded answers; from where were their progeny acquiring such outrageous behaviors?

Historian James Gilbert writes, "One theory caught hold," and "mass culture" was fingered as the culprit—"particularly in the guise of advertising, comic books, films, [television,] and other consumer entertainments aimed at youth." During the war and postwar years, juvenile delinquency became a hot political issue because it appeared that adolescent crime was on the rise. Gilbert attributes much of the apparent increase to broken families sustained by fathers heading off to war and mothers entering the workforce. He also suggests increased public interest in the topic meant that the popular press reported on it more frequently, consequently triggering police—now impelled by a concerned, fearful public—to monitor and arrest more teens on more charges heretofore not considered delinquent behaviors. Such activity contributed to a statistical increase in adolescent crime, thus "proving" a teenage crime wave had hit the nation. While most psychologists, criminologists, and sociologists suggested the root cause of juvenile crime could be found in the familial and social environment, "for many Americans," explains Gilbert, "mass culture . . . solved the mystery of delinquency. It was an outside force guided from media centers in New York and Hollywood. . . . It penetrated the home . . . [and] appeared to promote values contrary to many parents [thus] provok[ing] generational conflict. . . . As the movement to control delinquency grew in the early 1950s, one of the most important corollary developments was the impulse to investigate, control and censor mass culture."[78]

This abstraction of media impact is really at the heart of the 1953–55 U.S. Senate Judiciary subcommittee's probe of juvenile delinquency in America chaired first by New Jersey U.S. Senator Robert Hendrickson until 1954 and later by Tennessee U.S. Senator Estes Kefauver.[79] Television and general mass media were not mentioned in Senate Resolution 89 establishing the subcommittee, but the government investigation was given wide authority to delve into the "causes and contributing factors" of youth delinquency.[80] It was Senator Kefauver, then ranking minority leader on the four-member panel, who placed television and other mass media—movies, magazines, and comic books—on a roster of a dozen "special areas" considered "worthy of concentrated investigation because of their effects upon juvenile delinquency."[81]

Clearly, the broadcast business had some explaining to do. Chairman Hendrickson initially subpoenaed fourteen industry representatives to testify as to whether some television programs were harmful to children or adolescents, among them NBC-TV Vice-President Joseph Heffernan. Heffernan affirmed that "no responsible scientific data or opinion [exists] which fixes television as the cause of juvenile delinquency. There is a decided body of opinion that television . . . [has] no causal relationship to juvenile delinquency."[82] This corporate NBC-TV position had been seen in Helffrich's CART reports before and after Heffernan's 1954 testimony. As early as 1951, Helffrich quotes experts Dallas W. Smythe of the Institute of Communications at the University of Illinois, Lawrence Averil, director of psychology at Massachusetts State Teacher's College, and Mark May with the Yale Institute of Human Relations, who refute mass culture as the "link . . . to juvenile waywardness." Helffrich reports May's research in particular suggests that "conclusions on the behavior patterns of children cannot be solely confined to media influences since . . . other factors exist like the influence of parents, economic influences, world wide tensions, etc." Helffrich even used J. Edgar Hoover's well-worn argument that "broken homes, a lack of religion[,] ... inadequate school systems," and the like caused adolescent delinquency. When magazine or newspaper criticism stoked the argument that television violence negatively influenced children or juveniles—and in the 1950s, it happened regularly—Helffrich's NBC-TV CART reports invariably countered with the company line.[83]

> 1953: Television as a culprit [for juvenile delinquency] is not born [of] fact, and social scientists and others with responsible attitudes do not pin juvenile delinquency on us.... TV is [not] a vicious Pied Piper wooing kids to their doom.[84]

> 1959: ... Our adult population en masse isn't of necessity automatically qualified to pontificate on pet theories concerning the causes, neatly isolated, of juvenile delinquency. . . . Juvenile delinquency invariably comes down to a problem of adult delinquency.[85]

Also, in 1954, when publisher William Gaines succumbed to government pressure and "voluntarily" eliminated his company's "crime and horror" comic-book line,[86] Helffrich was outraged. In a CART report, he quotes Gaines disputing the premise that comics cause or "'stimulate juvenile delinquency.'" "On that point," beams Helffrich, "the facts bear him out." [87] Yet, despite the supportive statement, Helffrich still hedged his bet and made sure "a shot of some horror and sex comics"[88] was eliminated from a *Dear Phoebe* episode then filming at NBC-TV, Hollywood, and paradoxically remarks, "NBC ... avoids any [program] encouraging juvenile delinquency."[89] With one hand, Helffrich insists on realism. saying comics were not the harbingers of youthful crime, while, with the other, he removes the suspect cartoon magazines from view. Public relations appear to have animated Helffrich in these cases, not whether adolescents would be motivated to criminal deviance if they saw comic books displayed on television.

But of all areas of censorship, Helffrich was most concerned about race depicted on television. It can be argued that he was a moralist, activist, and well ahead of the curve on racial questions from 1948 to 1960.

7. Postwar Racial Discourse

*A*t the dawn of the U.S. civil-rights era, black stereotypes—the shiftless coon, termagant Mammy, servile Uncle Tom—remained the order of the day in popular American mass entertainment. These stereotypes were toned down considerably after the Second World War, but, with the exception of a few celebrated black entertainers and sports figures, such was still the case on radio and in motion pictures. Nonetheless, some believed commercial network television might be different. This chapter considers the remarkable work of NBC-TV's chief censor Stockton Helffrich in the area of race on early television.

Segregation was a contumacious institution in postwar America and particularly unyielding in the south after World War II.[1] Poll taxes, racial discrimination, and a half century of "separate but equal" ideology haunted the era. Even in the north, rabid strains of racism thrived from the 1930s to 1960s. Shameful discrimination by city zoning boards as well as by homeowners, real estate agents, and lending institutions resulted in de facto residential apartheid. This discrimination produced segregated neighborhoods, schools, public recreational facilities, and private shopping areas. Segregation in the "tolerant" northwest was not much better. In some Spokane, Washington, restaurants, "No Colored Patronage Solicited" notices were displayed, and a racist suggestion posted at the Idaho border read, "Nigger, Read This Sign and Run."[2] In virtually all regions of the nation after World War II, white people could still call an adult black man " boy"—even the President of the United States.[3] By the mid-to-late 1960s, race riots had fissured cities across the nation from Boston to Los Angeles.

Could TV break the stranglehold of American apartheid? In May 1950, *Variety* offered perhaps the overstatement of the decade on that question, with the headline, "Negro Talent Coming into Own on TV without Using Stereotypes: A Sure Sign That Television Is Free of Racial Barriers."[4] In a later *Ebony* interview, Ed Sullivan remarked television helped "the Negro in his fight . . . to win the guarantees [of] his birthright [by taking the civil rights battle] into the living rooms of America's homes where public opinion is formed."[5] To Sullivan's credit (and the occasional consternation of anxious advertisers), he regularly featured African American musicians, singers, dancers, and comedians on his popular variety program. Also, during television's experimental years—prior to the Second World War and into the early postwar years—black performers seemed to make significant inroads toward eliminating the color barrier. The medium's insatiate need for programs and talent meant that African American entertainers were seen regularly on local and network shows and had not yet been cast as caricatures as they were on radio and in movies.[6] Television's breezy attitude toward race before and immediately after the war, Donald Bogle argues, was due in large part to its early absence of significant audience—not enough people were watching to incite controversy and especially not yet in southern markets. Bogle claims at this juncture, television was still relatively free of "any particular social or political pressures . . . [and it was] not yet driven by the concerns of big advertisers."[7] But as millions of TV sets invaded American homes, and more network programming was consumed, commercial sponsorship along with the many restrictions it brought increased. Fear and discrimination by sponsors, abetted by commercial broadcasting's need for operating revenue from ad sales, could not be ignored. Moreover, racist programming prompted by the hegemonic ideology of the period worked to unconsciously reinforce American bigotry and intolerance for the first two decades of television's life.

Before advertising limited its possibilities, television, like radio before it, was envisioned as an electronic pathway to moral enlightenment. With the coming of television, proclaimed RCA's David Sarnoff would also come "a new world of educational and cultural opportunities . . . a new philosophy, a new sense of freedom, and greatest of all, perhaps, a finer and broader understanding between [sic] all the peoples of the world."[8] It was advertised as a "magic box," a window to the world, a portal to unimaginable possibilities. But television would not become a gateway to social utopia and instead worked to fortify consumptive lifestyles. In order to take quick advantage of a nation awash in pent-up savings after the war, big business needed a sweeping, cheap way to market products from bursting warehouses. TV led the way, with early television's business and programming models mirroring radio's template. And since racist attitudes permeated commercial radio entertainment for more then three decades by that time, it is not surprising that stereotypes of African Americans would appear on television as well. But some in TV were pushing to change that. One was the nation's first network television censor, Stockton Helffrich.[9]

Issues of Race

From the beginning of network TV programming, NBC had to contend with racist words and images in its telecasts. Helffrich, head of the network's Continuity Acceptance (CA) Department ordered cuts from all Hollywood films and cartoons replete with mocking stereotypes of African Americans. He banned any production that, in his words, "represented [a] too unrelieved picture of the crap-shooting, drinking, dope-taking, easy-living, shiftless, and knife wielding Negro,"[10] and frequently reminded NBC program management of its 1948 "policy against epitaphs designating races or creeds in any way known to be offensive."[11] As early as 1949, Helffrich wrote he was wary of intolerance in *The Horn and Hardt's Children's Hour,* seen on NBC-TV's New York station: "There has . . . been in the show some tendencies to go in for racial caricatures (particularly Negro)." Helffrich pledged to scrutinize the kiddy's show scripts "quite carefully in an effort to anticipate possible sources of public disapproval."[12]

To have his actions make sense in a postwar context, recall that Helffrich was a Communist before World War II and an active member of the Popular Front. He also marched in several of New York's always-controversial May Day Parades and organized Negro Youth Leagues at a Harlem settlement house.[13] Later, he renounced Communism, became an FDR liberal, and a union shop steward who organized white-collar and clerical employees against his own network.[14] Despite knowing Helffrich's well-known progressive leanings, NBC's top brass plucked him from the rank and file, elevating him to Continuity Acceptance—a middle-management, corporate public-relations position.[15] (For a more complete discussion of Helffrich's early life, see chapter 2 in the current volume.)

Of all his many censorial tasks, editing racist songs from TV programs proved quite daunting for Helffrich. He insisted the lyrics of many hundred-year-old Stephen Foster numbers be altered to meet what he saw as viewer prerequisites, concluding that if the words of those songs did not change, they would not be broadcast over NBC facilities.[16] The Foster songs to which Helffrich specifically referred are ones like "My Old Kentucky Home" ("Oh, the sun shines bright [on my] old Kentucky home/'Tis summer, the darkies are gay"),[17] "Old Folks At Home" ("Way down upon the Swanee Ribber . . . /Oh! darkies, how my heart grows weary/Far from de old folks at home"),[18] or "Massa's in de Cold Ground" ("Down in de cornfield/Hear dat mournful sound/All de darkeys am a weeping /Massa's in de cold, cold ground").[19]

Sensitivity on race issues evidently ran high in the Continuity Acceptance Department during the late 1940s and early 1950s. NBC-TV, through Helffrich, was plainly establishing a cautious but determined strategy to rid all network programming of racial stereotypes. Still, live television was unpredictable and could undo the best-laid plans. On *The Old Gold Amateur Hour,* a rancher from upstate New York performed a tune whose lyric contained the word *darky.* The singing farmer was ordered to cut the reference in rehearsal, and he did but ad-libbed it back into the live broadcast because the lights, cameras, and general commotion of live television made him nervous.[20] Helffrich reacted by stationing more censors on the show to monitor the "amateurs" just as he and his minions patrolled "professional" programs like the *Texaco Star Theater* and *Your Show of Shows.* Another song entitled "The Whip" was presented on the *Jack Carter Show* but only after the "careful deletion of a redundant reference to 'black and white,'" writes Helffrich.[21] He even required that the tune not be sung in a Negro "dialect," concluding, "the intent of the song is certainly not anti-Negro but rather anti-tyranny."[22] Nonetheless, complaint phone calls poured in from television cities around the nation. Through these experiences and others, Helffrich notes a sense of anxious change in viewer response of televised race portrayals: "On the whole problem of racial . . . minorities, we continue to have audience mail and like indications of a greater concern with these things . . . than used to prevail."[23]

After World War II, the cries of reform-minded activists in matters of race grew more intense. African American veterans demanded an end to de jure racism at home and demanded full integration of American society. Sustaining such postwar dissension were liberal political polices, a major rise in membership of civil-rights activist groups—like the National Association for the Advancement of Colored People (NAACP)

and the National Urban League (NUL)—and a growing, vocal, and organized black middle class. Also, whites in significant numbers, especially
in places like New York City and other urban centers, joined the cause
and pushed for racial change. This liberal ethos also meant television's
portrayals of ethnicity and race would now come under greater scrutiny,
and Helffrich recognized it earlier than most.[24]

NBC-TV/RCA Corporate Policy on Race

On October 6, 1950, Helffrich urged top network management to do
something about its superannuated, racist programming: "RCA [and]
NBC's public relations [have been adversely affected] by alienation of
the Negro audience through outdated editorial practice."[25] While there
is no specific documentation of the role Helffrich played in the corporate metamorphosis, in late November, apparently convinced of the
importance African Americans held for the future of the network, RCA
Vice-President John West, along with Syd Eiges, NBC VP for public
information, hosted a seminar for black leaders. More than fifty representatives of important urban newspapers as well as key officers from
the NAACP and NUL attended. Among those making presentations for
NBC-TV were Sylvester "Pat" Weaver covering programming, Ernest
de la Ossa explaining network hiring practices, and Helffrich outlining
editorial and censorship diligence. Helffrich later declared the seminar
an unqualified success, openly stressing in his Continuity Acceptance
Radio/Television (CART) reports that its only intent was "improvement
of RCA and NBC public relations" and "the need for alertness whenever
script material touches upon racial matters."[26] By early the next year,
plans were in place for significant programming changes at the network.

RCA began an overt public-relations initiative in January 1951 to
tap the burgeoning $15 billion "Negro market," one *Variety* called "the
most important, financially potent, and sales- and-advertising serenaded
'minority' in the land." Industry magazine *Sponsor* further validated
the potential African American marketplace by an article touting the
so-called forgotten 15,000,000 black consumers. Going even further,
Ebony called commercial television "an amazing new weapon which
can be all-powerful in blasting American's bigots."[27] But racial hatred
was an abiding feature of the American scene, and even promises of
untapped economic gain could not quickly change things.

Unthinking racial slurs and stereotypes continued to crop up in programs even as NBC-TV focused on wooing black middle-class viewers. For example, South Dakota U.S. Senator Karl Mundt thought nothing of using the phrase "Nigger in the woodpile"[28] on the nationally televised NBC-TV public-affairs show *The American Forum of the Air*.[29] Helffrich writes, Mundt's "ill advised adlib . . . brought in some fifty telephone calls" as well as objecting telegrams.[30] Later that same month, comic Jack Carter used a puppet to portray a stereotyped "Stepin Fetchit" character singing "Lazy Bones," a tune containing derogatory lyrics about sloth and fecklessness.[31] Later during the same show, in a sketch satirizing the 1937 film version of *King Solomon's Mines*, Carter's scripted line to an African American actor was to be: "Boy, I want you to call the other natives." However, the last word was not enunciated clearly, or so Carter claimed, and was heard on national television as "niggers." Embarrassed, Helffrich quickly distanced the network from Carter's gaffe pointing out that *that* particular "objectionable epitaph" was completely unacceptable in all NBC-TV scripts.[32]

To make amends for these continuing and costly errors, the network retained and regularly consulted public relations specialist Joseph Baker, an African American, whom Helffrich called an "authority . . . where the Negro people are concerned."[33] Baker modified NBC's formal television statement of "standards and practices" to assume the tone of President Harry S. Truman's 1947 special civil-rights committee report and later published book, *To Secure These Rights*.[34] The revised NBC-TV proclamation now noted that all programs would treat "aspects of race, creed, color, and national origin with dignity and respect."[35] Near the end of 1951, the National Association of Radio and Television Broadcasters, taking its cue from NBC-TV, also revised its code of good practices: "Racial or nationality types shall not be shown on television in such a manner as to ridicule the race or nationality."[36]

Blackface Minstrelsy on Television and Eddie Cantor

When minstrelsy died at the end of the nineteenth century, its blackface legacy was inherited by vaudeville, thus extending a powerful racist tradition a total of 120 years.[37] The elite vaudevillians who performed in blackface on the Keith-Orpheum and RKO circuits in the 1910s and 1920s make up a virtual *Who's Who* of early-twentieth-century show-biz celebrities: Al Jolson, Eddie Cantor, George Jessel, George Burns, Sophie Tucker, and Fanny Brice.[38] The deeply entrenched minstrel tradition prompted even Hollywood's biggest stars to don blackface in some movies of the 1930s and early 1940s: including Fred Astaire in *Swingtime*, Bing Crosby in *Holiday Inn* and *Dixie*, Judy Garland and Mickey Rooney in *Babes in Arms* and *Babes on Broadway*, and the Marx Brothers in *A Day at the Races*.[39] The minstrel mask was more than a racial expression; it acted as an odd signifier, and a top performer's calling card recoded to mean that grand, "traditional" entertainment was about to be presented.[40] Both Jolson and Cantor said on numerous occasions that they were anything but racist. Both openly refused to eat in restaurants that would not serve black performers, had long and abiding friendships with African Americans, and unreservedly advocated equal rights for blacks at a time when it was highly unpopular to do so. Each also said that singing and dancing in blackface gave them the emotional freedom they needed to take risks as performers.[41] Ultimately, the successes of Jolson and Cantor were built on the premise that audiences of the era did not consider watching a blackface performance on stage a racial travesty. Racism was so pervasive, so day-to-day unexceptional that it was seen and accepted as an unremarkable part of the American social fabric—at least by most whites.[42] Audiences perceived blackface entertainment with a similar indifference as vaudeville passed from the cultural scene by the mid-1930s.[43] Comedian Bob Hope once remarked, "When vaudeville died, television was the box they put it in."[44] It is not surprising then that Eddie Cantor, the now aging, former vaudevillian and radio headliner-turned-television star, performed his most-popular musical numbers in blackface on the nascent NBC-TV network.

When Cantor began his monthly hosting of *The Colgate Comedy Hour*, he was almost sixty years old.[45] At mid-twentieth century, Cantor was one of the most-popular and widely admired entertainers in the country, an "elder statesman" of show business with a career that spanned over forty-years in vaudeville, movies, recordings, and radio. In addition to being a passionate spokesman for suffering Zionist refugees who survived Hitler, he was a tireless fundraiser for the United Jewish Appeal and other liberal humanist causes and founder of March of Dimes. The showman certainly enjoyed his concurrent roles as performer, humanitarian, citizen of the world, and bona-fide icon in the entertainment industry.[46]

On the debut *Colgate* show, Cantor rendered a medley of his favorite tunes wearing blackface, a straw hat, and oversized glasses. With an audience share of nearly 50 percent, the New York–based telecast of September 10, 1950, beat Ed Sullivan's *Toast of the Town* show on CBS-TV—the early Colgate shows frequently beat Sullivan's program. Moreover, newspaper critics in major television cities were exuberant over Cantor's work. Nowhere, it appears, was there a note of disdain for the entertainer's blackface routine; on it, even Helffrich's CARTs were mute. When the *Colgate* show premiered, Helffrich was still less than a month away from writing his October 6, 1950, CART entry claiming that overt racism hurt NBC-TV. But Cantor's blackface routines did not abate. On another show in the *Colgate* series, Cantor did an Al Jolson impression—complete with nappy wig, exaggerated lips, and bugging eyes—which was labeled "'distasteful'" by a viewer whose comments Helffrich included in one of his reports. The complainant added, "'Most sponsors and audiences recognize this type of act as insulting to the Negro people of the United States.'"[47] In a later *Colgate* program, after Cantor performed what was described only as a "Negro dance number," a puzzled Helffrich muses, "There does seem to be an inconsistency between Eddie Cantor's obvious effort on behalf of tolerance in America . . . and his inclusion of somewhat dated versions of Negro life."[48] This riddle of Cantor's willingness to sing and dance in blackface while being a champion of human rights does at first glance seem inconsistent. But blackface at that time was perceived as theatrical convention, and most artists (and audiences) were able to disassociate patently racist performances from any abiding personal sense of racism, even though such performances only served to reinforce an invisible racist ideology.[49] One must also consider that sponsor Colgate-Palmolive was paying dearly for these expensive series of comedy spectaculars, one of NBC-TV's first successful counterprogramming of the Sullivan show on Sunday evenings.[50] Both network and sponsor desired to tap the attention of a vast audience that tuned in to enjoy Cantor's stage persona. Since he grew to fame frequently performing in the minstrel idiom, if Cantor wished to sing a song in his signature blackface on national television, who could (or would want to) stop him?—certainly not the network, the sponsor, or Chief Censor Helffrich. Not yet.

Helffrich also let it be known that NBC-TV's best interests would be served if all minstrel or blackface presentations were deleted. "The damage done to good will of the public toward talent and clients by this kind of thing is increasingly apparent," he patiently writes. Still, on the first anniversary of Jolson's death, comedian Danny Thomas did a salute to the minstrel showman in blackface that brought NBC-TV ferocious viewer complaints. The next week, on the popular *Kate Smith Show*, another blackface act was used that again begot stinging protests.[51] Now pushed beyond his limit, Helffrich declared he and his department would unceremoniously cut *all* racist portrayals on *any* NBC-TV show, admonishing writers and producers to steer clear of bigoted references to "avoid the possibility of a totally wasted effort."[52] And Helffrich and his editors delivered on their promise. Deleted from a *Kraft Television Theatre* drama were a reference to a "colored servant as 'that baboon,'" reveals Helffrich,, continuing, "and the order of her mistress 'you will bathe . . . I cannot have you smelling like a sow.'"[53] Also cut was a stereotyped line uttered by a policeman unjustifiably suspicious of an African American maid: "Maybe she's got a meat cleaver with her."[54] At NBC-TV's Chicago operation, Continuity Acceptance manager Harry Ward deleted racial clichés in hundreds of old movies purchased for television broadcast. One excised film scene depicted what Ward described as a "terrified Negro in frantic flight screaming, 'Help, help! Seventy thousand ghosts jumped in mah ear!'"[55] Ward's team also redacted dozens of comedies, cartoons, and silent films showing sycophantic black cooks, maids, and chauffeurs.

In the many *Our Gang* shorts, black skin was played for laughs. In one episode, the face of an African American infant is painted with white shoe polish; in another scene, Farina, a young African American character, wipes the sweat from his brow and black coloring comes off on his handkerchief. In still another, little Farina upsets a flour can on his head to look "white." In a Mutt and Jeff cartoon, Ward describes "'an unconscionable Negro stereotype with howling, gibbering cannibals.'" Guillotined from the popular *Gangbusters* crime show was a scene in which a black janitor was "scared and hopped up on gin." Cut from a *Fireside Theatre* script was "a billboard which would have featured Al Jolson in blackface." All racist notions, ideas, or images were cut, especially those that depicted African Americans as tambourine-shaking minstrels, derelict sociopaths wielding concealed weapons, simple-minded loafers, excessive drinkers, drugged-out zombies, addicted gamblers, infrequent bathers, and easily freighted stooges—that is, "Feets don't fails me now!" Helffrich admonishes his editors to "anticipate [these] kind[s] of [racial slurs] from writers and agencies," suggesting that "[such] sloppy and lazy cliché's are out of date, are not fair, and are anything but a pretty face of America to the rest of the world." He pointedly writes, "I can't very well poke my head in the sand to avoid reminding you not only of the century we are living in but of the nature of our audience."[56]

Such comments imply Helffrich was well aware of NBC-TV's multiethnic audience and the national and international political tensions surrounding race that engulfed the postwar era. In 1955, for example, Helffrich attended a meeting of the New York State Commission against Discrimination. Present at that gathering was Frederick O'Neal, a black pioneer in American theater, who likewise remarked, "That the absence of Negroes [on television shown as part of daily] . . . American life is something of which enemies of our . . . [nation] can take advantage."[57] Helffrich, of course, agreed and throughout the CART reports, frequently pointed to NBC-TV's far-sighted integration policy.

By mid-decade, NBC-TV demanded changes to any act that embraced racist stereotypes in any form. For this, the network endured angry protests from some of its biggest stars. *The Eddie Cantor Story* was about to open in cinemas around the nation, and NBC-TV Chicago and New York received several one-minute television commercials to promote the biopic. These ads, however, caused Helffrich and Continuity Acceptance significant problems. The advertisements depicted Keefe Brasselle—the actor portraying Cantor in the film—in blackface, an image now unfit for telecast over NBC facilities. Therefore, the network chose to air only the *non*blackface Cantor ad in its entirety and to "manufacture" a twenty-second commercial from the other unacceptable one-minute spot.[58] On the heels of this action, NBC-TV next demanded major changes to Cantor's first *Colgate Comedy Hour* show of 1954, originating from Hollywood.[59] Cantor again wished to sing his songs in blackface, a practice now deemed totally unacceptable by NBC-TV's west-coast management.[60] Cantor quit the show for good on May 16, 1954.[61]

The "Integration without Identification" Policy

As Helffrich worked to eliminate racial stereotypes of any single minority, he and others concurrently pushed into place a "radical" corporate programming strategy—radical, at least, for 1950s television. NBC-TV's plan, dubbed "integration without identification," would now work consciously to integrate television programs. The CART reports do not indicate how much of a hand Helffrich had in crafting the new policy, but it is clear that in 1949, he first wrote of public-relations problems the network encountered by broadcasting racist words or images.[62] By late December 1950, a companywide RCA racial initiative was being readied for the new year, which, as previously noted, included a comprehensive public-outreach effort to secure a foothold in the robust and thriving $15 billion African American marketplace.

One of RCA's first undertakings was to recruit more "Negro employees" at NBC-TV. In testimony before a subcommittee of the Senate Labor Committee during late summer 1952, RCA President Frank Folsom announced that blacks now held diverse NBC job titles that included director of community affairs, senior staff writer, assistant film librarian, announcer, scenic artists, and on-air performers. Folsom also reported that RCA had recently hired nine African American electrical engineers from Howard University, Columbia University, and Youngstown College among others. In late September 1952, Helffrich noted that key NBC managers "met with certain department heads to hypo the ["integration without identification"] program," which in turn was followed by meetings "attended by top Producers, Directors and their assistants."[63] An ebullient Helffrich comments, "Clearly, activities of Continuity Acceptance in deleting stereotypes are now being complimented by positive [management] actions creating an atmosphere in which further integration of talent regardless or color is the order of the day." That same month, RCA was awarded the first National Association of Colored Women citation in recognition of equitable employment in the broadcasting industry. By December, all pertinent members of the NBC production staff met with African American community leaders in Chicago. Early the next year, Mildred McAfee Horton—first woman director of RCA, NBC, and New York Life and seventh president of Wellesley College—declared NBC had "taken the lead in eliminating stereotypes which in the past has belittled certain races and minority groups." However, NBC-TV's program integration plan was not explained or promoted until a year later.[64]

The first direct CART report mention of NBC-TV's "integration without identification" policy was on January 12, 1953. Helffrich remarks that a conscious effort was now being made by management to integrate but never calls attention to Negro talent in all NBC programming. On a *Kraft Television Theatre* presentation a few months later, a black actor was distinctly seen among a few other white actors in a sweeping pan on the set of a newspaper bureau. "The camera very simply scanned the office," Helffrich explains, "catching quite incidentally . . . that one of the staff members was a Negro." This particular program is significant because the *Kraft* show was not an internally produced NBC-TV offering; Kraft's advertising agency had produced it. Because of that, Helffrich enthuses, "There was a good bit of gratification around the shop that an RCA/NBC [race] policy was spreading into agency production." But not all viewers took the liberal turn and saw television integration a positive thing. Many were afraid of what was considered aberrant "race mixing."[65]

Postwar segregation and racial fears were systemic, none more so than in the American south. Most southern politicians rejected television programs showing blacks and whites on an equal social status. Southern historian Pete Daniel explains that whites feared integration because it "would allow black males and white females to share the same social space" thereby leading to "interracial orgies" and mongrelized children.[66] Georgia Governor Herman Talmadge threatened a nationwide boycott of companies sponsoring "race mixing" programs so as "to clean up television before the situation becomes more offensive." The odd logic of race mixing was a cornerstone of Jim Crow, and "defending" women against almost certain sexual rape at the hands of a black man was frequently conflated with a white man's personal sense of masculine power, jingoistic patriotism, and the abiding horror of invisible Communism.[67] An improper glance or even the unintentional and harmless touching of a white woman by a black man could prompt outrage (or worse). An unidentified resident of East Saint Louis, a hotbed of bigotry and unrest since the 1917 race riots there left nine whites and hundreds of African Americans dead,[68] wrote to Helffrich complaining that he and his friends were "thoroughly disgusted" by what they saw on NBC-TV objecting to "mixed program[s] in which whites and Negroes take part. . . . Whenever your sponsors . . . find it necessary to put whites and blacks on the same program, it is . . . time to stop [that] show entirely. . . . If you must have Negroes, then have an all Negro performance. [Some] of my friends, as well as myself, shut off that part of the program, and even . . . recommend boycott[ing] the commercial lines represented by the sponsors. We intend to . . . do this so long as such programs continue."[69] Later, a Chicago viewer was equally upset, proclaiming it was all a lie that "the Negro community resents stereotypes." The viewer wrote that "the only persons challenging his statements '[were] the Communists and perhaps a handful of self-appointed leaders who are simply seeking publicity.'" Helffrich did not directly address this letter, but Ben Park, network TV program director for the NBC central division, did. In his reply, Park explains the reasoning behind RCA/NBC's "integration without identification" agendum.

> This emphasis on the preservation of human dignity is definitely not communist-inspired. . . . The so-called mass communications media are extremely potent in their ability to inculcate attitudes; we feel the least we can do is to avoid stereotyping and present human beings on the basis of their human attributes, good or bad. . . . [NBC-TV's "integration without identification"] policy has tended to accomplish two things. First, to state simply but effectively that Negroes bear the same general qualities of character and personality that exist among all the members of the human race, and whatever slight physical differences they have are not indicative of any inferiority. This is so apparent that it makes us a little ashamed of the past, and ashamed that we have to make a point of it. Second, generally speaking the policy to include Negroes in roles which they normally play in all walks of life has tended to increase the total number of opportunities available to them. In other words, instead of insisting always on casting an Irishman as a policeman, many programs will include a Negro in the role. The same goes for doctors, nurses, lawyers, cab drivers, laborers, and mechanics, as well as bootblacks, entertainers, and criminals. In short, we are attempting to cast Negroes as people.[70]

Those sentiments may have been veridical for NBC-TV, but it appears such concern for matters racial were less important to rival television networks during the same period—although it seemed NBC's competitors were coming around. Later that same year, for example, Helffrich noted that Frank Stanton, CBS president, was resigning from his Ohio State University fraternity because of the group's discriminatory practices. Stanton quit the Greek-letter society when he learned his college brotherhood barred membership to all persons "'not of pure Aryan blood.'" Helffrich, in an obvious and self-serving comment, writes, "For a couple of years now NBC has been pretty much alone in the leadership of a very conscious movement not only to eliminate stereotyping from our offerings but to integrate without identification member's of minority groups. . . . For a long time . . . our company's activity in the area has been pioneering in nature . . . [so] when we see our leading competitors beginning to take an interest it's obvious an excellent company policy is paying off."[71] Helffrich's commentary in this case may have been overstated for purposes of irony when one considers the unequivocally racist programs then being carried by the other two major networks.

Beulah and Amos 'n' Andy

Delta Sigma Theta—the celebrated African American service sorority founded by twenty-two African American women at Howard University in 1913—awarded citations to NBC-TV and its Lights Out program for the "conscious efforts by both RCA and NBC to advance . . . good relations with the Negro community." Helffrich proudly points to one episode of the psychological drama wherein "Negro actors assumed the roles of policemen." With evident satisfaction, he notes that it was obvious to the home viewer the patrolmen were "essentially . . . members of the force and only *incidentally . . . Negro[es]*. . . . Nowhere in the continuity was any racial identification involved" (italics added). A similar strategy was employed on another Lights Out show in which an African American was cast as a taxi driver, with Helffrich again asserting, "The fact that he was a Negro wasn't accorded any significance since he typified the hundreds of drivers who might be found cruising along any big city street." The images of black actors playing the quotidian roles of policemen or cab drivers, based upon Helffrich's notes, were curious, Promethean and well nigh incomprehensible to most television viewers of the era. Helffrich's verbiage certainly reflects that a detailed clarification was thought required for the seemingly imponderable casting of African Americans in incidental roles usually reserved for whites.[72]

Such concern for racial depiction did not appear to be the case at the two other major networks. In October 1950, *Beulah* premiered on ABC-TV. The sitcom holds the distinction of being the first nationally broadcast weekly television series starring an African American in the lead role. Distinguished actress Ethel Waters first played the central character, Beulah.[73] It was one of the very few images of African Americans on prime-time television during this period, which is perhaps why it so quickly came under fire—*Beulah* perpetuated the jolly, servile Mammy stereotype. Beulah, a middle-aged black domestic, worked for the somewhat-dysfunctional all-white Henderson family. Episodes revolved around life in the kitchen of Beulah's inept employers—her sensible, folksy ways, and down-home cooking that could repair just about any problem—and her interaction with other neighborhood blacks who also performed menial, blue-collar jobs for area white people. Television reviewer Jack Gould panned the show in the *New York Times*, as did some members of the black press, but its most severe critic was *New York Herald Tribune* columnist John Crosby. Crosby was particularly captious of Waters, arguing that she was, after all, a highly regarded actress and celebrated role model for the African American community. Crosby saw her participation in *Beulah* as a creative cul de sac and betrayal to Water's singular theatrical accomplishments and personal triumphs. Despite the rancor, *Beulah* never provoked the amount of bitter debate that *Amos 'n' Andy* generated, and it remained on the air until 1953.[74]

Amos 'n' Andy debuted on CBS-TV on June 28, 1951, a year after *Beulah* but became a lightning rod for organized protest.[75] The television show was modeled after the long-running and phenomenally popular radio program heard on NBC from 1928 to 1943 and again on CBS from 1943 through the mid-1950s. *Amos 'n' Andy*, set in Harlem, portrayed an all-black world in which a slow-witted cabby (and show narrator), Andy, and his gullible, cigar-champing friend, Amos, interact with the scheming carpetbagger, Kingfish, and his shrewish wife, Sapphire, alongside a spectrum of other stereotypical black characters. *Amos 'n' Andy* found its comedic voice in overstated black rural dialects, garish costuming, and exaggerated story lines that continually featured frauds or scams perpetrated on Andy and others by Kingfish.

Amos 'n' Andy's pedigree—deeply rooted in the minstrel tradition—caused the NAACP to launch lawsuits and boycotts against the show.[76]

At its 1951 summer convention in Atlanta, the NAACP officially condemned *Amos 'n' Andy* and all other television programs that featured
racist stereotypes.[77] In formal legal action brought against CBS-TV and
show sponsor Blatz Brewing Company, the NAACP presented over a
half-dozen objections to the *Amos 'n' Andy* television show, including
that the program tended "to strengthen the conclusion among unin-
formed and prejudiced people that Negroes are inferior, lazy, dumb,
and dishonest."[78] All that notwithstanding, bringing *Amos 'n' Andy* to
postwar television cannot be considered a programming miscalcula-
tion on the part of CBS-TV. The national mood on racism had yet to
change when the show went on the air, and its ratings were actually quite
good in the first year. *Amos 'n' Andy* "will be with us for a long time,"
wrote *Printers Ink*, and *Advertising Age* pointed out the program was
also well liked by black viewers, noting "most Negroes in this area do
not go along with the NAACP."[79] Historian Thomas Cripps contends
that the NAACP's efforts throughout the 1953 television season only
worked to "splinter" black unity against the show and "undercut" its
campaign against sponsor Blatz Brewing. CBS-TV moved the show to
a new time slot in the second season, causing the ratings to tumble,
so Blatz moved its sponsorship to the *Four Star Playhouse*, claiming
the anthology show brought "a higher-class image" to its product.[80] It
was not directly, therefore, the organized, angry public outcry against
televised racism that prompted the loss of sponsorship triggering the
network demise of *Amos 'n' Andy*; it was money and ratings. Clearly,
however, the NAACP played a central role in drumming up controversy
against Blatz—anathema to any television sponsor.[81]

Moreover, for some African Americans, *Amos 'n' Andy* was not perceived as a polemic on race as much as it was seen as an intraclass
problem. Sociologist Darrell Y. Hamamoto argues that "the real conflict
revolved around the anxiety of the newly arrived black middle class and
its ambiguous relationship to the upstart black underclass."[82] Cripps
concurs: "Into this world of newly felt . . . black middle-class consciousness, activism, and wealth descended *Amos 'n' Andy*, complete with
baggy pants, plug hats, foul cigars, pushy wives, misfired schemes and
mangled grammar. . . . Organized blacks were shocked, not so much
at what they saw but at the timing of its release in the year of liberal
'rededication,' at a cresting of black political consciousness."[83]

The national racial climate was slowly changing during the 1950s, but CBS-TV's and ABC-TV's programming remained tied to past perceptions of race. Only one network, NBC, tried something different. NBC-TV's early strategic decision to eliminate racial stereotypes was, indeed, a clear disruption of existing racial conventions and a forward thinking act of important cultural significance. In addition, Helffrich's CA department was responsible for a significant part of the network change. Television historian Jeff Kisseloff observes, "Helffrich lobbied forcefully, but unsuccessfully to keep *Amos 'n' Andy* off television," but Kisseloff provides no corroborating evidence, nor is there any mention of how Helffrich, an NBC-TV executive, could in any way directly influence CBS-TV from broadcasting the show. In addition, no mention of any such effort appears in Helffrich's 225 NBC-TV CART reports. However, evidence *does* show that Helffrich rejected the film series *Beulah* after its initial run on ABC-TV from 1950 to 1953. The distribution company handling the sitcom, Flamingo Films, was taking the series into syndication, and WRCA, NBC-TV's owned-and-operated station in New York, was offered the program.[84] "We turned [it] down," relates Helffrich.[85] He describes the show as "the usual so-called humor based upon racial peculiarities and is about dated these days as anything could get," and that there are "innumerable stereotypes [in the show,] garbling of English, etc.[,] plus 'subtle' condescension toward Beulah."[86]

At first blush, Helffrich's progressive humanism on race might be seen as heroic given the extant bigotry of the era. It is, after all, true that corporate documents show Helffrich recommended and helped facilitate a corporate policy change, insisting on program integration years ahead of the other networks, thus nudging NBC-TV toward multiculturalism before the concept had any social currency.[87] But a more critical reading suggests Helffrich's actions addressed social power inequities in TV programs by only censoring the symbols or expression of power. Merely expurgating bigoted speech did not and could not address the underlying problem: ubiquitous race discrimination in the United States promoted by morally corrupt political, economic, and legal systems. If Helffrich's palliative censorship worked at all, it worked to alleviate some symptoms manifest in racist broadcasts at the dawn of commercial television. Recall Helffrich was but a mid-level manager with highly proscribed corporate authority, a small cog in a large company machine. He changed what he could and no more. Cynicism easily prompts that NBC-TV's "integration without identification" policy may well have been adopted by the network to take advantage of a possible advertising windfall—as mentioned earlier, the postwar African American market was a massive $15 billion opportunity.[88] It was also good public relations and good business for NBC-TV to adopt a "pro Negro" policy before its broadcast competitors did. Seen this way, the network's early decision to eschew racial stereotypes was a strategic corporate move, not an authentic, disjunctive cultural act. But whether based on commerce or the disruption of early TV-programming tropes, methods of directly dealing with overt racism were at least put on the agenda and considered at NBC-TV thanks in part to Helffrich.

Still, more than business considerations alone animated Helffrich; a higher level of social consciousness appeared to be at play, and ethical principles were regularly invoked in his CART reports. For example, Helffrich repeatedly used the notion of human dignity to frame questions about race on television. "An obvious way to spot racist programming," he writes, was to have "an attentive ear cocked toward those who express hurt." Helffrich says he maintained an "automatic" wariness toward racial clichés like "Irish drunks, Italian gangsters, avaricious Jews, [and] Lazy Negroes. . . . When you get right down to it, the simplest rule of thumb [for spotting racist programming] is summed up in the word 'dignity.' . . . You may not please everybody depending on preconceived prejudices behind the point of view, but in terms of your own conscience as a broadcaster you are in pretty good odor. . . . Remember that in the broadcasting business the potential to do something harmful or beneficial to racial amity is conceivably greater than in any other medium at this time. . . . Broadcast of a racial fallacy is so immediate, so pervasive, so irretrievable, so shared coast-to-coast, border-to-border, as to be of enormous significance."[89]

And the above quote shows the crux of it: Helffrich identified and linked *speech* with *action*, and he then expurgated symbolic racial discourse using some notion of "moral censorship" guided by his passionately liberal ideology. And Helffrich's program suggestions *were* humanistic improvements—albeit cosmetic ones—to early TV fare. The chief censor plainly saw his job not only as preventing hurtful speech but also as gatekeeper, philosopher, teacher, public-relations agent, and catalyst encouraging progressive ideas on national television, despite viewer and sponsor protest. Researcher Patrick Garry discusses the phenomenon, explaining that "persons who do not traditionally advocate censorship" will sometimes do so, not to restrict personal freedoms, they say, but to "improve social conditions."[90]

William Clotworthy, a standards-and-practices editor who worked at NBC-TV in the 1970s, says Helffrich "left a legacy of thought on racial matters" at the network that was talked about more than twenty years after his departure.[91] Clearly, Helffrich's influence and social conscience in areas of race and ethnicity were foundational, though obviously not fully realized during his twelve-year tenure as chief censor at NBC-TV.

Of the many areas of censorship under the jurisdiction of Continuity Acceptance, the one that caused Helffrich and his team the most trouble by far was commercials, difficult to police and control in early network sponsorship and television advertising.

8. Of Truth and Toilet Paper

*f*rom its postwar beginnings, major ad agencies and national sponsors were cautiously interested in television's commercial potential. Most saw immediate and striking results when they "test purchased" ad time in the local New York, Chicago, and Los Angles markets. But since there were few TV broadcast outlets at the time, sponsors of the era budgeted most of their ad dollars for other media. It was a time broadcast historian Erik Barnouw calls "a strange twilight period . . . [for television. Because o]nly twenty-four cities had two or more stations; most cities had only one station, or none."[1] In late 1947, only one out of every 853 Americans owned a television set.[2] Ad-agency strategy, therefore, was to continue spending a major sponsor's budget in network radio while preparing to make the leap to TV.[3]

There was also an important technical consideration for advertisers: the coming of coaxial cable. In 1946, American Telephone and Telegraph (AT&T) engineers perfected the coax—a wire in which one conductor wraps around another enabling the unit to transmit multiple sources of data, from telephone conversations to a radio broadcasts to TV pictures. Historian James L. Baughman explains, "When regular network broadcasts commenced in 1947 and 1948, the coaxial cable [that hooked individual stations to the networks] only reached the largest northeastern cities."[4] Before coaxial technology, "bicycling" kinescopes or sending filmed programs via courier or mail linked cities like Houston, Pittsburgh, Milwaukee, and Saint Louis into crude celluloid networks.[5] By September 1951, high-frequency coaxial transmission lines and microwave units connected both coasts and made available true web-delivered programming to many southern cities as well.[6] With the crucial circuitry in place, TV was finally ready to sell *real* "network airtime" to national patrons. Stockton Helffrich's censorship diary, what was termed the Continuity Acceptance Radio/Television (CART) reports, begin *before* this full national electronic infrastructure was in place.

Helffrich's early memos, therefore, concern themselves with questions of advertising and program content, decency, and appropriateness for the local New York market, later for all the NBC owned-and-operated stations (O&Os) including Washington, D.C., Cleveland, Chicago, and Los Angeles, and later still for the entire NBC-TV network. The programming impact of having New York City at the early hub of network operations—as well as being the center of the U.S. advertising world—cannot be overstated. With seven stations broadcasting in metropolitan Manhattan, television appeared to be viable and ready to be subsidized by advertising dollars.[7]

Commercially supported television was seen also as natural extension of radio's blueprint and was tacitly accepted upon the medium's postwar commercial arrival. There was, however, considerable public hostility toward television advertising.[8] In research conducted during the early 1960s, four out of ten persons surveyed agreed that "commercials are ordinarily in poor taste and very annoying," 43 percent indicated a preference for TV without commercials, and 63 percent complained there were too many commercials that were interruptive and too long. There were howls that television ads were "dishonest," "dull," "boring," and "repetitive." There was also the matter of sinfulness, vulgarity, and "bringing the bathroom into the living room," with ads for beer, cigarettes, deodorants, bras, and girdles.[9] How should this contentious area be handled? Helffrich and his corps of Continuity Acceptance (CA) editors stood at the network gateway to reply.

Brassieres and Undergarments

Many product groupings were considered totally unacceptable for early television advertising including, among others, toilet paper, laxatives, depilatories, acne creams, and deodorants. In 1948, NBC-TV also refused to accept advertisements for girdles and brassieres on its network. Helffrich et al. considered corsets and bras "not a particularly timely classification for the new medium."[10] NBC-TV, it must be understood, was not hostile to these products per se, just concerned about audience reaction to such marketing on commercial television and about the potential public-relations problems and backlash such messages could pose to the nascent industry. These products stirred concerns because of their association with human reproductive organs and bodily functions, areas of abiding taboo never to be spoken of in mixed company or in front of children.[11]

For example, when asked what commercial content was disconcerting on television, a survey respondent remarked, "Bras and girdle [ads that] talked about the lift and separation," concluding, "That's embarrassing when there's teen-age boys around. . . . [I]t starts the imagination."[12] Nonetheless, one of Helffrich's early memos make clear that he saw a possible future for bra and girdle promotion and explains that "a classification of this type can be better absorbed in the framework of a come-of-age television schedule."[13] That sense of uncertainty, of not knowing what kind of ads the television viewer would bear, was a central tension as the industry was inventing itself. Based upon their experience with radio advertising, early television practitioners knew if they first limited "controversial" ads to certain parts of the day, such a scheme would gradually spur audience acceptance. And, true to form, six months later, in late January 1949, NBC television had already reconsidered dropping its advertising ban on bras and girdles but only during local broadcasts and in specific time periods. Helffrich writes, "Possible [commercial] treatments . . . [may] be acceptable and we have indicated with certain reservations a willingness to examine suggested presentations."[14]

By November 1949, NBC-TV Continuity Acceptance took a chance on a girdle commercial deemed "in pretty good taste." It "featur[ed] a demonstration of the girdle on a life-like dummy," describes Helffrich, "followed by a dissolve . . . to a live model attractively outfitted in a negligee bearing a marked similarity facially and by stance to the dummy seen earlier." Still, there was some "tampering" by CA: Helffrich insisted the girdle had to cover the dummy's thighs. If there was even the hint of a "crotch shot," as he put it, tulle—fine silk netting used in veils and scarves—had to be used to mask the "offense" of exposing a female "thigh between the bottom of the girdle and top of the hosiery." Helffrich's final caveat had the ad restricted to daytime broadcast "and on a woman's participation show basis only."[15]

By early February 1950, speculation was that Maidenform Brands Inc., a brassiere company, would soon be allowed to advertise bras on an NBC-TV Saturday-night program. Chief rival CBS-TV was the first to accept a bra commercial—showing it three days a week on its afternoon *Vanity Fair* fashion broadcast—it was therefore assumed evening ads for women's undergarments could not be far behind. The "controversial" CBS-TV afternoon bra commercial was uninspired and straightforward: a female spokesperson sat before cameras holding samples of the company's brassieres while exhorting their virtues. "The first [bra]," writes Helffrich, "was a flesh colored number . . . [the spokesperson's] only particularly graphic remarks [were] that Maiden Form 'supports from below' . . . [with] the accent on 'uplift.'" Next came a strapless black bra dubbed the "Hold Tight," that again referred to the undergarment's support and comfort. Helffrich stated the product was "perfectly in line for a women's weekday daytime show . . . [but still] undesirable [for] nighttime network programming," and NBC-TV ad sales agreed, as did head of NBC television programming, Sylvester "Pat" Weaver. So, while no specific network code forbid such sponsorship, Helffrich's rule-of-thumb precedent restricted such advertising to before 4:30 P.M. or earlier.[16] "Placement at any other times would be poor programming," he concludes.[17]

But what *if* a bra manufacturer wished to advertise on a specific show at a later time? Lilyette brassieres' division of Maidenform desire to display its foundation-garment line only on Faye Emerson's nighttime NBC-TV program asked just such a question. By May 1950, Emerson's new show—*Fifteen with Faye*—seen Saturdays from 10:30–10:45 P.M.,[18] had only been on the network for about a month, but her earlier CBS-TV shows and many other television guest appearances had already caused considerable controversy with certain viewers and critics. But Emerson's program—a breezy, celebrity chat show on trends in fashion, theater, and New York café society in general—was not the problem, her glamorous gowns were.[19] On television, Emerson always wore revealing designer frocks with dramatic plunging necklines, which became her trademark.[20] As the new visual medium took its first steps, Emerson's décolletage became the subject of popular and industry newspaper coverage, sparked photo layouts in *Life* and other publications,[21] and inspired comedians' jokes—one quipping "Emerson put the 'V' in TV."[22]

The *New York Times* reports on a 1950 television broadcast in which Emerson is said to have accidentally exposed her whole bosom causing a particularly heated national discussion over plunging necklines.

Emerson put the controversy to a vote by her viewing audience, and 85 percent—split evenly between men and women—said she should not stop wearing her celebrated tops.[23] All the more reason Lilyette wanted to associate itself with Emerson's poitrine, intending to advertise its fetchingly named Cue-T-Bra. Lilyette's ad copy stressed its brassiere's "ingenious . . . self-adjusting straps [that] lift each bust individually [for] . . . contour separation."[24] Despite sales-department and sponsor pressure, NBC-TV and Helffrich again turned away the nighttime brassiere business for daytime-television placement. In this case, Helffrich appears more concerned about local press reaction than home-viewer anger: "It would be hard to conceive of [bra] claims of this type on a show like Faye Emerson's getting by without a tweaking from [New York newspaper television critics] Gould, Crosby, et al." These TV critics wielded considerable sway in a television market like New York, and their critical comments undoubtedly influenced early network television.[25]

The exhibition of brassieres on live models was initially out of the question on television so dummies were used, but the industry magazine *Sponsor* reported CBS-TV considered changing its display standards to real women.[26] "A tasty idea," remarks Helffrich, "and I guess it remains to be seen whether or not it is actually done."[27] Whatever would happen one thing was clear: NBC-TV would not be a trailblazer in this area. As it turned out, the upstart ABC-TV network used a live model. Moreover, Helffrich noted, ABC permitted the ad to be broadcast during "family viewing" time—considered evenings until 9:30 P.M., eastern time, 8:30 P.M., central time, and 9 P.M. elsewhere. On Friday evening, October 20, 1950, the Hi/low Witchery and Disguise Bra was displayed on a live model to network audiences. Helffrich comments, "I haven't caught this particular pioneering effort but called my counterpart at ABC, Grace Johnson, to get her side of the story. She insists the plug was handled in good taste [and] says they have had only one adverse letter." Nonetheless, the *New York World Telegram* was critical of the "event" as was John Crosby, TV critic for the *New York Herald Tribune*, who wrote that using a live model "accentuates the—uh—positive, if I make myself clear, and I'm afraid that I do." On balance, the commercial was praised by entertainment industry publications *Variety*, *Radio Daily*, and *Cue*. Helffrich, again toeing the conservative company line, notes, "NBC . . . is taking a wait and see attitude."[28]

Sensitivity to bra advertising persisted throughout the 1950s. In mid-November 1957, NBC-TV preempted the popular *Perry Como Show* for a special, *Holiday in Las Vegas*, sponsored by Exquisite Form Bra. In what is described only as "a situation" having occurred, a puzzled Helffrich writes, "There have been enough phone calls and letters on [this] . . . broadcast to suggest *something*. But what? . . . Parallels and precedents notwithstanding, polite phrasing and poetic persuasion aside, [the brassiere ads] bothered certain viewers . . . [more w]omen more than men, in mail I personally have seen." Helffrich ticks down a list of potential reasons for the clear audience revulsion: the Las Vegas locale perhaps; maybe because full-bosomed actress Jayne Mansfield was featured in the show despite, he says, the "careful avoidance of the contiguity of the commercials themselves and program material." Perchance, muses Helffrich, it was the "cumulative feelings brought to the program by certain viewers . . . I truly do not know, nor do some very mature colleagues working with me. I do know that I . . . am concerned over such critical reaction . . . which articulates itself around words like 'indecency' and 'embarrassing' in the family viewing circle."[29] And it was puzzling indeed. Newspapers and magazines of the era continually ran large display ads for all manner of brassieres and girdles, but the women featured wearing them were *illustrations*, not photographs. If a photo of a bra-clad female was too close to the real thing, the use of a live, moving brassiere model on television would be considered a near obscenity for many or at the very least a deeply offensive breech of taste. It is important to recall that gazing upon the female breast in this era was a taboo of enduring power, one wrapped in sex, lust, guilt, shame, and all the baser emotions to which "decent" people should not be tempted or exposed.

Bra-ad complaints persisted into at least the early-to-mid-1960s, prompting Helffrich in his final NBC CART to ask: "Is it or is it not 'poor taste in advertising' to advertise a brassiere on television?" He quotes a *Printers' Ink* column that proclaimed horror over an Exquisite Form Bra commercial's "'close-up of [a] bosom that filled the entire screen and went into clinical details about a gadget in front put there to adjust the fit.'" Helffrich explains what was actually presented was a special-effect shot of the garment itself "as *if* filled out by the anatomical matter it was designed to fit," not a close-up of a breast itself. In a direct and pointed defense, Helffrich writes, "The exploration of how and how not to advertise brassieres . . . [is a discussion that] examines 'good taste' as a euphemism for evasion. . . . 'Personal undergarments' advertising, invariably relates itself to alleged damage to children, presumes a direct contribution to delinquency, and so on. If the handling is provocative, cheap, or essentially dishonest in its appeal: agreed. Otherwise, nonsense; arrant, head-in-the-sand, silly nonsense. . . . Avoidance of television commercials concerning brassieres in effect would be avoidance of reflection in television of a major cultural preoccupation: the bosom fetish. Better a passing reference to the fact that those 'personal undergarments' are designed to fit than television pretence denying their existence."[30]

Here, Helffrich speaks to the essence of the matter: a brassiere was not merely a functional piece of female underclothing, it was an erotic symbol, part and parcel of a culturally constructed American breast fetish. Bra ads by their nature hyperfocused the ongoing societal obsession with the female bosom. Advertising such an obsession on the ubiquitous new medium of television made sexual propriety an explosive social issue that held economic and political consequences for the networks. Television in general and brassiere commercials specifically provided many outlets for "inappropriate" gazing of the female breast. At midcentury, ads like these were regarded as yet another repudiation of a "system of sexual controls"—social strictures that, observes cultural historian Beth Bailey, "few were willing and able to publicly reject."[31]

Deodorants

Of all the personal toilette products advertised on postwar television, deodorants caused Helffrich and NBC the most concern. The concern mimicked radio listeners' past aesthetic objections to commercials for personal-grooming products.[32] Helffrich states that deodorant products were "generally not acceptable [on television]" as an NBC Code classification—although NBC radio enjoyed a long and profitable experience with Lifebuoy deodorant soap. Still, despite its somewhat odious radio legacy Helffrich concedes there were "conceivable ways in which deodorants could be handled acceptably on television, but our imaginations can likewise picture some pretty unacceptable treatments."[33] He adds if a sponsor or agency could produce a deodorant ad that NBC considered in good taste, there would be "no reason to assume categorically the we wouldn't be unwilling to at least give it a look."[34] For example, Helffrich refused the airing of Dial soap commercial until the producing ad agency agreed to delete "an excessive number of mentions of the word 'odor.'"[35] By August 1949, all NBC-TV O&O stations had approved the broadcasting of deodorant commercials, but the category was still banned from full network advertising by programming boss Weaver who favored "holding the line" on axillary products.[36]

Even though personal-hygiene goods found their way onto WNBT-TV, NBC's New York O&O, local presentation was still heavily policed and scrutinized. Of course, as advertisers experimented with video marketing, Helffrich did not hesitate to suggest ways to sell questionable products. For instance, offering ad agencies ideas on how to sell Clorets gum—a breath deodorant—Helffrich advises, "The general rule . . . on all these personal products is to have the copy stress the enhancement of one's life derived from the use of the product rather than to itemize ad nauseum the results from failure to use the product."[37] An example of one such "failure" was included in the commercial copy Helffrich deleted from *The Kathi Norris Show*, a local daytime talk program.[38] The underarm roll-on spot for Yodora read: "'Every other deodorant had either caused a pimply rash or dried to a hard crusty mess.' There were other equally choice lines about 'unsightly arm pits,'" Helffrich says, concluding, "[The commercial] was extremely negative . . . [and] derogatory to Yodora competition."[39] The same problems persisted for Heed deodorant, the presentation of which was, according to Helffrich, not only "unfairly derogatory to [its] competition but . . . concentrated [its] copy on the dire results bound to catch up with anyone who does not use Heed." The commercial reads in part:

MAN—(*heavy voice*): They're whispering all over town.

TWO GIRLS—(*gossipy tone*): Mary lost her man because of *that.*

Helffrich notes, "The copy thereafter builds [with] . . . more emphasis on '*that*' until '*that*' sounds pretty dreadful. (We are not making a pitch for everyone to go around unwashed, but neither do we think NBC would get any orchids for irritating everybody with copy of this type)."[40]

The same reasoning applied to Five-Day Deodorant Pads, another personal product that ran afoul of NBC-TV standards. After previewing the commercial, Helffrich frets that the copy had a much too "negative stress, unfairly hitting the competition." Its theme of "no muss, no fuss, no mess" was unsettling to CA because of one key sentence: "'Throw away the pad, throw away with it hundreds of thousands of odor forming bacteria that other deodorants leave under your arm.'" Helffrich labels this "an unnecessary dreary claim," christens it "bunk," and points out, "No deodorant advertiser suggests an avoidance of soap and water before application of the product."[41]

Helffrich's insistence that Five-Day change the tone of its "tasteless" deodorant campaign flew in the face of sure-fire "negative" marketing strategies that had persisted in broadcasting since at least the late 1920s. NBC-TV CA would have none of it and at least for a while effectively blocked the winning albeit negative ad technique. But after being turned away by the CA department on what Helffrich called "principle and . . . precedent," the Five-Day Deodorant Pad interests "appealed" to NBC-TV's top management, and the censor's decision was overturned. The questionable commercial was suddenly deemed in "good taste" because management determined that the underarm "application [of the Five-Day Deodorant Pad was shown] *without movement*" and was, therefore, "well done" since it was patterned after the magazine ad exhibiting a pretty girl administering the product. The decision was clearly capricious, and the actual reason for the network's change of heart may be that NBC-TV simply wanted a share of the ad buy. Helffrich relates, "We learned subsequently that NBC was alone in its initial opposition [to Five-Day], CBS and all the other leading broadcasters [had accepted] the material."[42] Not that this episode drained the CA department of its vigilance on poor taste in deodorant commercials. As late as June 1954, NBC rejected "three Arid [commercials] in toto," Helffrich says. "They showed . . . a drawing [of] a circle around the armpit of a dress, representing the area destroyed by perspiration, and then ripping the dress apart."[43] No appeal occurred this time, and the spots were not broadcast.

This notion of bodily odor control and social reserve is rooted in seventeenth- and eighteenth-century Europe. French bourgeois society drew up extensive codes of manners and cleanliness as a reaction to the boorish pomp and hierarchy of King Louis XIV's court.[44] However, from about the time of the American Revolution, the fermented ideas of British royalty, most notably the writings of Lord Chesterfield, shaped the

Yankee sense of self-restraint and propriety.[45] Spurred by industrial and hygienic innovations of the late nineteenth century, the Victorians built upon Lord Chesterfield's earlier notions of cleanliness and self-control and brought forth new, more complex standards for bodily restraint, this time based upon reason and character. Such Promethean rules were the markers against which social deviance would now be measured and condemned. But, just in case character and reason were in short supply, the Victorians also sought to regulate personal behavior by identifying and restricting what they perceived as deviant in word or deed by the "lower" immigrant class. By employing the legal power of the state, invoking the guilt and morality of evangelical Protestantism, or simply implying class or teleological distinctions, the Victorians left a significant censorious legacy. After years of debilitating economic depression, repeal of prohibition, and the tumult of global war, some strictures eased, but most Americans still clung to many previous ideas of what constituted the "social graces." And television advertising breathed new life into lingering prewar attitudes of good taste.

Laxatives, Toilets, and Toilet Paper

Given postwar American television's concern with bodily odor, laxative advertising was simply out of the question on the NBC-TV network and its locally owned and operated broadcast stations. The concern, comments Helffrich, was "not that laxative advertising [had] never been handled by NBC radio or TV but . . . if it can be lived without . . . makes for a less graphic bombardment of the viewer."[46] Nonetheless, laxative ads *were* considered and accepted by the NBC O&Os, and a few experimental commercials, though seriously circumscribed, were broadcast on WNBT-TV, New York. In Helffrich's early CART reports, bowel purgatives appear to be permissible so long as certain appropriate limits were "maintained on the number of advertisers in this classification at any given time."[47] But other problems cropped up with commercial copy that overstressed the laxative effects of products not necessarily categorized or manufactured as an intestine purifier per se. For instance, an ad about refreshing Duffy Mott prune juice was cut from two to one "laxative mentions," and an alarmed network management, says Helffrich, insisted to be "appraised of the extent at any given time of this kind of advertising over NBC facilities."[48] But early laxative ads would not have a smooth time of it on television—no pun intended. Helffrich later writes that a "leading [New York ad agency had] been pressing NBC-TV for facilities to advertise a well-known laxative. . . . The thing [was] discussed in detail on a management level and rejected." On July 20, 1953, NBC sales director Jack Herbert explained that NBC-TV had "no laxatives on the television network and after weighing the pros and cons, we have decided against accepting any laxative for television advertising at this time. The subject of acceptability . . . has come up . . . time and again, and we have taken the position [such advertising] might offend the sensibilities of the audience or the stations themselves. . . . [W]e feel . . . [it inadvisable] . . . to open the door to this product classification on the television network. . . . [I]f we accept laxative advertising from one client, we will have requests . . . from others."[49] By the fall of 1953, the laxative advertising ban was extended to *all* NBC O&O stations.

But, as seen with other ad categories like those of girdles and brassieres, no decision was ever final because postwar television advertising was in flux. Just a year after the laxative ban, NBC program chief Weaver called together a committee to explore the matter of physic advertising on television. Helffrich quotes Weaver saying, "Company practice for this classification . . . should parallel radio," which permitted such advertising. Besides, Helffrich writes, "The acceptance of laxative [commercials] on television [was] not contrary to [NBC's] published polices or the National Association of Radio and Television Broadcasters (NARTB) code." Both Weaver and Helffrich agreed that *all* ads should be decided by their own merits, that CA guidelines should never supersede "good judgment," and that NBC reserved final say on what is acceptable or offensive.[50]

The frequency of laxative ads or overstatements of the cleansing power of prune juice posed fewer problems to NBC-TV than the exhibition of certain toilette activities. For example, in the case of the laxative Sal Hepatica, the brief display of a toilet in the commercial had to be deleted. Helffrich explains that a television ad picturing "a pajamaed man in front of a bathroom medicine chest" was okay but it was important to keep "out of camera range [the] shot of popular plumbing."[51] An eight-second ad for Vanish, a bathroom-bowl cleanser, was not permitted on the air because the drawing on its label depicted "a series of dots plunging downward to the bowl of a toilet."[52] Harry Ward, head of the CA department at NBC-TV in Chicago, reported that he turned down "a prospective local TV sale from a fellow who makes transparent Lucite toilet tanks. . . . What manner of quirk[,] . . . caprice or depravity would prompt one to buy [such a thing?"][53] In another unusual turn of events, Dow Chemical Company wished to advertise a line of its many subsidiary products on the popular NBC-TV drama *Medic*—considered by some media historians as a "pioneer in TV realism."[54] The show frequently used actual doctors and nurses in its cast and in September and October 1955 was the first television series to exhibit an actual childbirth.[55] Broadcasting the birth of a human baby was one thing, but Dow wished to advertise plastic toilet seats on the show, an image NBC-TV simply could not countenance. Helffrich observes, "Anticipated demurs all along the line materialized on this . . . and my hunch is the issue won't be pressed further."[56] It was not. In this case, NBC management imagined its audience as priggish and unaccepting of such images based on past aesthetic taboos. Social historian Julie L. Horan traces such priggishness to the Victorian era's denial of "natural emotions and bodily functions. . . . [W]hen it came to relieving themselves, the Victorians went to great lengths to hide the action." Nineteenth-century furniture, she points out, was designed to obscure from view the unplumbed toilet bowl. "The furniture produced was reminiscent of James Bond's toys," Horan explains. "Gadgets and secret doors were hidden in every corner of this seemingly innocuous cupboard" all to conceal the sight of the "offensive" chamber pot.[57] Clearly, such tradition was not given up gracefully when it came to witnessing flushable plumbing in television commercials at mid-twentieth century. And the taboo was not just confined to commercials; it spilled over into popular NBC-TV programming as well. Milton Berle in his autobiography tells the story of Sharkey, a seal who was prevented from doing his big trick on television: balancing a small potty on the tip of his nose.[58] Images of lavatory vessels, even one that a sea mammal could counterpoise on its snout, would simply not be sanctioned for television viewing.

For NBC-TV, toilet *paper* was also considered a "borderline" product for television advertising in 1950. DuMont Television Network and ABC-TV had approved shooting scripts and concomitant scheduling of the tissue product, but Helffrich had "recommended against acceptance."[59] So fearful of public and political reaction, NBC-TV even hesitated to *say* the words *toilet paper* on the air. Northern Paper Mills, manufacturers of such tissue and other paper products, requested ad time through local NBC spot sales, with Helffrich suggesting Northern's commercials "concentrate . . . their attention on . . . towels, napkins, or facial tissues with only incidental visual showing of the fourth . . . product, toilet paper. . . . [A]n audio reference [could be made] stating that in addition to the facial tissues or napkins or towels 'Northern Paper Mills . . . manufacturer . . . other high grade tissue products;' the toilet paper at that point would be seen."[60] This obtuse and timid approach was not acceptable to Northern, whose only reason for experimenting with television was to clearly advertise its line of toilet tissue. Nonetheless, NBC-TV and Helffrich were content to consistently turn away potential income that might have been generated by toilet-paper advertising. In a 1954 CART report, Helffrich notes editorial deletions caused the "outright loss of revenue . . . on behalf of Charmin Toilet Tissue" but insisted that toilet paper "continues as a classification of business the Management thinks NBC had best do without."[61] NBC's refusal of toilet paper advertising is an example of how it imagined its audience would react and the public-relations problems it might bring. Such prudishness was but another nod to the nineteenth-century legacy that eschewed acknowledgment of personal wiping after toilette activities. According to the Scott Paper Company, another manufacturer of bathroom tissue, Victorian-era "toilet paper was [first] sold from behind the drugstore counter. . . . Women would ask for [it] by brand name or lower their eyes and say, 'I'll have one of *those*, please.'" Horan submits such behavior indicates "toilet paper reminded genteel citizens of the base needs of the body."[62] Clearly, people of class and deportment were circumspect about purchasing the product and did not wish to see advertisements for it.

By 1956, bathroom tissue had assumed a higher profile in local drugstores and supermarkets, and commercials for it were on track as a viable category for local spot sales. Nonetheless, Helffrich et al. were still concerned about the images that had to be conjured to sell toilet paper. "For one thing," Helffrich grouses, "the proposed [bathroom] setting [for the toilet-tissue commercial] was so specifically preoccupied with the more related plumbing, and for another, the wording of the claims seemed to linger like a fetish . . . creating graphic mental images." In a letter to the ad agency, Helffrich's New York office

CA chief, Carl Watson, wrote, "Video-wise I think we can allow for a shot of the bathroom and even some occasional panning to take in the towel racks, shower curtain, soap dish, washbowl and the tub, but feel that any additional panning should avoid bringing the actual toilet into evidence," adding, "If, by way of showing the washbowl or some other section at the same level, the top of the water closet is also in evidence, I am sure it will not be objectionable." Helffrich concludes, "All of this is a little too much and needless to say in for modification before . . . the folks at home get to see it."[63]

Innocuous toilette activities like teeth brushing were also considered highly taboo by some in postwar America. Helffrich, quoting a letter from the *Washington Post*, opines about an audience member "upset over a toothpaste commercial." The viewer wrote that tooth brushing is the "sort of toilet activity . . . usually done in one's private bathroom . . . [and this ad carries that] disgusting act too far. I turned off the program as I hope many others will do if [station's] continue feeding the public such filth."[64] Labeling as "filth" the act of tooth brushing in a television commercial exemplifies the depth of feeling such images provoked in some Americans and tells much about viewers' cultural relationship to bodily restraint at mid-twentieth century.

Depilatories and Skin-Care Products

Network television ads for hair-removal products were yet another suspect commercial category at NBC-TV. By 1950, the female depilatory Nair was approved as "safe and effective" by the Food and Drug Administration, the Better Business Bureau, and the American Medical Association.[65] Nonetheless, advertising for Nair and other women's hair-removal products was still restricted to local NBC O&O stations and only on daytime network television for which the audience was constructed as primarily female. *The Kathi Norris Show*—a weekday afternoon women's program on NBC-TV's New York station, WNBT—was thought the perfect place for a "trial acceptance" of the new depilatory cream labeled Irma. Helffrich had used the show in the past for brassiere advertising and thought Norris could handle the commercial "in good taste" so long as the "plug refrain[ed] from [a] demonstration of application."[66] Helffrich had difficulty with a television demonstration of the depilatory wiping hair from women's legs, underarms, or faces. He rejected one cosmetic hair remover's claim to expertly eliminate female facial whiskers because, said Helffrich, the ad featured the "depiction of lathering up a bearded lady."[67]

This kind of so-called "negative" television ad was highly policed by Helffrich and his local CA departments and was never seen on the NBC-TV network. A negative commercial to Helffrich was one that conjured a social picture of dire personal consequence to those who did not buy and use a given manufactured product. Such was the case in declining the account of the acne medication Clearasil. Helffrich writes, "NBC Management feels on deodorant, laxative and other advertising of a personal nature that public acceptance depends entirely on the positiveness of approach." Again stating NBC-TV's unwillingness to accept a commercial that "details what happens through failure to use a product instead of discussing positively the enhancement to one's life through the use of the product." NBC-TV refused the proposed Clearasil commercial on three counts: its approach was "negative [and] it used the word 'pimple,'" which, determined Helffrich, was far too "graphic [a] description . . . [of] externally caused skin blemishes," violating a network policy of not "pitching a sales message exclusively to adolescents." Helffrich explains the decision was made "on the basis of medical . . . and public relations . . . advice," calling the "depictions of the physiological differences of adolescents . . . borderline and inadvisable." He held up a competitive skin care product, Cuticura, as an example of a commercial with wider message appeal than solely adolescents and one that would successfully make the transition from radio to television.[68] Cuticura later fell out of favor as an exemplar of good taste in blemish medication when the manufacturer submitted an idea about cannibals who would not eat a teenager because her skin was craggy with pustules and blackheads.[69] The "acne war" was heightened in early 1951 when competitor ABC-TV agreed to air a Clearasil commercial showing a teen with one substantial and obvious skin blemish. The CA department nonetheless held firm with Helffrich explaining that NBC-TV "favored representing the skin condition more by mood and copy then by apparent disfiguration."[70]

The ever-vigilant NBC-TV CA Department found and expunged all manner of "bad taste" in commercials. In 1948, a television ad could show a person sneezing, but the *sound* of the sneeze was not permitted. A natural, synchronized sneeze would, according to NBC-TV CA, constitute a breach of taste. Therefore, in both Vicks Vaporub and Vicks Vatronol commercials, "silent sneezes" accompanied by judiciously written copy on cold-symptom relief were the only acceptable option.[71] It would also be in bad taste to show people getting in and out of bed in order to sell Pequot sheets and pillowcases,[72] refer to so-called detergent hands as "reddened, rough . . . cracked and bleeding,"[73] and schedule antacid announcements for Tums and Bromo-Seltzer during mealtimes.[74] Among other early commercials for which Helffrich refused advertising on NBC-TV was Absorbine Jr. (for "pre-occupation with symptoms of athletes foot"),[75] Preparation H (for "telling us the product's [ingredients would] shrink . . . hemorrhoids"),[76] Doan's Pills, a bladder and kidney nostrum (for "bad acting" and "dreary copy"),[77] and Polident, a denture cleaner (for "bad taste in general").[78] Helffrich, therefore, not only acted as a de facto Federal Trade Commission commissioner—inspecting commercial copy and storyboards for legitimacy and veracity—but as a sort of *supra* creative director to some of America's largest ad agencies and advertisers. It was ultimately Helffrich who decided if it was bad acting, questionable images, or depressing copy that made a commercial unacceptable.

Truth in Advertising

The NBC-TV CART reports from 1948 through 1960 indicate a consistent preoccupation with the probity of television commercials, suggesting "truth in advertising" was a central concern to most viewers and critics of television. Helffrich expended much of his energy scrutinizing storyboards and finished commercials and writing about the veracity, puffery, and legitimacy of advertiser's marketing declarations.[79] When ads used the word *free* in their commercials, for example, Helffrich suggested instead the phrase "without additional expense" or "at no extra charge."[80] The Hotel New Yorker, advertising locally, once offered a "free" calendar to guests; Helffrich changed the statement to "a gift" done so, he explains, "to comply with the prevailing FTC attitudes on the use of the word 'free.'"[81] The number of commercial copy changes in which Helffrich and the CA department participated is long and ponderous. From demanding Snow Crop ground coffee stop referring to instant coffee as a "trick,"[82] to correcting the inference that a Sonotone hearing aid was the antidote for deafness,[83] to toning down Philco's rather expansive claim of having made a record player providing "the greatest fidelity in all the history of recorded music,"[84] NBC-TV censors clearly had their hands full.

Helffrich and the CA Department were particularly sensitive to commercials advertised on the popular children's show *Howdy Doody*. For example, one sponsor, Ovaltine—a vitamin-fortified chocolate powder—claimed that when the product was mixed with milk and drunk, it "cured" laziness in children.[85] Another extravagant and worrisome claim was that Ovaltine contained "more vitamin C than . . . a pound of steak." Helffrich was concerned the commercials could cost NBC-TV and the advertiser "public good will from parents who find their children unwilling to eat a pound of steak." Programming chief Weaver even weighed in on the controversy, stressing "caution with ad copy pushing to children what are basically adult considerations."[86] Helffrich frequently had NBC-TV top management support for his occasionally costly decisions. Journalist and former ABC-TV vice president Bert Briller recalled having lunch with Helffrich in early August 1955. Briller watched in shock as an otherwise teetotaling Helffrich drank a double martini because, he writes, the censor "had [just] turned down a campaign for a headache medicine, and the client announced that it was taking the $2,000,000 budget to another network."[87] Helffrich and Watson did not think there was sufficient clinical proof that the pain reliever was any better than its competitors. Helffrich determined "the [ad] copywriter . . . had gone overboard . . ."[88] In truth, the advertiser wished to use the therapeutic study deceptively. Apparently, the pain reliever was tested only on women with postpartum depression, so NBC asked its medical advisers if the test could be extrapolated to general aches and pains, as the sponsor's copy was doing.[89] The answer was no, yet the offending advertiser balked. Later, the FTC issued a consent order compelling the manufacturer to amend its disingenuousness with "corrective" and more forthcoming commercials.[90]

Cigarettes and Tobacco Advertising

For all his "vigilant" work—even though some labeled it severe and faultfinding—Helffrich could not touch one product, at least not with any degree of success: cigarettes. Since the beginning of network radio, cigarettes held a secure and privileged position at NBC, and by as early as 1949, cigarette advertising accounted for 19.4 percent of all television revenue. In only his second CART report, Helffrich naively raised "strong objections" to a tobacco commercial that featured an "exaggerated picturization . . . of the lesser degree of [throat] irritability found in Phillip Morris cigarettes." Both CBS-TV and NBC-TV told the agency handling the account such a treatment was forfeiting credibility.[91] Little did Helffrich or his colleagues know this was not a single misstep but a new and calculated technique for cigarette advertising. The tobacco companies actually encouraged consumers to use "healthfulness" as the standard by which to judge cigarettes. This rather-bizarre retailing approach occurred as a reaction to dozens of postwar scientific and popular articles that presented new research linking smoking to lung cancer, strokes, and myriad diseases. The tobacco companies dismissed the news as a "health scare" but, write marketing professors Richard W. Pollay and Timothy Dewhirst, so-called motivation researchers and advertising gurus "advised the industry to shift from explicit verbal assertions of health toward implied healthfulness, an approach that incorporated the use of visual imagery."[92]

Aware of the growing reach of television, Helffrich became concerned over a questionable commercial planned by Camel cigarettes. The suggested copy read, "A thirty-day nationwide test of hundreds of Camels smokers revealed not a single case of throat irritation due to smoking Camels." Helffrich requested from the ad agency "an outline of their proposed visual treatment [of the commercial] in order to avoid . . . exaggeration."[93] What happened next is a matter of speculation since research reveals no further mention of Camel cigarettes in *any* CART report after September 30, 1948. This may have been because Camels were the first cigarette brand to deeply insinuate itself into NBC-TV programming.

The R. J. Reynolds Tobacco Company, makers of Camel, sponsored the first daily television newscast, *The Camel News Caravan* with host John Cameron Swayze—essentially a "talking head" seen Monday through Friday evenings for fifteen minutes. NBC-TV began primitive "newscasts" on February 16, 1948, with *The Camel Newsreel Theatre* broadcasting a ten-minute Fox-Movietone Newsreel. NBC-TV also experimented with a weekly fifteen-minute newscast sponsored by Esso gasoline. The Camel newsreel program lasted only a year, and on Valentines Day 1949,

The Camel News Caravan with Swayze debuted. The program was on NBC-TV for seven and a half years.[94] As they had with radio, television sponsors in the early days directed the content of the shows they "owned." And as such, Camel cigarettes required that their news show cover certain topics—football for men, fashion for women—and avoid shots of "no smoking" signs, anyone puffing on cigars (with the exception of British Prime Minister Winston Churchill)[95] and any video of *actual* camels. An actual drooling, vile-smelling, sludge-spitting dromedary was, for some reason, not considered "as attractive as the sponsor's logo," an artist's rendering that was apparently a more fetching depiction of a camel.[96] Reuven Frank, later president of NBC-TV News, was a young writer on the *Camel* show and recalls that big tobacco totally dominated the budding network news operation: "What Camel wanted Camel got . . . because they paid so much. . . . The money from Camel cigarettes supported the entire national and worldwide structure of NBC Television News—salaries, equipment, bureau rents, and overseas allowances . . . with enough left over to allow for some other programs."[97]

Other cigarette brands were cited and discussed during the first six years of the CART reports, but after 1953, no brand was ever specifically mentioned again. The last one to be directly accused of using "alarmist copy" was Kool cigarettes. Helffrich wrote that the commercial inferred Kool had "some effect on [colds], flu, grippe, etc.,"[98] and throughout the 1950s, Kool was positioned as a cigarette that had remedial qualities since its filter tip contained the "taste of menthol."[99] The ad also presented what Helffrich characterized as "an epidemic scare," to wit:

> ANNOUNCER: (*Newsy—Important*) City after city reports colds, raw, rasping throats, grippe and flu! Intelligent Americans who hear these alarming facts will understand why they, too, may want to switch to *Kools* cigarettes. So when you've got a cough?—smoke *Kools*! Throat raw?—smoke *Kools*! Got a cold?—smoke *Kools*!"[100]

A righteous Helffrich and company angrily rejected the above ad. But it was a Pyrrhic victory for CA because the judgment only applied to NBC owned-and-operated *radio* stations; NBC's O&O television properties and its network operations were unaffected by the decision.

Under such conditions, NBC-TV CA had little say in the ad copy of certain cigarette advertisers, and considerable latitude was taken. For example, Helffrich permitted a Lucky Strike commercial in an early televised football game that had Bob Stanton, an NBC staff announcer, saying, "Just before the opening kickoff, I'm going to get set with a Lucky Strike cigarette," and "While we're waiting for the play to resume, how about joining me in some real deep-down smoking enjoyment."[101] In addition, other questionable claims made it on the air. "We have from Brown and Williamson Company," writes Helffrich, "substantive data that 39,468 dentists recommend Viceroys to their patients who smoke."[102] Yet, occasionally the CA department still balked at some tobacco-company assertions. A cigarette named Cavalier, for instance, in a proposed network-radio commercial averred the "flavor and lightness" of the tobacco blend meant "no heavy . . . back away breath with Cavalier."[103] It is unclear whether the ad was rejected on the basis of its dubious veracity or its connection to bodily/mouth odor—an area in which Helffrich rarely wavered. He also railed against the ad agency that produced the popular *Old Gold Show* on NBC radio. The September 14, 1951, program was interrupted by a presidential address with the announcer saying, "Our program is being cut short so that we may bring you the address of President Truman from San Francisco. I suggest you light up an Old Gold and relax as you listen to the president." Helffrich reprimands, "Such a tie-in [is] in bad taste . . . and we have an assurance from the agency involved that this kind of thing will be avoided in the future."[104] It may appear the CA chief had at least some persuasive power over the cigarette companies, but when one looks closely, one sees Helffrich's small victories occurred only on NBC radio, not in network television.

Helffrich also played referee to the childish complaints of competing cigarette sponsors. The "highly competitive claims" of Old Gold cigarettes caused "resentment on the part of another [unnamed] NBC cigarette client," writes Helffrich. "Some tempering had been accomplished . . . but somehow Old Gold still got in some [unflattering] cracks" about its competition.[105] On another occasion, Lucky Strike was outraged with an ad featuring a man writing down his New Year's resolutions, one of which was quitting cigarettes. A spokesman for the tobacco company snapped it was "a slap at smoking."[106] Often, comedian's jokes about cigarettes were considered "overly acidic" by the tobacco companies and viewed as unfair. "Please watch," scolds an unenthusiastic Helffrich to its on-air talent.[107] Even the powerful Milton Berle and his *Texaco Star Theater* were edited on behalf of the cigarette interests. Berle planned a burlesque lampooning cigarette commercials and, relates Helffrich, "It seemed to [the NBC] Management figures with whom we checked ... [Berle's sketch was] too ridiculous and slapstick to be taken seriously, but NBC tobacco advertisers thought differently."[108] The piece was cut.

In 1952, *Reader's Digest* ran an influential article titled "Cancer by the Carton," and by early the next year, a widely circulated medical report by Dr. Ernst L. Wynder heralded a definitive link between cigarette smoking and cancer. Over the next two years, dozens of prominent articles appeared in the *New York Times* and other major publications including *Good Housekeeping, Woman's Home Companion, The New Yorker,* the *Nation,* and *Look.*[109] In 1953, sales of cigarettes went into an unusual, sudden decline, "evidence," states historian Karen S. Miller, "that the public increasingly believed there existed a link between smoking and disease."[110] By 1954, Helffrich suggested "reevaluation" of cigarette advertising in light of the "considerable controversy" that plagued some of NBC's leading tobacco accounts. His CART report included a newsmagazine *TIDE* article that associated smoking with lung cancer. Helffrich writes that the deadly link created "a complex problem [both] for the cigarette interests and for the media carrying their advertising."[111] As the cigarette companies panicked, internal memos from the industry-funded Tobacco Institute Research Committee allude to the antismoking publicity as the "1954 emergency."[112] According to a tobacco-industry insider, advertising expenditures leapt from $55 million in 1952 to about $150 million by 1959, most of it spent on television commercials and public relations "damage control."[113] With its fierce political lobby, the powerful public-relations firm of Hill and Knowlton easily able to spin the scientific debate,[114] and legions of contentious lawyers, the cigarette industry was not one with which to trifle. And, given the astonishing amount of money they exhausted on television, any CA questioning of outrageous cigarette claims fell silent. Helffrich was an antismoking advocate but, as a company executive and chief censor, clearly abetted NBC management's desire to keep important cigarette money flowing into network coffers. In an interesting aside, Helffrich's widow claims it may have been an operative for Action on Smoking and Health (ASH), then a New York–based antismoking organization, who first alerted the Federal Bureau of Investigation (FBI) of Helffrich's past Communist ties. She cited the informant as Warren Braren, a past associate of Helffrich, who claimed the CA chief was not doing enough to stop cigarette commercials on NBC-TV.[115]

Hard Liquor, Illegal Plugs, and Beer Advertising

Decades of angry, organized contentiousness citing the morality of drinking hard spirits and the excesses of the Volsted Act—also know as the National Prohibition Act passed by Congress in 1919—convinced distillers that broadcasting would be an inhospitable place for their message. In 1936, the liquor industry voluntarily barred radio ads promoting the consumption of all whiskey and other hard liquors. Twelve years later, the ban was extended to television and expanded at NBC-TV (for a while) to cover all soft drinks being sold as high-ball mixers. In mid-May 1950, Helffrich turned down spirits distributor Heublein's wish to advertise their Cock and Bull Ginger Beer, a fizzy ginger-ale product, as a mix with any of their various whiskeys.[116] But only six months later, Helffrich approved a Hoffman Beverages spot that *specifically* sold carbonated soft drinks as mixers for alcohol. In explaining his stunning reversal, Helffrich declares, ambiguously, that the Hoffman commercial went only "very slightly beyond precedent," and besides, the Hoffman spot was also being seen on competing television facilities. The apparent reason CA accepted the spot on an "experimental basis" was simply not to lose another significant buy to the competition.[117] NBC-TV also waited cautiously on embracing wine commercials and again took its cue for acceptance from its network competitors. By the summer of 1950, NBC-TV's new policy was to accommodate wine advertisements but only, Helffrich warns, if the visuals were "restricted to the most genteel deportment." CA would not pass a wine commercial that featured a "background of carousing [or] inferr[ed] therapeutic uplift ... [the spot should just] empha[size] ... simple and pleasurable refreshment."[118]

Despite numerous network sanctions against advertising spirits on television and notwithstanding the industry-imposed ban, references for hard liquor were still heard and seen on NBC-TV's most popular shows. Many times, the CA Department found and deleted the names of well-known call-brand liquors—in both packaging and plugs—that were placed in favorite programs. On Milton Berle's *Texaco Star Theater*, for example, a set dressed with whiskey bottles displaying the brand name labels Imperial and Carstairs were removed.[119] On Phil Silvers's *Arrow Show* of January 20, 1949, deleted were plugs for the whiskey blends Four Roses and Lord Calvert.[120] Sid Stone, the Berle show's old-time pitchman, had a liquor gag removed even though his reference was to the product's slogan, not the brand name. Cut was the joke: "Why only last week a 'Man of Distinction' bought one of those [electric] bulbs, and since then he's been lit every night."[121] The "Man of Distinction" reference was connected to a long-running (albeit snobbish) print campaign of a well-dressed celebrity, clutching a whiskey apéritif made with Lord Calvert.[122] Frequently during rehearsals of the Berle show, CA cut any unacceptable plugs, but Berle on many occasions would "accidentally" ad-lib them back in during the live telecast. Such was the case on the June 12, 1951, *Texaco* show. CA deleted scripted plugs for Four Roses and Liggett Drug Store, but unauthorized "mentions" for Lord Calvert and Greyhound Bus Lines were inserted during the broadcast.[123]

Plugola—the conscious, planned mention of a product or service for money, not part of the paid advertising schedule—was quite common during the early days of television, too. The words *plugola* and *payola* often used interchangeably would not enter the common parlance until the late 1950s after the quiz-show scandals that rocked the broadcasting industry. Helffrich never referred to the practice as "plugola" in his CART reports. He called it "graft," and its practice was maddening to him and his network CA team. Although Berle was a major abuser, product plugging was common on many of NBC-TV's more popular shows. In 1951, vaudeville comic Ed Wynn plugged Arthur Murray Dance Studios and Good Humor Ice Cream without censure, and the comedy team of Dean Martin and Jerry Lewis ad-libbed plenty of free mentions for Mixmaster electric mixers, Danny's Hide-A-Way (a New York saloon), and the Copacabana night club where they frequently appeared. "In many cases," Helffrich writes, "writers and talent may be getting paid off in one form or another for gratuitous trade plugs integrated into material." He demands the practice stop before "public awareness and trade press criticism . . . reflects badly on the talent and on NBC."[124] As a point in fact, a Nassau County community paper took a crack at comic Joey Fay's appearance on a 1951 Berle show: "Radio and TV gag writers have found a new way to make a buck if they can get away with it. The gimmick is to mention a commercial product in a gag. Standard price is $250 a mention. On Berle's show the other night, Joey Fay had a five-minute bit in which he mentioned five products. That was a quick $1,250 some writer made on the deal."[125]

Irving Grey, Berle's manager, denied the charges as unfounded. Nonetheless, to combat future problems and shift responsibility, NBC-TV decided to count any trade-name plugs against commercial time allotted to a given program's sponsor. This usually slowed or stopped the practice since the show's sponsor would investigate being charged for time it did not purchase. But NBC-TV also took a "can't beat 'em, join 'em" tack. The network's legal department, for example, suggested if television personalities were going to plug products illegally anyway, why not at least plug the ones already advertised on NBC? Lawyers issued a memo explaining that since "S.O.S. scouring pads are advertised on NBC and Brillo pads are not . . . if the [on-air talent] uses a [name] brand merely incidentally, it is preferable that . . . any specific brand [plugged] . . . be S.O.S."[126] Even Helffrich winks at offending comics, saying that a few network "sponsors [had] taken umbrage over the fact that trade name competitors of theirs not bankrolling NBC programs were publicized in topical gags and such on leading . . . shows, [so] watch it, huh?"[127]

Helffrich was also concerned about props or backdrops that featured the sponsor's trade name, slogan, or product. Frequently reminding the television audience who paid for a program (by using a background or embroidered curtain) did not accrue goodwill for the sponsor.[128] On the contrary, it was believed constant insinuation of a sponsor's name or slogan in early television programs worked to anger and upset viewers, a situation Helffrich and company sought to avoid. "On camera shots of such materials should be fleeting, not too frequent, and mindful of the need of maintaining a proper program balance," says Helffrich, exhorting that broadcasting codes restricted showing the sponsor's name, product, or slogan on "stationary backdrops in television presentations . . . [and] may be used only incidentally" while not encroaching on the show.[129] But solving such problems were easy compared to those posed by beer advertisers.

Television beer commercials had fewer "prop or plug" dilemmas than hard liquor, most likely because beer and wine *could* be advertised. However, beer faced other problems. As early as 1949, federal law prohibited any malt beverage from advertising its curative or therapeutic effects[130]—a cuff at folklore that claimed alcohol had "medicinal qualities." Later, in 1955, the government outlawed the use of "non-caloric" or "non-fattening" themes in beer ads (there was no equivalent to so-called light or low-carbohydrate beers on the market at that time).[131] Of course, Helffrich and CA made certain all federal and state laws concerning alcohol advertising were followed and enforced a blanket NBC-TV policy stating that "beer commercials [must] avoid any barroom atmosphere, inebriation, or hilarity in anyway undignified or condoning looseness."[132] Because of that CA dictum, beer ads were prohibited from showing a person actually *drinking* the beverage on the air. "Some beer clients," writes Helffrich, "get across the refreshment angle by attractive picturization of beer being served but [do] not carry it over into the quaffing of the beverage."[133] Pouring beer, gazing at it, even holding it was permitted, but sipping it on television was verboten. This "invisible beer-drinking" code in commercials is still practiced today in malt-beverage retailing, says the Beer Institute, the industry's Washington D.C.–based government and public-relations body established in 1986. According to the institute, guideline 11 of its thirteen marketing codes states, "Beer advertising . . . should not depict the act of drinking." The code also instructs beer advertising may "not portray sexual passion, promiscuity or any other amorous activity as a result of consuming beer" and "should not depict Santa Claus" in any ad or commercial.[134]

What, then, prompted all this fuss over beer commercials? Why such extreme behavior regarding alcoholic beverages on the part of Helffrich and the CA? Network and beer-industry fear of government reprisal appears to the major reason. Prohibition's stated goals were to reduce crime and corruption, solve class-based immigrant and urban social problems, reduce the tax burden created by prisons and poorhouses, and improve health and hygiene in the United States by eliminating its root cause—demon drink. The angry, prolonged struggle between the "wets" and "drys" after passage of the Eighteenth Amendment in 1920, and its subsequent repeal in 1933, was still fresh in the national memory in the 1950s. Some even thought the "noble experiment" would rebound after the Second World War.[135] Television's first congressional inquiry in 1952—an investigation originally called to determine the effects of TV programs that featured immorality, crime, and violence—included many witnesses who used the hearings as a forum to deplore the evils of drinking. Mass communication researcher Keisha L. Hoerrner found committee reports included a mountain of testimony from the American Temperance Society, the Woman's Christian Temperance Movement, and the National Grand Lodge of the International Order of Good Templars. These witnesses never mentioned violent content but rather concentrated their remarks on the harmful and unhealthy effects of television commercials that promote alcohol consumption to adults and children.[136] Clearly, postwar temperance advocates were still the kind of determined minority that commanded the attention of Helffrich and NBC-TV.

Humorous treatments of drinking, alcoholism, or alcoholics were suspect on NBC-TV, too. A questionable alcohol ad or even a comedian's joke about intemperance and its effects could bring a torrent of angry missives labeling NBC-TV irresponsible and acting without regard for the public good—and, indeed, during the 1953 holiday season, that is exactly what happened. Comic Sid Caesar once repeated his celebrated sketch "A Drunkard's Fate" on *Your Show of Shows* to angry letters of protest. The network did not hear complaints on the skit's first airing, causing Helffrich to write, "This tends to indicate that generally speaking our audience is not so much anti-beer and drinking as particular about when and how our program material touching upon same is presented."[137] Not surprisingly, 1952 statistics from NBC's research and planning division bear out Helffrich's assertion, revealing that nearly 60 percent of America families consumed beer, and 97 percent of those beer consumers drank at home. In addition, big breweries were now aligning themselves with major grocery chains and respectable food companies. In early 1950s print ads, Pabst beer teamed with Campbell's pork and beans, Swift's hot dogs, and Ritz Crackers in a "Picnic Values" promotion.[138] The alcoholic-beverages industry spent millions "normalizing and domesticating the consumption"[139] of its products, and television and print advertising was its vanguard. With the flood of postwar products, the money to buy them, and ubiquitous pro-drinking marketing, Prohibition was made to seem like a quaint idea from grandma's era. Rarely was it framed as an earnest social and moral movement undertaken to eradicate the scourge of alcohol. Indeed, by 1956, Pabst was crowing, "It's Beer, Mama, and TV . . . 3 ingredients of a recipe for successful living."[140]

Protecting the Institution

NARTB Code Review Board—established in 1952, also the year NARTB introduced its Television Code—responded to a total of 1,663 letters of viewer disapproval from January to October 1956. Of that sum, only 1 percent labeled television programming "immoral," 2 percent condemned its "excessive violence," and 3 percent decried a lack of "decency and decorum" on the air. There were also scattered comments on inappropriate children's and Western programming, representing .3 percent of the aggregate. The overwhelming complaint—93.7 percent of all objections—was television advertising.[141] Astonishingly, by the time the NARTB published the above statistics, over five hundred television stations were on the air serving forty million households. About 85 percent of American homes were watching approximately five hours of programming a day,[142] with advertisers already spending nearly a half-billion dollars a year on television.[143]

Given the millions watching, a few thousand complaints in the scheme of things could have been considered statistically insignificant, but they were not. The NARTB, NBC-TV, and the other networks expended an inordinate amount of time, energy, and resources responding to the comparative few who disapproved of one thing or another on early television. Why? Because it appears some viewers "counted" more than others. If the protests of certain "well-connected" individuals or small, organized groups reached the desks of important advertisers, competing media, or powerful politicos, significant dilemmas followed. Without network and industry public-relations intervention, serious revenue loss or political problems could arise. For those relatively few complaints, then, a sizeable censorship coterie was established and maintained by NBC-TV at an annual cost of over one-quarter million dollars per year.[144]

Helffrich insisted that sponsors and their agencies act "responsibly" and keep their commercial claims believable. "Too many advertisers," Helffrich states, "still practice weasel-wording, a calculated risk policy which helps to erode public confidence in advertising generally." Employing specific codes and regulations, he reasons, would protect the institution of advertising from itself and shield the broadcast institution from guilt by association and collusion. He admonishes both broadcasters and commercial interests to "think first of their responsibilities to the viewers . . . and [industry] self-regulatory activities in the protection of said audience will automatically protect broadcasters and broadcast advertisers." While laudable, Helffrich's naïve notions were ultimately self-defeating. To be sure, many ad agencies accepted or negotiated CA regulations, but many others opposed the idea of commercial-content control, saying it was not in the best interests of their clients. For that reason, advertisers often grudgingly or half-heartedly submitted to CA the required product-efficacy documentation. Helffrich, of course, saw such tepid, incomplete, or poorly tested evidence as "too flimsy for reasonable souls to accept." Clearly, it was not in either faction's nature to yield to the other. "'We have checked this with our lawyers,'" twaddled the ad agencies, "'and are assured that it will get by the FTC. No need for you to inquire any further.'" Such practices were infuriating to Helffrich and company. NBC-TV CA was convinced that advertisers were their own worst enemies and their arrogance helped "explain the recurring criticism not only of broadcast advertising in particular but broadcast practice in general." Helffrich, ever the mediator, tried to persuade both sponsors and NBC sales that each had a public responsibility in addition to their bottom line concerns. "Too many broadcasters, like advertisers," he chides, "still regard a reasonable concern for the interests of the customers who make up the audience as less important than the legitimate profit-making role of broadcasting and broadcast advertising." Helffrich also suggests that "overcommercialization" may be "a convenient catch-all for . . . viewer resistance . . . directed at the . . . believability of many [television ads]," concluding, "Critics of the length and frequency of commercials may very well be criticizing content."[145]

In a textbook on television advertising and production to which Helffrich contributed, the censor laments, "There is something inherently wrong . . . about a copy platform that screams of threatening shortages of a commodity for the sole purpose of moving it rapidly off shelves. . . . [An advertiser] has to include a very real consideration for the goodwill of the prospective buyers."[146] To make sense of his certainty from the perspective of our redoubtable postmodern world, one must understand Helffrich's sensibilities of right and wrong, his perceptions of the era, and his intuition of what the culture would bear were believed as true and generalizable. Audience mail, telephone calls, and feedback from his many community speeches only confirmed his suspicions, guided his decisions, and helped him construct a very specific yet wholly imagined audience. It was this construction, this *idea* of the home viewer that drove CA department decisions from 1948 to 1958. By 1960, however, things had changed.

By the time he retired from NBC-TV, Helffrich actually called for the abolishment of his job. The medium was maturing, and Helffrich saw television with new cultural boundaries to cross and important social taboos to address.

Conclusion: A Prescient Vision

*I*t is undeniable that from about the time he began work at NBC in 1933 and throughout the Great Depression, Helffrich grew into an unapologetic progressive activist. But Helffrich's politics at that time were more *Grapes of Wrath* than *Communist Manifesto,* more "Steinbeckian than Marxian," more fellow traveler than hard-liner. Although a bona-fide member of the Communist Party, Helffrich was not an unyielding ideologue. Interviews with those closest to him reveal Helffrich "sentimentalized the poor, the immigrant, the Negro, and the working class" as did his heroes—popular poets of the age Pete Seeger and Woody Guthrie, whose songs exalted the poor and disenfranchised.[1]

The Popular Front era and dawning of the New Deal marked what historian Wayne Hampton calls an "unprecedented glorification" of the workingman and workingwoman in literature and art. Helffrich was as well an erstwhile poet and former college literature major; he aligned himself with the artistic, intellectual New York crowd, most of whom shared his romanticized views of the common man. Richard Crossman, former Member of the British Parliament and editor of *The God That Failed*—a work that traces the attraction of Communism to prominent writers of the era—wrote of the intellectual allure of Marxism in both Europe and the United States in the 1930s and 1940s. Between the time of the October Revolution and the Stalin-Hitler Pact, countless numbers of atypical converts were drawn to the consummate promise of Communism. Crossman notes that such neophytes were "people of quite unusual sensitivity [that had . . .] a heightened perception of the sprit of the age, and *felt* more acutely than others both its frustrations and its hopes." Such a cohort, observes Crossman, made for the "most abnormal [of] Communists."[2] This is not to say there were no Communist hard-liners at the core of the Communist Party of the United States of America (CPUSA), for there most assuredly were. These calculating, scarlet-red ideologues schemed to undo the American political and economic system from within. However, encircling the

CPUSA's perimeter was the Popular Front, an impressionable, idealistic, and cerebral lot with which Helffrich closely identified. They believed that political demonstrations, songs of protest, and organizing for the good of the collective were the new patriotic expressions of America's "radical" heritage—but as historian Richard M. Fried points out, the nation's *"anti-radical* tradition [ran] at least as deep" with both sides in persistent conflict.[3]

It was during the early 1930s that Helffrich became involved with socialist-lawyer-turned-union-organizer Murray Berman and the American Labor Party, an offshoot of the Popular Front.[4] From the Union Settlement Association in New York City and for most of the "Pink Decade,"[5] Helffrich helped organize groups like the Young Communist League, the Young People's Socialist League, and the Negro Youth League. Despite his undeniable progressive bent, this book has argued that Helffrich did not bring a "Communist agenda" to NBC-TV network censorship per se; no absolute socialist political imprimatur is apparent in his work. Rarely are politics or economic policies overtly mentioned or discussed in his Continuity Acceptance Radio/Television (CART) reports. It is nonetheless clear that upon arriving at NBC each day, Helffrich did not remove his liberal mantle and put on a conservative corporate coat. Although overtly subversive or radical political ideology cannot be detected in his CART reports, Helffrich's writings and content decisions indicate an unambiguous and persistent progressive-humanist bent in most—but not all—areas of censorship. As was mentioned earlier, for example, Helffrich was not as kind to homosexuals as he was to other minorities, a position that appeared to change by the end of his tenure at NBC-TV.

By accepting a corporate management position in network television and recanting Communism, Helffrich's actions may be seen as a man who put aside some of his youthful political ideals and embraced the "American system" after the war—a system that appeared to be working. He had, after all, witnessed a significant change in the nation's social conditions from the Depression era and evidently believed that his corporate position as chief TV censor could engender further cultural transformations. For Helffrich, most stereotypes of 1950s mass culture had to be shattered, and his work played a significant part of this complicated negotiation after the war. Moreover, the period marked a transition between an older, neo-Victorian social system of gendered hierarchy, and the postwar's more liberal cultural order.[6] Helffrich's social outlooks were much more subtle and pluralist than had been realized. His CART reports suggest he frequently followed his progressive "gut" in delicate areas of morality. He also called his expurgations of insensitive, stereotyped portrayals of the mentally ill and African Americans on television "censorship by common sense." However, what seemed commonsensical to Helffrich was not always widely shared. His resolutely progressive views in most areas were, perhaps, not as perceptible in the liberal, creative communities of New York or other urbanized TV cities, but there is little doubt Helffrich's ideas on postwar integration was troubling to many southern segregationists. When one considers the race hatred and bigotry extant in the postwar era, Helffrich's progressive humanism on racial equality was really quite heroic, albeit not fully realized. Nonetheless, it was he who first called for an NBC-TV corporate-policy change, insisting on program integration years before the other networks. Helffrich's earlier progressive political activities might even be considered prologue to his abiding sense of obligation to blacks, immigrants, and the mentally ill and his insistence on removal of their stereotyped portrayals on television. As his hundreds of CART reports make evident, at NBC-TV, Helffrich used his power of censorship more as a scalpel than a cleaver.

And near the end of his tenure, Helffrich's CART reports assume the tone of a reluctant censor-philosopher. Helffrich writes, "We *need* controversy to grow as a nation. We need controversy and airing of our troubles to help us live with ourselves as we really are." In the same CART, he asks, "Would anything . . . too horrifying happen if censors . . . were faced more often with submissions . . . less 'safe' than the run of the mill?" adding, "Isn't it true that almost anything can be said or done if it is said or done with good and honest intent?" That last comment is not as naïve as it sounds. One need remember Helffrich still carried the hope of immense possibility for television, despite what he saw as intractable commercialization.[7]

From 1948 to 1958, Helffrich witnessed, participated in, and shaped a great flourishing of the medium—a palpable and exciting "golden age." As the industry now contemplated its second decade, Helffrich may have visualized the dawning of a second golden age and sensed that this renaissance could happen only by less timidity on behalf of sponsor, program supplier, and network. Helffrich's perception of what television *might* be caused him to declare that censors needed to live "more dangerously" in the coming 1960s,[8] suggesting it was easy to be *against* something, and challenged every NBC-TV editor to consciously be *for* something as well.[9] "You have to take some calculated risks if you stand [on principle]," says Helffrich, "even if you actively displease a peripheral few ... [I]t's part of the price for advancing the common and responsible good."[10] Helffrich was plainly summoning more ambitious television and encouraging future censors to permit ideas that would stun and illuminate audiences despite obvious corporate or cultural costs.

As his time as NBC-TV's chief censor drew short, Helffrich proffered a long list of "some of the realities and issues extant in the world [that television] cannot completely ignore." In his final CART report of January 27, 1960, he submitted an extraordinary list of topics as items ripe for exploration by the TV medium. Helffrich made it clear that his surprising inventory was, as he put it, "not a taboo list, an approved list, or even a suggested list," further cautioning that using such notions as grist for television programs did not mean condoning them. "But," he asks, "how are the very standards we talk about for the young to be achieved if material affecting those standards is usually concealed?" Herewith is a truncated catalogue of Helffrich's thoughts for future television programming (in either dramas or "panel discussions"—never fodder for comedy programming): dope addiction, birth control, unwed mothers, premarital and extramarital sexual relations, polygamy, nudity, momism, miscegenation, sadism, violence, including fratri-, infanti-, patri- and suicide, white-collar crime, tax evasion, euthanasia, the Santa Clause myth, lip-service religion, irreverence and atheism, and interfaith friction. This is an astonishing index suggested for exploration by postwar network television. Yet, while his stances on stereotyped portrayals of African Americans and on those suffering from mental illness are clear, Helffrich's early position on televised discussions or portrayals of homosexuality teetered between unfriendly and hostile. Nonetheless, his final CART also suggested national television's second decade was obliged to present programs dealing with all manner of sexual variation, as well as the deeply tabooed subjects of incest and transvestitism. He comments, "You cannot at one and the same time in any medium of artistic expression hope to capture the intelligent without exposing the innocent to considerations alleged to be better understood by adults."[11]

A few years before his death, Helffrich told author Jeff Kisseloff that he used to argue with lawyers at the American Civil Liberties Union about censorship. "They took the position that there ought to be built into [network censorship] self-obsolescence," he explains, "that we would eventually cease to exist. . . . I came to that conclusion myself by the end of my career: that even a little bit of censorship is bad."[12] The censor had become a heretic in his own house.

After twenty-seven years at NBC-TV, Helffrich resigned in 1960 to take a position with the National Association of Broadcasters (NAB) Code Authority office in New York City, a job he held for twenty years. The NAB—a trade and lobbying association representing commercial networks and local TV stations—promoted the code as an industry self-regulation document. At the Code Authority, Helffrich acted as a sort of super censor, heading up a clearinghouse that decided local and network standards and practices—although its emphasis focused more on editing questionable commercials than deleting or changing entertainment programming.

Helffrich retired from the Code Authority at the age of sixty-nine, and two years later, in 1982, the NAB Code and its regulatory apparatus ceased to exist. A federal judge ruled that some portions of the code openly colluded to limit the commercial time of advertisers, which was seen as a violation of the Sherman Anti-Trust Act. When network advertising no longer came under the aegis of the code, the following occurred: the preclearance of commercials for children's advertising was suspended; some local advertising, formerly prohibited by the code, was accepted; a heavier burden was placed on advertising agencies to police and regulate their activities; there was no interest on behalf of NAB stations to reformulate the code; and efforts increased by the Children's Advertising Review Unit (as well as censors at the ABC, CBS, and NBC-TV networks) to uphold the standards of the former NAB code for youth-targeted advertising.[13] Not long after the 1982 ruling, the NAB suspended all code operations. This book specifically limits itself to the work of Helffrich at NBC-TV from 1948 to 1960, although there is abundant source material awaiting future scholars to provide a clear picture of Helffrich's contributions at the Code Authority during the volatile 1960s and 1970s.[14]

Helffrich lived his next seventeen years in retirement after leaving the Code Authority in 1980. When he died at the age of eighty-five, he had spent more than half his life as a professional radio and television censor and arbiter of taste.[15] He would undoubtedly be stunned but not surprised at the television offerings seen today. It took more than four decades, but every one of Helffrich's "outrageous" ideas above (with perhaps the possible exception of completely demythologizing Santa Claus) became grist, in some form or another, for the television mill. Subscriber-based cable companies and satellite-delivered television systems (some boasting more than five hundred channels) convey arrant commercial-supported programming to audiences sliced into razor thin demographic and lifestyle cohorts.

And in the case of pay-per-view and premium channels like Home Box Office and Showtime, even advertisers' sway no longer enters into the equation. Programming from premium pay television is literally without boundaries exploring everything from full-frontal nudity to powerful adult language, lurid sex, and brutal violence. Just to compete in this brave new TV world, all major U.S. commercial broadcast networks—ABC, CBS, Fox, NBC, UPN/WB—have found it necessary to offer shows almost as audacious as cable.[16] On November 21, 2002, for example, a few days after CBS-TV broadcast the *Victoria's Secret Fashion Show Special*—essentially a group of young women parading about in sexy, revealing lingerie—Federal Communications Commission Commissioner Michael J. Copps issued a statement, saying, "It's time for the Commission to change its definition of 'indecency.'"[17] Copps later said that the Victoria's Secret show was one of two programs that generated so much angry e-mail that the FCC's computer servers "crashed." He said, "There are hundreds, sometimes a thousand, two, three, four thousand e-mails that come in overnight from around the country, expressing their revulsion at what has been on TV the night before."[18]

Viewers also complained the adult drama *Nip/Tuck*—an FX cable network offering in the early 2000s—was one of the most dangerous shows on television. L. Brent Bozell III, president of the Christian-based Parents Television Council, wrote that the program "revolves around graphic sex, a surfeit of nudity and screaming-orgasm acting. It features routine obscene language, with no bleeps. In addition to beatings, killing, and torture, it favors gut-churning graphic operation scenes that make the most graphic 'CSI' look like a calm episode of 'Mr. Wizard.'"[19] The controversial offering from the FX network premiered on July 22, 2003, to critical acclaim despite its over-the-top sexuality, gory depiction of plastic surgery, and rough language.[20] Billed by the producers as "a disturbingly perfect drama,"[21] *Nip/Tuck* is about a plastic-surgery practice and the two doctors who own it. The opportunity to comment upon America's obsession with youth culture, notions of perfect beauty, and sex in general is the usual focus of *Nip/Tuck*, but it was not merely social commentary or mature sensuality that agitated some viewers, it was the *other* subject matter discussed. In show 6 of the first season, for example—one titled "Megan O'Hara"—a woman desires reconstructive breast surgery after a mastectomy. By the tenth episode, she is dying of a cancer relapse, and her would-be plastic surgeon turned lover drives her to a hotel and helps her commit suicide. Recall how sensitive Stockton Helffrich was to TV stories dealing with the subject of deliberately killing oneself; he feared copycat suicides, potential lawsuits, and negative public relations for the network over shows like this.[22] In the *Nip/Tuck* episode in question, the doctor not only feeds sleeping pills to his dying patient/lover but also helps her place a plastic bag over her head to encourage faster asphyxiation.[23]

But a few thousand complaints cannot top the commotion begun by the infamous "wardrobe malfunction" of pop singer Janet Jackson. Some cultural analysts say when singer Justin Timberlake yanked on Janet Jackson's leather bodice at the 2004 Super Bowl halftime show exposing her bejeweled areola—an image that lasted for about eighteen video frames or approximately three quarters of a second—early-twenty-first-century media censorship came roaring back with a vengeance. However, if history teaches anything, it is that major cultural shifts usually occur slowly and develop from a confluence of events. While it appears the Jackson incident served to trigger a sociopolitical avalanche, it did so only because sociopolitical conditions were ripe for it. To illustrate with a physical example: if the slope of a snow-covered mountain is situated at the precise angle, and the temperature, wind speed, and other myriad variables are spot on, only then could some otherwise minor event (i.e., a loud yell or firearm report) set off an avalanche.[24] However, to prompt such dramatic change like a smothering snow slide (or, say the social consequences from a "wardrobe malfunction"), all predicable elements must act in concert to eventually reach what structural engineers call the "angle of repose," or what happens when one leans too far back in a chair. Mathematicians and economists graph it as the "point of inflexion," the position on a curve at which the tangent crosses the curve itself. One may call it "the straw that broke the camel's back." In other words, it is the process by which change or upheaval is brought about through an ostensibly inconsequential act or addition.

It seems reasonable to argue, then, that a sociocultural convergence of events in the early twenty-first century—such as, the spread of a national conservative political agenda since the Ronald Reagan administration, the ascendancy of the Christian right, and two George Bush presidencies—set the stage for the ferocious reaction to the Janet Jackson episode.[25] C/Net News reported that officials at TiVo—a subscription service that permits viewers to pause and "rewind" live television—said Jackson's breast flash "was the most-watched moment to date on its device." TiVo users watched the incident nearly three times more than any other moment during the Super Bowl broadcast, confirmed TiVo management.[26] We also must factor that the singer bared her breast during Super Bowl 38, one that Neilsen ratings estimate was watched at least in part by 89.6 million during any given *minute*.[27] Combine the symbolic nature of "seeing" Jackson's breast with a massive audience, and all self-appointed moral guardians and their watchdog groups had a powerful wedge issue (and enough political outrage) to ride the controversy for more than a year.

Clearly, each of the above reasons and myriad others were contributing factors to the uptick in media expurgation in the early 2000s. But if one conjures latent censorship as, say, a dormant, incurable virus—a sort of herpes-simplex encephalitis in the body politic—some prodrome would be needed to spark it back to virulence. Jackson's "wardrobe malfunction" may plausibly be identified as the spark. Clearly, the Jackson incident was a flashpoint but not for a *new* culture war just a *continuing* one. And punishment came swiftly in its wake. The FCC was flooded with more than one half million complaints over the breast flash. CBS-TV and its twenty owned-and-operated stations were fined

$27,500 *each* (an unheard total of $550,000),[28] and the FCC ended the year by posting a record $7.7 million in indecency fines. Free-speech enthusiasts were horrified while so-called watchdog groups claimed the fines were not high enough. Four years later, the Third Circuit Court of Appeals in Philadelphia reversed the massive fine against all the CBS stations, concluding the "FCC was arbitrary and capricious" in changing its decades-old policy of *not* holding "fleeting" nudity as indecent.[29]

That then is the story I wanted to tell, one that honestly considered and tried to make sense of the legacy of censorship left by Stockton Helffrich and the NBC-TV Continuity Acceptance Department he ran during its foundational postwar years. While many essential areas of censorship were covered in detail—sex, violence, language, race, and advertising among them—there is certainly abundant room for future scholarship in this area. For example, looking at Helffrich's decisions through the lenses of various public-relations theories would make a most helpful contribution and could put into greater focus the value and productivity of corporate censorship. More research is also needed to determine the exact affiliation between Helffrich and NBC top management, David Sarnoff among them. These relationships may be the key to understanding why Helffrich, an admitted, documented, former Communist (who could have provided authorities with names, dates, and details), was never deposed by the Federal Bureau of Investigation, House Un-American Activities Committee (HUAC), or any government investigative body during the United States' second "Red Scare" from 1947 to 1957.[30]

Censorship is and has always been a phenomenon clearly power based, driven by both peril and preservation. Through the millennia, it has been the way of emperors and popes, latter-day governments, corporations, and, yes, TV censors. When historicized, it leaves instructive testimony: That which is censored helps us understand the confluence of elaborate social issues and power arrangements at particular moments in time. The practices and standards developed by NBC-TV's Stockton Helffrich better help us understand not only the emerging television industry but also the political, social, and religious climate of the 1950s. Moreover, the logic of early TV censorship insisted that any cultural questioning or heresy permitted wide distribution to a heterogeneous population would ultimately damage that population, leaching power from elite authorities, causing destabilization and potential harm to the overall good. But Helffrich's later thesis appeared to be exactly the opposite. His final CART report (mentioned above) suggested that too much censorship would not prevent but provoke destabilization and be an agent to wound societal good. If network television was permitted to be bold enough to present more programming about the human condition—even the unseemly and perverse—Helffrich believed America would be the stronger for it.

While it is true his call for less timidity and more artful and "dangerous" expression in programming came later in his career, as early as 1950 Helffrich insisted on deletion of stereotyped portrayals of African Americans, immigrants, and the mentally ill—ideas that remained consistent throughout his professional life. That said, his early CART reports also occasionally appear defensive, patriarchal, even contradictory—for example, he worked to tone down or eliminate excessive television violence and later validated the essential place of brutality in dramatic storytelling. Helffrich also first seemed prudish in terms of female undergarment advertising, citing it as an affront to gentility. Later, he quoted a university study that argued television developed critical-thinking skills in children, and he advocated the medium as "a prerequisite [for students] in the study of the world in which they live ... bra commercials included."[31] Helffrich's change in attitude on these issues could reflect his developing recognition of the unstable, evanescent culture of the 1950s, or perhaps they were a glimpse of his true colors. Whatever prompted what might be seen as Helffrich's evolving philosophy, by 1960 bra advertising was still considered risky for TV in certain day parts, and censorship of female undergarment commercials remained intact.

Marxist theory would suggest that censorship is and has always been a tool of class power, a component of hegemonic patriarchy and false consciousness. In most cases, network censorship was *demanded* by a definable home-viewing audience during television's formative postwar years. The work of Stockton Helffrich argues that censoring certain images and ideas is also a deeply human, anxiety-centered, creative reflex rooted in notions of protection and salvation. There is one thing of which we can all be certain and history has consistently affirmed: Censorship in all its cultural forms will endure.

NOTES
INDEX

Notes

Abbreviations

NBC Files   National Broadcasting Company Inc., State Historical Society of Wisconsin

NCCM   National Council of Catholic Men Collection, Department of Archives and Manuscripts, Catholic University of America, Washington, DC.

Introduction: Context and Beginnings of TV Censorship

1. Jan de Vries, *Heroic Song and Heroic Legend* (Manchester, NH: Ayer, 1988); Geoffrey Horrocks, *Greek: A History of the Language and Its Speakers* (Boston: Addison-Wesley, 1997).

2. Bono qtd. in Frank Aherns, "Clear Channel Fined $775,000 for Radio Indecency," *Washington Post*, 28 January 2004, C7.

3. Ibid. The FCC fined radio giant Clear Channel Communications Inc. $775,000 for twenty-six violations of federal indecency standards during seven morning-show segments that aired on the "Bubba the Love Sponge" program in July, November, and December 2001.

4. The following figures were compiled via LexisNexis and FCC record searches made by the Center for Public Integrity, an investigative-journalism Internet site. More than $2.5 million in indecency fines were leveled against Stern. John Dunbar, "Indecency on the Air: Shock-Radio Jock Howard Stern Remains 'King of All Fines,'" *Center for Public Integrity*, 4 April 2004, http://www.publicintegrity.org/telecom/report.aspx?aid=239 (accessed 3 May 2005).

5. "Censorship Invades the Animal Kingdom," *TV Guide*, 4 January 1958, 12–15.

6. NBC Program Policies, March 1936, folder 397, NBC Files, State Historical Society of Wisconsin, Madison, WI. Hereinafter referred to as NBC Files.

7. "Are We Growing Profane?" *Literary Digest*, 112, January 1932, 23.

8. Roy C. Whitmer to John F. Royal, memo, 8 April 1932, folder 332, NBC Files; NBC program script, "Radio Is Human, Too," April 1938, folder 398, NBC files.

9. NBC, "Working Manual for Continuity Acceptance under NBC Program Policies," 1939, folder 396, NBC files. See also Janet MacRorie, "Report of Department Continuity Acceptance for the Year," 17 December 1935, folder 65, NBC files.

10. Don E. Gilman to Janet MacRorie, memo, 16 March 1938, folder 332, NBC Files.

11. Ibid.

12. Janet MacRorie, Sidney Strotz, Philips Carlin, and Clarence L. Menser, memos, 12–21 December 1940, folder 332, NBC Manuscripts, NBC Files.

13. Douglas B. Craig, *Fireside Politics: Radio and Political Culture in the United States, 1920–1940* (Baltimore, MD: John Hopkins University Press, 2000), 264–67, 269, 271–72.

14. Susan Smulyan, *Selling Radio: The Commercialization of American Broadcasting, 1920–1934* (Washington, DC: Smithsonian, 1994), 119.

15. Albert F. McLean Jr., *American Vaudeville as Ritual* (Lexington: University of Kentucky Press, 1965), 118.

16. Irving Howe, *World of Our Fathers* (New York: Harcourt, 1976), 558.

17. Milt Josefsberg, *The Jack Benny Show* (New York: Arlington, 1977).

18. J. Fred MacDonald, *Television and the Red Menace: The Video Road to Viet Nam* (New York: Praeger, 1985), 340–41.

19. Estelle Edmerson, "A Descriptive Study of the American Negro in United States Professional Radio, 1922–1953" (unpublished master's thesis, University of California, Los Angeles, 1954), 108, 354. See also Robert Pondillo, "Rod Serling's Hegemony Zone," (unpublished conference paper, University of Wisconsin–Milwaukee, 1997), 10.

20. MacDonald, *Don't Touch*, 350.

21. Michele Hilmes, *Radio Voices: American Broadcasting, 1922–1952* (Minneapolis: University of Minnesota Press, 1997), 91; James Baldwin, *Nobody Knows My Name* (New York: Dell, 1962), 133–34; MacDonald, *Don't Touch*, 341; Eric Lott, *Love and Theft: Blackface Minstrelsy and the American Working Class* (New York: Oxford, 1995); and Scott L. Malcomson, *One Drop of Blood: The American Misadventure of Race* (New York: Farrar, 2000), 320–45.

22. Anthony Tollin, *Too Hot for Radio* (New Rochelle, NY: GAA, 1997), 5–6.

23. Ibid. See also MacDonald, *Don't Touch*, 344; Erik Barnouw, *A Tower in Babel: The History of Broadcasting in the United States to 1933* (New York: Oxford, 1966), 229–30; and Freeman F. Gosden and Charles J. Correll, *All about Amos 'n' Andy* (New York: Rand McNally, 1929), 43–44.

24. Hilmes, *Radio Voices*, 88. Hilmes adds that in the radio scripts, "there are many references to elements and activities whose significance lies in racial stereotypes." 88.

25. Ibid., 305n43. See also Stanley Lieberson, *A Piece of the Pie: Blacks and White Immigrants since 1860* (Berkeley: University of California Press, 1980), 367.

26. Hilmes. *Radio Voices*, 89, 91.

27. Barnouw even suggests that the show was responsible for selling millions of dollars worth of radio sets; sales rose from about $6.5 million in 1928 to over $8.5 million in 1929. See Barnouw, *Tower in Babel*, 229–30.

28. Toni Morrison, *Playing in the Dark: Whiteness and the Literary Imagination* (Cambridge, MA: Harvard University Press, 1992), 9.

29. Erik Barnouw, *The Golden Web: The History of Broadcasting in the United States, 1933–1953* (New York: Oxford University Press, 1968), 16–17.

30. MacDonald, *Don't Touch*, 346–49.

31. Tollin, *Too Hot for Radio*, 12.

32. Mae West, *Goodness Had Nothing to Do with It* (New York: Manor, 1976), 111. West's book was ghostwritten by Stephen Longstreet, and there are doubts about its accuracy.

33. Although author credit on the sketch is given to legendary radio writer Arch Obler and billed as a "light hearted travesty," Able Green and Joe Laurie Jr. contend it was actually "the brainchild of the J. Walter Thompson ad agency." *Show Biz from Vaude to Video* (New York: Holt, 1951), 470.

34. Tollin, *Too Hot for Radio*, 15–16.

35. Elizabeth McLeod, "Old Time Radio Moments of the Century," *Original Old Time Radio*, 1994–2009, http://old-time.com/mcleod/top100.html (accessed 15 June 2001).

36. Qtd. in Tollin, *Too Hot for Radio*, 15–16.

37. Qtd. in Emily Wortis Leider, *Becoming Mae West* (New York: Da Capo, 1997), 341–42.

38. Tollin, *Too Hot for Radio*, 16.

39. Qtd. in Leider, *Becoming Mae West*, 341–42.

40. "The American People," 75th Cong., *Congressional Record* 83 (January 14, 1938): 560.

41. Qtd. in Tollin, *Too Hot for Radio*, 16.

42. The *New York Times* wrote, "Sex ain't what it used to be, or maybe Miss West isn't." 27 January 1938, 17.

43. Mary Beth Hamilton, *"When I'm Bad I'm Better:" Mae West, Sex, and American Entertainment* (Berkeley: University of California Press, 1997), 227–28.

44. MacDonald, *Don't Touch*, 107.

45. Janet MacRorie, *Report of Department of Continuity Acceptance for the Year 1935*, box 93, NBC Files.

46. Alan Havig, *Fred Allen's Radio Comedy* (Philadelphia, PA: Temple University Press, 1990), 112.

47. First draft, NBC Program Standards, 1938, folder 5, box 93, NBC files.

48. Dorothy Kembel to Ken R. Dyke, memo, 11 May 1938, folder 28 ("Bristol Myers" folder 1938), box 59, NBC files.

49. Hilmes, *Radio Voices*, 200–212.

50. Janet MacRorie to John F. Royal, memo, 2 February 1938, folder 28 ("Bristol Myers" folder 1938), box 59, NBC files.

51. Janet MacRorie to I. E. Showerman, memo, 20 December 1938, folder 28 ("Bristol Myers" folder 1938), box 59, NBC files.

52. Jack Gould, "L'Affaire Allen," *New York Times*, 27 April 1947, sec. 2:9.

53. Havig, *Fred Allen's*, 102.

54. "Allen to Stay On Despite Censors," *Variety*, 5 February 1947, 1.

55. *Variety*, 23 April 1947, 1.

56. Havig, *Fred Allen's*, 103.

57. Fred Allen, *Treadmill to Oblivion* (Boston: Little, Brown, 1954), 212. See also "NBC—Cantor Feud Breaks Out Anew as Censor Menser K.O.'s Besser's Act," *Variety*, 21 June 1944, 2.

58. Allen qtd. in Ben Gross's newspaper column in Havig, *Fred Allen's*, 104.

1. Stockton *Who*?

1. Ernest K. Lindley, "Is There a Real Danger of War," *Newsweek*, 15 May 1950, 27.

2. Qtd. in Thomas C. Reeves, *America's Bishop: The Life and Times of Fulton J. Sheen* (San Francisco: Encounter Books, 2001), 208.

3. David Marc and Robert J. Thompson, *Television in the Antenna Age: A Concise History* (Malden, MA: Blackwell, 2005), 53.

4. Lynn Spigel, *Make Room for TV: Television and the Family Ideal in Postwar America* (Chicago: University of Chicago Press, 1992), particularly chap. 2.

5. Fred Inglis, *Media Theory: An Introduction* (Cambridge, MA: Blackwell, 1990), 81.

6. NBC CART, 24 September 1948, folder 1, box 1, NBC files.

7. NBC CART, 15 February 1950, folder 3, box 1, NBC files. NBC Continuity Acceptance "headquarters" for the network and all company owned-and-operated stations

was room 294 at 30 Rockefeller Center, New York City. CA later moved its offices to the seventh floor, same building.

8. Hilmes, *Radio Voices*, 21. See also Matthew Murray, "Television Wipes Its Feet: The Commercial and Ethical Considerations behind the Adoption of the Television Code," *Journal of Popular Film and Television* 21 (Fall 1993): 128–38.

9. Michael Ritchie, *Please Stand By: A Prehistory of Television* (Woodstock, NY: Overlook, 1994), 197.

10. William Boddy, *Fifties Television: The Industry and Its Critics* (Urbana: University of Illinois Press, 1993), 155–64.

11. Louis Chunovic, *One Foot on the Floor: The Curious Evolution of Sex on Television from* I Love Lucy *to* South Park (New York: TV Books, 2000).

12. James Lull, *Media, Communication, Culture: A Global Approach*, 2nd ed. (New York: Columbia University Press, 2000), 13–17.

13. Heather Hendershot, *Saturday Morning Censors: Television Regulation before the V-Chip* (Durham, NC: Duke University Press, 1998), 1.

14. James L. Baughman, *The Republic of Mass Culture: Journalism, Filmmaking and Broadcasting in America since 1941*, 2nd ed. (Baltimore, MD: Johns Hopkins University Press, 1997), 30.

15. Erik Barnouw, *The Image Empire: A History of Broadcasting in the United States from 1953* (New York: Oxford University Press, 1970), 65–80; *Television Factbook 1960, Supplement to Television Digest* (Radnor, PA: Triangle, 1960), 18; Cobbert Steinberg, *TV Facts* (New York: Facts on File, 1985), 85–86. Radio, for example, took more than thirty years to achieve the diffusion and saturation rate of TV.

16. "TV and the Taproom Trade," *Television Digest*, 17 January 1948, 5.

17. Anna McCarthy, "'The Front Row Is Reserved for Scotch Drinkers': Early Television's Tavern Audience," *Cinema Journal*, 34, no. 5 (Summer 1995): 32; and Tim Brooks and Earl Marsh, *The Complete Directory to Primetime, Network and Cable TV Shows: 1946–present*, 6th ed. (New York: Ballantine, 1995), xiii.

18. Green and Laurie, *Show Biz from Vaude to Video*, 532.

19. Alex McNeil, *Total Television: The Comprehensive Guide to Programming from 1948 to the Present*, 4th ed. (New York: Penguin, 1997), 44–45, 332, 388, 421–23, 481.

20. Steven D. Stark, *Glued to the Set: The 60 Television Shows and Events That Made Us Who We Are Today* (New York: Delta, 1997), 9–17.

21. Matthew Murray, "NBC Program Clearance Policies during the 1950s: Nationalizing Trends and Regional Resistance," *Velvet Light Trap*, spring 1994, 37–48. See also Spigel, *Make Room for TV*; William Boddy, *Fifties Television: The Industry and Its Critics* (Urbana: University of Illinois Press, 1990).

22. House Subcommittee on Interstate and Foreign Commerce, *Hearings: Radio and Television Programs*, 92nd Cong., 2nd sess., 5 June 1952, 83.

23. Spigel, *Make Room for TV*, 114.

24. Eric F. Goldman, *The Crucial Decade: America 1945–1955* (New York: Knopf, 1956); and Michael Vlahos, "The End of America's Postwar Ethos," *Foreign Affairs* (Summer 1988): 1091–107; and Carl N. Degler, *Affluence and Anxiety, 1945–present* (Glenview, IL: Scott, 1968), 9.

25. Elaine Tyler May, *Homeward Bound: American Families in the Cold War Era* (New York: Basic Books, 1988), 94.

26. Qtd. in Elaine Tyler May, "Explosive Issues: Sex, Women, and the Bomb," in Lary May, ed., *Recasting America: Culture and Politics in the Age of Cold War* (Chicago: University of Chicago Press, 1981), 161.

27. Gallup poll, July 2–7, 1954, qtd. in John Kenneth White, *Still Seeing Red: How the Cold War Shapes the New American Politics* (Boulder, CO: Westview, 1997), 4, 287.

28. George H. Gallup, *The Gallup Poll: Public Opinion, 1935–1971*, 3 vols. (New York: Random, 1972), 2:881, 889, 916, 919.

29. William Faulkner qtd. in Allen Freeman, "Echoes of the Cold War," *Historic Preservation*, January/February 1994, 86.

30. Ted Gupp, "The Doomsday Blueprints," *Time*, 10 August 1992, 32–35.

31. "Wonderful to Play In," *Time*, 5 February 1951, 12.

32. Richard Gid Powers, *Secrecy and Power: The Life of J. Edgar Hoover* (New York: Free Press, 1987), 288–89.

33. Pope Pius XI qtd. in Goldman, *Crucial Decade*, 130.

34. Cardinal Francis Joseph Spellman qtd. in Jack Newfield and Mark Jacobson, eds., *American Monsters: 44 Rats, Blackhats, and Plutocrats* (New York: Thunder's Mouth, 2004), 132–40.

35. Joseph McCarthy, "Speech at Wheeling West Virginia," in William Chafe and Harvard Sitkoff, eds., *A History of Our Time: Readings on Postwar America*, 2nd ed. (New York: Oxford University Press, 1987), 64–67.

36. Richard H. Rovere, *Senator Joe McCarthy* (New York: Harper-Collins, 1979), 7. See also Newfield and Jacobson, *American Monsters*, 284–93.

37. Stevenson qtd. in Robert A. Taft, *A Foreign Policy for All Americans* (Garden City, NY: Doubleday, 1951), 118–19.

38. J. Ronald Oakley, *God's Country: America in the Fifties* (New York: Barricade Books, 1990), 119–20.

39. Alan Ehrenhalt, *The Lost City: The Forgotten Virtues of Community in America* (Chicago: Basic Books, 1995), 280.

40. Oakley, *God's Country*, 320.

41. Eric Goldman, "Good-bye to the Fifties—and Good Riddance," *Harper's*, January 1960, 28.

42. "Words and Work," *Time*, 20 September 1954, 65.

43. Oakley, *God's Country*, 320.

44. Peter Lyon, *Eisenhower: Portrait of the Hero* (Boston: Little, Brown, 1974), 477.

45. Lawrence S. Wittner, *Cold War America: From Hiroshima to Watergate* (New York: Praeger, 1974), 123.

46. Oakley, *God's Country*, 320.

47. The line was written by ad copywriter Al Scapone. For a full discussion, see Patrick Peyton, *All for Her: The Autobiography of Father Patrick Peyton, C.S.C.* (Garden City, NY: Doubleday, 1967).

48. See Reeves, *America's Bishop*, 31, 167–70.

49. Oakley, *God's Country*, 321. See also Martin E. Marty, *Modern American Religion: Under God, Indivisible, 1941–1960*, vol. 3 (Chicago: University of Chicago Press, 1996), x.

50. William Lee Miller, "Piety along the Potomac," *Reporter*, 11 August 1954, 25.

51. Oakley, *God's Country*, 153.

52. Robert S. Ellwood, *The Fifties Spiritual Marketplace: American Religion in a Decade of Conflict* (New Brunswick, NJ: Rutgers University Press, 1997), 63–101, 70–71.

53. Hilde T. Himmelweit, preface, in Himmelweit, A. N. Oppenheim, and Pamela Vince, *Television and the Child. An Empirical Study of the Effects of Television on the Young* (London: Oxford University Press, 1958), xiii.

54. Wilbur Schramm, Jack Lyle, and Edwin B. Parker, *Television in the Lives of Our Children* (Stanford, CA: Stanford University Press, 1961), 67.

55. Charles A Seipman, *Radio, Television and Society* (New York: Oxford University Press, 1950), 341.

56. The metaphor of "television as menace" has had durable appeal over the years and is also mentioned in Daniel J. Boorstin, *The Image: A Guide to Pseudo-Events in America* (New York: Vintage Books, 1961), 240; Jerry Mander, *Four Arguments for the Elimination of Television* (New York: Quill, 1978), 45; and Bob Hodge and David Tripp, *Children and Television: A Semiotic Approach* (Cambridge: Polity, 1986), 1.

57. Oakley, *God's Country*, 7.

58. U.S. Bureau of the Census, *Historical Statistics of the United States: Colonial Times to 1970* (Washington, DC: GPO, 1975), 716.

59. John O'Sullivan and Edward F. Keuchel, *American Economic History: From Abundance to Constraint* (New York: Watts, 1981), 197, 213. See also Harold G. Vatter and John F. Walker, *History of the U.S. Economy since World War II* (Armonk, NY: Sharpe, 1996), 3–23.

60. Barbara Norfleet, *When We Liked Ike: Looking for Postwar America* (New York: Norton, 2001), 13–14.

61. Christopher H. Sterling and John M. Kittross, eds., *Stay Tuned: A Concise History of American Broadcasting*, 2nd ed. (Belmont, CA: Wadsworth, 1990), 657; and Stark, *Glued to the Set*, 14.

62. Guy LeBow and Los Angeles watchdog group qtd. in R. D. Heldenfels, *Television's Greatest Year: 1954* (New York: Continuum, 1994), 145–47.

63. Thomas Lane qtd. in "TV Censorship Board Proposed," *Variety*, 7 March 1951, 36.

64. Ezekiel Candler Gathings qtd. in "TV's Hottest Problem: Public Relations," *Sponsor*, 16 June 1952, 27–29.

65. "Television Rescues the Home?" *America*, 5 February 1949, 473.

66. Ed Madden to Jules Herbevaeux, telegram, 17 March 1953, folder 12, box 569, NBC files.

67. "Inside Stuff—Television," *Variety*, 6 December 1950, 3.

68. Francis J. Haas qtd. in "St. Louis Clergyman Raps Suds, Ciggies, Sponsors of Ballgames; Hurts Kids," *Variety*, 23 May 1951, 35; "Hell pipeline" quote in "TV 'Doing Work of the Devil' in Homes via 'Sex Diodes,' Catholic Bishop Asserts," *Variety*, 9 May 1951, 24.

69. The Miracle Case is a nickname for the legal case *Joseph Burstyn Inc. v. Wilson*. For a discussion, see Gregory Black, *The Catholic Crusade against the Movies, 1940–1975* (New York: Cambridge University Press, 1997); and Gregory Black, *Hollywood Censored: Morality Codes, Catholics and the Movies* (New York: Cambridge University Press, 1994).

70. "Catholics Urge Legion of Decency to Clean Up TV Programs for Kids," *Variety*, 14 March 1951, 1; "Catholic Archbishop Warns Televiewers," *Christian Century*, 26 December 1951, 1499.

71. Francis Joseph Spellman qtd. in "Cardinal Sees Evil in Films, Radio, TV," *New York Times*, 2 December 1950, 2.

72. "Church Censorship of TV Programming Seen in Priest's Sermonizing," *Variety*, 31 January 1951, 1.

73. For more information on the National Catholic Welfare Conference, see Francis I. Nally, "What Is the NCCM," 1953–54 file, NCCM Reports and Proceedings, collection 10, National Council of Catholic Men Collection, Department of Archives and Manuscripts, Catholic University of America, Washington, DC. Hereinafter documents in this archives will be designated by NCCM. See also Howard J. Carroll, *Memo: Proposed Meeting on Television*, folder 18, box 10, collection 10, NCCM.

74. "TV Classification Plan Studied by National Council of Catholic Men," 27 July 1951, folder 18, box 35, collection 10, National Catholic Welfare Conference News Service, NCCN News Service (Domestic), NCCM.

75. "Boston Prelate Blasts TV Comics for 'Committing (Video) Suicide,'" *Variety*, 28 February 1951, 26.

76. "Catholics Urge," 1.

77. "Senate Probes B'cast Industry" and "Benton Bill 'Dangerous' to AM-TV Saz Fellows; Threat to Freedom," *Variety*, 10 October 1951, 22.

78. "Church of TV Programming Seen in Priest's Sermonizing," *Variety*, 31 January 1951, 1. Networks, of course, had their own standards and program rules. The Hays office, led by William Harrison Hays Sr., former Harding Administration Postmaster General and Republican Party National Chair, was also known by its formal name: The Motion Picture Producers and Distributors of America (MPPDA). The MPPDA, or Hays office, was a "self-regulatory" (i.e., self-censoring) body set up by the major U.S. film studios in 1922. Parts of the Hays office censorship code were used as models for early network television censorship.

79. "NARTB Special Committee at Work on Code to Clean Up TV Programs," *Variety*, 1 August 1951, 24; "TV Producers Prep Code to Clean Up Pgms.," *Variety*, 25 July 1951, 27; "TV May Get Legion of Decency," *New York Times*, 31 August 1951, 35.

80. Father J. D. Masterson to Bishop Timothy Manning, 26 May 1953, attached to Bishop Timothy Manning to Monsignor Harold Carroll, 28 May 1953, folder 19, box 35, collection 10, NCCM.

81. "'$64,000 Challenge' Now Set to Make Debut on March 25," *Broadcasting-Telecasting*, 5 March 1956, 26.

82. Father Tom Chapman to NCCM office, San Alfonso Retreat House, West End, Long Branch, NJ, 24 February 1956, folder 21, box 35, collection 10, NCCM; Reverend Paul M. Lackner, *The Role of NODL*, 1938, folder 7, box 2, NCCM Records, 1920–75, NCCM; and *The Fifth Annual Television Report*, 1949, folder 22, box 35, collection 10, NCCM.

83. Paul F. Tanner to Archbishop John. F. O'Hara, 13 March 1956, folder 21, box 35, collection 10, NCCM. See also Charles A. McMahon to Episcopal Committee for Motion Pictures, Radio and Television, memo, "The Need for the Coordination of Lay Action in the Fields of Motion Picture and Television," 1951, NCCM.

84. Pope Pius XII, *Miranda Prorsus*, statement to Italian bishops, television, 1 January 1954, folder 20, box 35, collection 10, NCCM. See also *Miranda Prorsus*, folder 2, box 35, collection 10, NCCM.

85. Television Study Meeting, questionnaire and itinerary, 21–22 April 1958, folder 22, box 35, collection 10, NCCM; National Catholic Welfare Service, Conference News, *TV Classification Plan Studied by National Council of Catholic Men*, 1951, file 18, box 35, collection 10, NCCM.

86. Ehrenhalt, *Lost City*, 24.

87. Murray, "NBC Program Clearance Policies," 37–48.

88. David Sarnoff, "The American System of Broadcasting and Its Function in the Preservation of Democracy" (address, Town Hall Luncheon, Hotel Astor, New York City, 28 April 1938).

89. Boddy, *Fifties Television*, chaps. 2, 6, 7, 9, passim.

2. The Early Years

1. Stockton Helffrich, interview by Jackie Austin, 1 March 1987, Helffrich residence, Jackson Heights, New York, private collection. Austin, Helffrich's daughter, videotaped interviews with members of her immediate family (e.g., father and mother, Stockton and Delores; stepmother, Sophia "Maxie"; and family friend, Lillian Berman) to act as a historical document for her children.

2. Biographical information was gathered from family accounts, Helffrich's personal documents, and Federal Bureau of Investigation records. See Stockton Helffrich, FBI file 100-336937, 1950.

3. Other later NBC pages that went on to fame and fortune in the entertainment or news media include: Michael Eisner, Dave Garroway, Willard Scott, Regis Philbin, Steve Allen, and Ted Koppel. See "Early Career Programs (East Coast Page Programs)," *NBC*, http://www.nbcunicareers.com/earlycareerprograms/pageprogrameast.shtml (accessed 15 September 2009).

4. The phrase is derived from "The Long Gray Line," referring to the color of the uniform worn by U.S. Army cadets at West Point. John Grant, James Lynch, and Ronald Bailey, *West Point: The First 200 Years* (Guilford, CT: Globe Pequot, 2002), 26.

5. Sophia "Maxie" Helffrich, Helffrich's widow, interview by author, 11 March 2000, Helffrich residence, Jackson Heights, New York.

6. Helffrich, personal papers, and Samuel Kaufman, "Interesting Previews of the World's Greatest Broadcast Metropolis," *Radio News*, December 1933.

7. Stockton Helffrich, interview by Austin, 1 March 1987. In a later interview, Sophia "Maxie" Helffrich indicated Stockton "held the pen" for the NBC tour-guide group, writing most of the tact manual and typing it on his Underwood typewriter.

8. Richard Finley Krauser, Helffrich's stepson, interview by author, 11 March 2000, Helffrich residence, Jackson Heights, New York. The brothers from eldest to youngest are: Lawrence Stockton Helffrich, Allen Boone Helffrich, Ralph Stockton Helffrich, Oliver Boone Helffrich, and Stockton Helffrich. Stockton had no middle name and claimed to be quite relieved his parents had not given him one. The recurring "Stockton" appellation pays homage to a distant relative from Helffrich's mother's side, Richard Stockton of New Jersey, a signer of the American Declaration of Independence. The paternal "Boone" appellative descends from a marriage to the brother of Daniel Boone, the famous frontiersman.

9. Sophie Helffrich and Krauser, interview by the author; Stockton Helffrich, interview by Austin; Delores (Helffrich) Smith, videotaped interview by Jackie Austin, 27 July 1986, Oregon, WI.

10. Patrick Marnham, *Dreaming with His Eyes Open: A Life of Diego Rivera* (Berkeley: University of California Press, 1998), 248–60. See also Daniel Okrent, *Great Fortune: The Epic of Rockefeller Center* (New York: Viking, 2003), 287–320.

11. Marnham, *Dreaming*, 265. In 1934, a smaller rendition of the controversial Rockefeller Center mural was repainted and renamed "Man, Controller of the Universe." It may still be seen in Mexico City at the Placio de Bellas Artes.

12. Ibid., 255; Okrent, *Great Fortune*, 302–18.

13. Stockton Helffrich, interview by Austin.

14. See Brian J. Cudahy, *Under the Sidewalks of New York: The Story of the Greatest Subway System in the World* (New York: Fordham University Press, 1995).

15. See Judith Ann Trolander, *Settlement Houses and the Great Depression* (Detroit: Wayne State University Press, 1975); Berman, interview by Jackie Austin, 7 October 1987, Oregon, WI. See also Domenica M. Barbuto, *American Settlement Houses and Progressive Social Reform: An Encyclopedia of the American Settlement Movement* (New York: Onyx Press, 1999); Jane Addams, *Twenty Years at Hull House* (Whitefish, MT: Kessinger, 2004).

16. Berman, interview by Austin. See D. S. Howard, *The WPA and Federal Relief Policy* (New York: Russell Sage Foundation, 1943); John O'Connor and Lorraine Brown, eds., *Free, Adult, Uncensored: The Living History of the Federal Theatre Project* (Washington, DC: New Republic, 1978); Lionel C. Bascom, ed., *A Renaissance in Harlem: Lost Essays of the WPA, by Ralph Ellison, Dorothy West, and Other Voices of a Generation* (New York: Amistad, 1999); and Clifford Odets, *"Waiting for Lefty" and Other Plays* (New York: Grove, 1993).

17. Robert S. McElvaine, *The Great Depression: America, 1929–1941* (New York: Times Books, 1993), 6–23.

18. Michael Denning, *The Cultural Front: The Laboring of American Culture in the Twentieth Century* (New York: Verso, 1997), 4–5. See also Cedric Belfrage, *The American Inquisition: 1945–1960* (Indianapolis, IN: Bobbs-Merrill, 1973), 19.

19. M. J. Heale, *American Anticommunism: Combating the Enemy Within, 1830–1970* (Baltimore, MD: Johns Hopkins University Press, 1990), 106.

20. Lovett and Steffens qtd. in ibid., 106–7.

21. Ellen Schrecker, *Many Are the Crimes: McCarthyism in America* (New York: Little, Brown, 1998), 12–13. Some scholars consider Schrecker sympathetic toward and an apologist for the Communist Party in America.

22. Vivian Gornick, *The Romance of American Communism* (New York: Basic Books, 1977).

23. Harvey Klehr, *The Heyday of American Communism: The Depression Decade* (New York: Basic Books, 1984), 26–68. See also Theodore Draper, *The Roots of American Communism* (New York: Viking, 1957), 11–196.

24. Maurice Isserman, *Which Side Were You On? The American Communist Party during the Second World War* (Middletown, CT: Wesleyan University Press, 1982), 206–8.

25. Schrecker, *Many Are the Crimes*, 13. See also Klehr, *Heyday*, 26–68, and Frasier M. Ottanelli, *The Communist Party of the United States: From the Depression to World War II* (New Brunswick, NJ: Rutgers University Press, 1991), 17–48.

26. Schrecker, *Many Are the Crimes*, 14–15.

27. Berman, interview by Austin. See also Joshua Freeman, Nelson Lichtenstein, Stephen Brier, David Bensman, Susan Porter Benson, David Brundage, Bret Eynon, Bruce Levine, and Bryan Palmer, *Who Built America: Working People and the Nation's*

Economy, Politics, Culture and Society: From the Gilded Age to the Present, vol. 2 (New York: Pantheon, 1992), 435, 499. Murray Berman organized the Printing Pressman's Union, while his wife, Lillian, a lifelong Communist, was an officer in the state office workers union.

28. Stockton Helffrich, FBI file.

29. Stockton Helffrich, FBI file. Helffrich's FBI file indicates he was a registered member of the ALP in 1942 and was mentioned in the "records of the Queens Country Communist Party" in May 1944.

30. Stockton Helffrich, interview by Austin.

31. Peggy Dennis, *The Autobiography of an American Communist: A Personal View of a Political Life, 1925–1975* (Berkeley, CA: Hill, 1977), 34; Berman, interview by Austin; Schrecker, *Many Are the Crimes,* 16; Isserman, *Which Side Were You On?* 16, 23; Gornick, *Romance of American Communism.*

32. Jackie Austin, interview by author, 11 January 1999, Madison, WI.

33. Smith, interview by Austin.

34. Austin, interview by author. See also Schrecker, *Many Are the Crimes,* 20–21; Gornick, *Romance of American Communism,* 130–35, and Robert Conquest, *The Great Terror: A Reassessment* (New York: Oxford University Press, 1990).

35. Stockton Smith, interview by Austin. Delores also explained her overwhelming sadness at losing her child was tied to her abiding belief that "getting married and having kids was the most important thing a woman can do with her life."

36. Dan vander Vat, *The Pacific Campaign: The U.S. Japanese Naval War, 1941–1945* (New York: Touchstone, 1992), 3–4.

37. Stockton Helffrich, interview by Austin; John Patrick Diggins, *The Proud Decades: America in War and Peace, 1941–1960* (New York: Norton, 1988), 36–37. Because the Japanese set up strategic communication bases on Guam and Wake islands, intercepting and decoding messages were essential to the Allied powers' Pacific Theater strategies.

38. Vander Vat, *Pacific Campaign,* 352–62; Diggins, *Proud Decades,* 37. The Leyte Gulf naval engagement was fought over three days, October 23–26, 1944.

39. Jackie Austin's given name is "Delores Stockton Helffrich," after her mother.

40. Austin, interview by author. During this his wartime duty, Helffrich says he "began to veer toward pacifism but not as an activist." Jackie Austin, interview by author; and Stockton Helffrich, videotaped interview by Austin.

41. Diggins, *Proud Decades,* 36.

42. Joan E. Childs, *The Myth of the Maiden: On Being a Woman* (New York: Health Communications, 1995); Anna Field and Laura Ziv, "I Had a Nervous Breakdown and Nearly Lost My Mind," *Cosmopolitan,* 1 October 1997, 272–73; Carol A. B. Warren, *Madwives: Schizophrenic Women in the 1950s* (New Brunswick, NJ: Rutgers University Press, 1991), 23–24, 128–32. Depression and suicide ran in Delores's family. Her father was an alcoholic, her mother battled depression, and her Aunt Elizabeth jumped to her death from the second floor of her home. Smith, interview by Austin. For an excellent, albeit technical, account of mental illness in the United States, see Gerald N. Grob, *The Mad among Us: The History of the Care of America's Mentally Ill* (New York: Free Press, 1994), and Stephanie Coontz, *The Way We Never Were: American Families and the Nostalgia Trap* (New York: Basic Books, 1992), 32.

43. Warren, *Madwives,* 23–24, 128–32.

44. "From tanks to Cadillacs in two months" was the mantra of General Motors. See Douglas T. Miller and Marion Nowak, *The Fifties: The Way We Really Were* (Garden City, NY: Doubleday, 1977), 106–23.

45. Kenneth T. Jackson, *Crabgrass Frontier: The Suburbanization of the United States* (New York: Oxford University Press, 1985), 232–33, Diggins, *Proud Decades*, 22–34, and Miller and Nowak, *Fifties*, 106–23.

46. Stephen B. Goddard, *Getting There: The Epic Struggle between Road and Rail in the American Century* (New York: Basic Books, 1994), 179, Jackson, *Crabgrass Frontier*, 168–71. See also Eric Schlosser, *Fast Food Nation: The Dark Side of the All-American Meal* (Boston: Houghton, 2001), 8, 16, 22.

47. Mary F. Corey, *The World through a Monocle: The New Yorker at Midcentury* (Cambridge, MA: Harvard University Press, 1999), 8. See also Jackson, *Crabgrass Frontier*, 232–33, Diggins, *Proud Decades*, 22–34; Miller and Nowak, *The Fifties*, 106–23; and Michael Harrington, *The Other America* (New York: Macmillan, 1962), 2–6.

48. Diggins, *Proud Decades*, 14–22.

49. Stockton Helffrich, interview by Austin.

50. Thomas K. McCraw, *American Business, 1920–1960: How It Worked* (Wheeling, IL: Davidson, 2000), 126.

51. The *Committee for* and later the *Congress of* Industrial Organizations (CIO) was more a political and social union movement that organized workers by industries, concentrating on gaining the right to bargain collectively for wages, benefits, hours, and working conditions. Denning, *Cultural Front*, 21–51.

52. "All Star Program," *White Collar Mike*, 1 August 1946, 1.

53. "Top NBCer Says: Biggest Network Whitecollarites Need Guild," *White Collar Mike*, 1 August 1946, 1.

54. "Counting Noses: NBCers Agree with Helffrich," *White Collar Mike*, 1 August 1946, 1.

55. "Top NBCer Says," 1.

56. Ibid.

57. "New CBS Classifications Would Tilt Wages 25–100%," *White Collar Mike*, 1 August 1946, 1. NBC office workers sought parity with their CBS and WMCA brethren, who had already voted to unionize.

58. Stockton Helffrich, FBI file.

59. Austin, interview by author.

60. Austin said the trash-can "gift" incident was seen as "a statement against him, against the role he was taking in supporting union organizers," the conclusion was that it was "very unseemly behavior at that level of management."

61. The Mutual Broadcasting System (MBS) had also rejected the coming of a white-collar union. Bert Briller, "Conscience of the Industry," *Television Quarterly* 26, no. 1 (1997): 52–57; Stockton Helffrich, interview by Austin.

62. Schrecker, *Many Are the Crimes*, 19–20.

63. John D'Emilio, *Sexual Politics, Sexual Communities: The Making of the Homosexual Minority in the United States, 1940–1970* (Chicago: University of Chicago Press, 1983), 40–91.

64. Joseph R. Starobin, *American Communism in Crisis, 1943–1957* (Cambridge, MA: Harvard University Press, 1972), 195–205, and Schrecker, *Many Are the Crimes*, 19–20.

65. Stockton Helffrich, *Sweet and Sour: A Collection of the Poetry of Stockton Helffrich* (New York: Self-published, 1980), preface, acknowledgments, 1–4.

66. Berman interview by Austin.

67. Stockton Helffrich, FBI file.

68. Berman. interview by Austin.

69. Richard H. S. Crossman, ed., *The God That Failed: Andre Gide, Richard Wright, Ignazio Silone, Stephen Spender, Arthur Koestler, and Louis Fischer and Their Disillusioned Return* (New York: Bantam Matrix, 1949). Each of these men embraced Communism with a religious zeal, then rejected it upon learning that terror and tyranny were the movement's ultimate goals.

70. Will Herberg, "After Communism—What?" *Reconstructionist*, 7 April 1950, 29–32. In this article, Herberg declares ex-Communists and fellow travelers had now become unappeasable opponents to the cause in which they once unswervingly believed.

71. Stockton Helffrich, FBI file.

72. Kenneth Bilby, *The General: David Sarnoff and the Rise of the Communications Industry* (New York: Harper, 1986), 252.

73. Stockton Helffrich, FBI file.

74. Stockton Helffrich, interview by Austin.

75. W. O. Somin, *The Glove*, box 22–23 (18 December 1949–25 December 1949), NBC-TV Masterbook 89, 1, 6, 7, 18, Film and Television Archive, Library of Congress, Washington, DC. See also McNeil, *Total Television*, 456–57; Brooks and Marsh, *Complete Directory of Prime Time Network and Cable TV Shows*, 564–65.

76. Somin, *Glove*, 7.

77. Stockton Helffrich, FBI file.

78. See Richard Gid Powers, *G-Men: Hoover's FBI in American Popular Culture* (Carbondale: Southern Illinois University Press, 1983). Of particular interest are Powers's chapter 11, the postwar "Shift in the Bureau's Image," and chapter 12, "FBI Public Relations during the Fifties and Sixties."

79. Marty Jezer, *The Dark Ages: Life in the United States 1945–1960* (Boston: South End Press, 1982), 83–84; Coontz, *Way We Never Were*, 33; May, *Homeward Bound*, 94–95; Robert S. Ellwood, *1950: Crossroads of American Religious Life* (Louisville, KY: Westminster John Knox Press, 2000), 14–15; David Caute, *The Great Fear: The Anti-Communist Purge under Truman and Eisenhower* (New York: Simon and Schuster, 1978), 422–23, 491–98; Carl N. Degler, *Affluence and Anxiety: 1945–Present* (Glenview, IL: Scott, Foresman, 1968), 36–42.

80. Albert E. Kahn, *High Treason: The Plot against the People* (New York: Lear, 1950), 329–32. See also Lisle A. Rose, *The Cold War Comes to Main Street: America in 1950* (Lawrence: University of Kansas Press, 1999), 33–34; Robert A. Goldberg, *Enemies Within* (New Haven, CT: Yale University Press, 2001), 32; Brooks and Marsh, *Complete Directory of Prime Time Network and Cable TV Shows*, 101, 368, 800; McNeil, *Total Television*, 93, 297, 644, 739.

81. Miller and Nowak, *Fifties*, 28.

82. Ellwood, *1950*, 2–4.

83. Samuel A. Stouffer, *Communism, Conformity and Civil Liberties* (Garden City, NY: Doubleday), 1955, 40–46, 158–64.

84. John Cogley, *Report on Blacklisting II: Radio-Television* (New York: Fund for the Republic, 1956), 23, 29–31, 206–9. See also Barnouw, *Golden Web*, 269.

85. Cogley, *Report on Blacklisting II*, 2.

86. Ibid, 122. The quote is from the *New York Times*, 1 August 1955.

87. Sig Mickelson, *The Decade That Shaped Television News: CBS in the 1950s* (Westport, CT: Praeger, 1998), 63. See also Cogley, *Report on Blacklisting II*, 123–24.

88. J. Fred MacDonald, *Television and the Red Menace: The Video Road to Viet Nam* (New York: Praeger, 1985), 22.

89. Mickelson, *Decade That Shaped Television News*, 67.

90. Briller, "Conscience of the Industry," 57.

3. The NBC-TV Program Policies Manual

1. "Be Careful on the Air," *Sponsor*, 10 September 1951, 60.

2. *Responsibility: A Working Manual of NBC Program Policies* (New York: National Broadcasting Company, 1948), passim. This manual was found in Helffrich's personal papers.

3. Hans Magnus Enzenberger, Daniel Bell, Martin Malia, David Horowitz, William Pfaff, Russell Jacoby, and Simon Leys, "Marx Reconsidered:—A Symposium," *Los Angeles Times Book Review*, 8 February 1998, 12–13.

4. *Responsibility*, 5–6.

5. Susan Smulyan, *Selling Radio: The Commercialization of American Broadcasting, 1922–1934* (Washington, DC: Smithsonian Institution Press, 1994), 7.

6. William Boddy, *Fifties Television: The Industry and Its Critics* (Urbana: University of Illinois Press, 1993), 155, 159.

7. Robert Alan Aurthur, Rod Serling, Irve Tunick, et al., *The Relation of the Writer to Television* (Santa Barbara, CA: Center for the Study of Democratic Institutions, 1960), 11–12.

8. *Responsibility*, 6. See also Gregory D. Black, *The Catholic Crusade against the Movies, 1940–1975* (New York: Cambridge University Press, 1997), 248.

9. *Responsibility*, 7.

10. Dennis K. Davis and Stanley J. Baron, "A History of Our Understanding of Mass Communication," in Davis and Baron, eds., *Mass Communication and Everyday Life: A Perspective on Theory and Effects* (Belmont, CA: Wadsworth, 1981), 19–52.

11. James L. Baughman, "'The World Is Ruled by Those Who Holler the Loudest': The Third-Person Effect on American Journalism History," *Journalism History* 16, no. 1–2 (1989): 12–19. See also H. Rojas, D. V. Shah, and R. J. Faber, "For the Good of Others: Censorship and the Third-Person Effect," *International Journal of Public Opinion Research* 2 (1996): 163–86.

12. *Responsibility*, 8. See also Black, *Catholic Crusade*, 250.

13. Stephanie Coontz, *The Way We Really Are: Coming to Terms with America's Changing Families* (New York: Basic Books, 1997), 35–37.

14. Stephanie Coontz, *The Way We Never Were: American Families and the Nostalgia Trap* (New York: Basic Books, 1992), 24, 167.

15. Coontz, *The Way We Really Are*, 36.

16. *Responsibility*, 11.

17. John C. Burnham, *Bad Habits: Drinking, Smoking, Taking Drugs, Gambling, Sexual Misbehavior and Swearing in American History* (New York: New York University Press, 1993), 208.

18. *Responsibility*, 8.

19. *Journal of American Medical Association* 268, no. 8 (26 August 1992): 78.

20. Mary F. Corey, *The World through a Monocle:* The New Yorker *at Midcentury* (Cambridge, MA: Harvard University Press, 1999), 184, 195.

21. Coontz, *Way We Never Were*, 36.

22. *Responsibility*, 8.

23. See Christopher Anderson, *Hollywood TV: The Studio System in the Fifties* (Austin: University of Texas Press, 1994), and R. D. Heldenfels, *Television's Greatest Year: 1954* (New York: Continuum, 1994).

24. *Responsibility*, 12.

25. Henry Hampton and Steve Fayer, *Voices of Freedom. An Oral History of the Civil Rights Movement from the 1950s through the 1980s* (New York: Bantam, 1990), 1–35, passim.

26. Ralph Ginzburg, *100 Years of Lynchings* (Baltimore, MD: Classic Black Press, 1988), 238–51.

27. Hampton and Fayer, *Voices of Freedom*, 77–79.

28. David McCullough, *Truman*, qtd. in William T. Martin Riches, *The Civil Rights Movement: Struggle and Resistance* (New York: St. Martin's, 1997), 16.

29. Melanie Kaye-Kantrowitz, "Jews in the U.S.: The Rising Costs of Whiteness," in Marianne Adams, Warren J. Blumenfeld, Carmelita Rose Gastaneda, and Heather W. Hackman, eds., *Readings for Diversity and Social Justice: An Anthology on Racism, Sexism, Anti-Semitism, Heterosexism, Classism, and Ableism* (New York: Routlege, 2000), 138–44.

30. Leo C. Rosten, ed., *Religions of America: Ferment and Faith in an Age of Crisis* (New York: Simon and Schuster, 1963), 441–42; U.S. Bureau of the Census, *Historical Statistics of the United States: Colonial Times to 1970* (Washington, DC: GPO, 1975).

31. *Responsibility*, 12.

32. Ibid.

33. Mike Gallagher qtd. in Peter G. Horsfield, *Religious Television: The American Experience* (New York: Longman, 1985), 5, 7–8, cited in Roger Kahle "Religion and Network Television" (master's thesis, Columbia University, 1970), 3–4.

34. Federal Communications Commission, *Public Service Responsibility of Broadcast Licensees* (Washington, DC: GPO, 1946). The factors were balanced programs gained from carriage of sustaining (i.e., "unsponsored") programs, carriage of local, live talent shows, carriage of programs dealing with important public issues, and elimination of advertising excess.

35. Walter B. Emery, *Broadcasting and Government: Responsibilities and Regulations* (Ann Arbor: University of Michigan Press, 1971), 319.

36. The nineteen program categories are: children's programs, contests, crime and mystery, defamation, direct appeals for funds, impersonations, insobriety, living persons, marriage, narcotic addiction news, physical and mental afflictions, politics, profanity and obscenity, professional advice, public affairs and controversy, racial considerations religion, and sex. *Responsibility*, 5–12.

37. Oakley, *God's Country*, 302.

38. Benita Eisler, *Private Lives: Men and Women of the Fifties* (New York: Watts, 1986), 129.

39. Alfred C. Kinsey, *Sexual Behavior in the Human Male* (Philadelphia, PA: Saunders, 1948), passim. It should also be pointed out that much of Kinsey's data collection was suspect.

40. Alfred C. Kinsey, *Sexual Behavior in the Human Female* (Philadelphia, PA: Saunders, 1953), passim.

41. Albert Ellis, *The American Sexual Tragedy* (New York: Stuart, 1954), 256–59; William Manchester, *The Glory and the Dream: A Narrative History of America* (Boston: Little, Brown, 1974), 478–80.

42. *Responsibility*, 12.

43. Ehrenhalt, *Lost City*, 14, 32, 280.

44. *Responsibility*, 12.

45. Steven Mintz and Susan Kellogg, *Domestic Relations: A Social History of American Family Life* (New York: Free Press, 1988), 182–83.

46. Qtd. in Coontz, *The Way We Never Were*, 35.

47. *Broadcasting Yearbook* (Washington, DC: Broadcasting, 1950), 16.

48. *Responsibility*, 13.

49. John Patrick Diggins, *The Proud Decades: America in War and Peace, 1941–1960* (New York: Norton, 1988), 99.

50. *Responsibility*, 14.

51. See Barbara Goldsmith, *Other Powers: The Age of Suffrage, Spiritualism, and the Scandalous Victoria Woodhull* (New York: Harper Perennial, 1998), 28–39; Thomas J. Schlereth, *Victorian America: Transformations in Everyday Life, 1867–1915* (New York: Harper Perennial, 1992); and Jeffery Sconce, *Haunted Media: Electric Presence from Telegraphy to Television* (Durham, NC: Duke University Press, 2000).

52. Burnham, *Bad Habits*, 4.

53. Jim Tester, A *Western History of Astrology* (Rochester, NY: Boydell, 1996), 200, 204–5.

54. Peter Whitfield, *Astrology: A History* (New York: Abrams, 2001), 191; Keith Thomas, *Religion and the Decline of Magic* (New York: Oxford, 1971), 641–68.

55. Brooks and Marsh, *Complete Directory of Prime Time Network and Cable TV Shows*, 107–8; McNeil, *Total Television*, 97. *The Bigelow Show*, sponsored by the Bigelow Carpet Company, was a split half-hour program. Dunninger did one segment, Winchell and friends the other.

56. Joseph Atmore to author, 14–18 June 2002, Murfreesboro, TN. For a brief article on the life and career of Dunninger, see "Joseph Dunninger," "Magician's Hall of Fame," *Magic Web Channel*, 2000–2009, http://www.magicwebchannel.com/hall_dunninger. htm (accessed 16 June 2002).

57. Brooks and Marsh, *Complete Directory of Prime Time Network and Cable TV Shows*, 108.

58. *Responsibility*, 12, 14.

59. Thomas K. McCraw, *American Business, 1920–2000: How It Worked* (Wheeling, IL: Davidson, 2000), 129.

60. Smulyan correctly points out, "The consensus on national radio became an important building block in the construction of the American commercialized broadcasting system." *Selling Radio*, 12.

61. David Sarnoff, "The American System of Broadcasting and Its Functions in the Preservation of Democracy," Town Hall Luncheon address, Hotel Astor, New York City, 28 April 1938, 10–15.

62. *Responsibility*, 23–24.

63. *NBC Radio and Television Broadcast Standards* (New York: National Broadcasting Company, 1951).

64. "Code for Radio-TV," *Broadcasting-Telecasting* 40, no. 26 (25 June 1951): 27.

65. "NAB Becomes NARTB," *Broadcasting-Telecasting* 40, no. 10 (5 March 1951): 36. On January 1, 1958, the NARTB reverted to its original acronym, NAB, and has remained so to this day.

66. *New York Times*, 20 April 1951, 22.

67. Thad Brown, speech, American Television Society, 28 November 1951, qtd. in Morgan, "Television Code," 86.

68. Morgan, "Television Code," 86, 106.

69. "Strong Medicine," *Broadcasting-Telecasting* 40, no. 24 (10 December 1951): 77, 97.

70. *Responsibility*, 11; "The Television Code of the NARTB," repr. in *Radio/Television Daily: 1953 Television Year Book, Sixteenth Annual Edition* (New York: Radio Daily, 1953), 815.

71. *Motion Picture Code* qtd. in Raymond Moley, *The Hays Office* (New York: Bobbs-Merrill, 1945), 243; and "TV Code," 803–13.

72. NBC Code, 10; *Responsibility*, 5.

73. "TV Code," 811.

74. NBC Code, 4; *Responsibility*, 5–7.

75. NBC Code, 51; "Radio Code," *National Association of Broadcasters, Standards of Good Practice* (Washington, DC: National Association of Broadcasters, 1948), 4.

76. NBC Code, 18.

77. "Radio Code," 4.

78. Ibid., 5; NBC Code, 18–20.

79. NBC Code, 28.

80. Morgan, "Television Code," 123.

4. Sin, Sex, and TV Censorship

1. Donald Webster Corey, *The Homosexual in America: A Subjective Approach* (New York: Greenburg, 1951), 284–85.

2. Oakley, *God's Country*, 302.

3. Beth Bailey, *From Front Porch to Back Seat: Courtship in Twentieth Century America* (Baltimore, MD: Johns Hopkins University Press, 1989), 77.

4. Beth Bailey, *Sex in the Heartland* (Cambridge, MA: Harvard University Press, 1999), 46.

5. Mary F. Corey, *The World through a Monocle:* The New Yorker *at Midcentury* (Cambridge, MA: Harvard University Press, 1999), 3–11. See also Douglas T. Miller and Marion Nowak, *The Fifties: The Way We Really Were* (Garden City, NY: Doubleday, 1977), 147–81.

6. Albert Ellis, *The Folklore of Sex* (New York: Boni, 1951), 13. For a complete listing of all works studied, see 289–302.

7. Ibid., 272.

8. Alfred C. Kinsey, Wardel B. Pomeroy, Clyde C. Martin, and Paul H. Gebhard, *Sexual Behavior in the Human Male* (Philadelphia: Saunders, 1948), passim.

9. Robert T. Michael, John H. Gagnon, Edward O. Laumann, and Gina Kolata, *Sex in America: A Definitive Study* (New York: Little, Brown, 1994), 15–23. See also Paul D. Brinkman, "Dr. Alfred Kinsey and the Press" (PhD diss., Indiana University, 1971), passim.

10. NBC CART, 14 December 1948, folder 1, box 1, NBC Files.

11. NBC CART, 25 July 1949, folder 2, box 1, NBC Files.

12. Ibid.

13. NBC CART, 5 October 1951, folder 4, box 1, NBC Files.

14. Kinsey, Pomeroy, Martin, and Gebhard, *Sexual Behavior in the Human Male*, passim.

15. Michael Gagnon, Laumann, and Kolata, *Sex in America*, 17–19.

16. John D'Emilio, *Sexual Politics, Sexual Communities: The Making of a Homosexual Minority in the United States, 1940–1970*, 2nd ed. (Chicago: University of Chicago Press, 1998), 37.

17. Donald B. Hileman, "The Kinsey Report: A Study of Press Responsibility," *Journalism Quarterly* 30 (1953): 434–35; Paul D. Brinkman, "Dr. Alfred Kinsey and the Press" (PhD diss., Indiana University, 1971), passim. See also Bailey, *From Front Porch to Back Seat*, 83. Quoting from *Time, Ladies Home Journal*, and *Look*, she argues the popular press also reflected a note of caution in their reportage of Kinsey.

18. NBC CART 26 August 1953, folder 6, box 1, NBC Files.

19. D. H. Monro, "Theories of Humor," in Laurence Behrens and Leonard J. Rosen, eds., *Writing and Reading Across the Curriculum*, 3rd ed. (Glenview, IL: Scott, Foresman, 1988), 349–55. See also Simon Critchley, *On Humour* (London: Routledge, 2002), 2–6.

20. See Brooks and Marsh, *Complete Directory of Prime Time Network and Cable TV Shows*, 56; and McNeil, *Total Television*, 57.

21. Harriet Van Horne, review of *Armstrong Circle Theatre*, *New York World Telegram and Sun*, qtd. in NBC CART, 22 September 1953, folder 6, box 1, NBC Files.

22. Kinsey Pomeroy, Martin, and Gebhard, *Sexual Behavior in the Human Male*, 585; and Alfred C. Kinsey, Wardel B. Pomeroy, Clyde C. Martin, and Paul H. Gebhard, *Sexual Behavior in the Human Female* (Philadelphia, PA: Saunders, 1953), 233.

23. NBC CART, 22 September 1953, folder 6, box 1, NBC Files.

24. Caroline Burke, "It's Not TV Censorship: Case History of a Classic," *Variety*, 3 January 1951, 102. The four plays produced from 23 July 1950 to 3 September 1950 were *Hedda Gabler, Richard III, Uncle Vanya*, and *Six Characters in Search of an Author*.

25. Another example from the *Masterpiece* show: edited was the 27 August 1950 production of Shakespeare's *Othello*. The original line penned by the famous Bard is, "Villain, be sure thou prove my love *a whore!*" Italicized words were changed to *wanton*. See also NBC CART, 6 September 1950, folder 3, box 1, NBC Files.

26. Aurthur, Serling, Tunick, et al., *The Relation of the Writer to Television*, 15.

27. Erik Barnouw, *The Sponsor: Notes on a Modern Potentate* (New York: Oxford University Press, 1978), 57.

28. Joanne Meyerowitz, *How Sex Changed: A History of Transexuality in the United States* (Cambridge, MD: Harvard University Press, 2002), 51–98.

29. Christine Jorgensen, *A Personal Autobiography* (New York: Bantam, 1968), xi.

30. D'Emilio, *Sexual Politics*, 40.

31. Jorgensen, *Personal Autobiography*, xi, 37, 155.

32. In her memoir, Jorgensen claims to have met and stayed at the Kinsey's home in 1952 and "enjoyed a friendly conversation with him until his death in August of 1956." Jorgensen, *Personal Autobiography*, 201–2.

33. NBC CART, 12 January 1953, folder 6, box 1, NBC Files.

34. NBC CART, 11 January 1954, folder 7, box 1, NBC Files.

35. NBC CART, 12 January 1953, folder 6, box 1, NBC Files.

36. On June 28, 1969, a series of riots broke out between gay/transgendered people and New York City police at the Stonewall Inn, a Greenwich Village gay bar. It is considered a watershed event for the gay-rights movement out of which came the Gay Liberation Front. See also David Carter, *Stonewall: The Riots That Sparked the Gay Revolution* (New York: St. Martin's, 2004).

37. George W. Henry, *All the Sexes: A Study of Masculinity and Femininity* (New York: Rinehart, 1955), 291. See also Harold Wentworth and Stuart Berg Flexner, *Dictionary of American Slang* (New York: Crowell, 1960).

38. Henry, *All the Sexes*, 291.

39. D'Emilio, *Sexual Politics*, 1–22.

40. NBC CART, 14 December 1948, folder 1, box 1, NBC Files. Helffrich provided no example of what was cut from the show or why the deletion was unacceptable.

41. NBC CART, 28 February 1949, folder 2, box 1, NBC Files.

42. NBC CART, 1 September 1949, folder 2, box 1, NBC Files.

43. NBC CART, 27 September 1949, folder 23, box 1, NBC Files.

44. NBC CART, 8 November 1950, folder 3, box 1, NBC Files.

45. NBC CART, 14 June 1950, folder 3, box 1, NBC Files.

46. NBC CART, 18 October 1950, folder 3, box 1, NBC Files.

47. NBC CART, 17 October 1951, folder 4, box 1, NBC Files.

48. NBC CART, 26 April 1951, folder 4, box 1, NBC Files.

49. NBC CART, 28 May 1951, folder 4, box 1, NBC Files.

50. Ibid. For other deletions to sexual references in audience warm-up activities, see also NBC CART, 14 June 1950, box 1, folder 3, NBC Files.

51. Leviticus 20:13 reads, "If any man layeth with mankind, as he layeth with a woman, both of them have committed abomination; they both shall surely be put to death." Another oft-used passage taken from the Christian Bible to decry the wickedness of same-sex eroticism is from the Book of Romans 1:26–27.

52. Richard Godbeer, *Sexual Revolution in Early America* (Baltimore, MD: Johns Hopkins University Press, 2002), 105–12. See also Robert F. Oaks, "Things Fearful to Name: Sodomy and Buggery in Seventeenth-Century New England," *Journal of Social History* 12 (1978): 268–81.

53. Jonathan Ned Katz, *Gay American History: Lesbians and Gay Men in America* (New York: Plume, 1992), 16–24.

54. U.S. Senate Committee on Expenditures in Executive Departments, *Employment of Homosexuals and Other Sex Perverts in Government*, 81st Cong., 2d sess., 1950, 1–5.

55. Ibid.

56. Qtd. in Stephen J. Whitfield, *The Culture of the Cold War*, 2nd ed. (Baltimore, MD: Johns Hopkins University Press, 1996), 43.

57. Literally dozens of volumes trace McCarthyism's rise and fall and its misguided, albeit politically productive, union of homosexuals with Communism. See Whitfield, *Culture*; Richard H. Rovere, *Senator Joe McCarthy* (New York: Harper and Row, 1973); Ellen Schrecker, *The Age of McCarthyism: A Brief History with Documents* (Boston, MA: Bedford/St. Martin's, 1994) and *Many Are the Crimes: McCarthyism in America* (Boston: Little, Brown, 1998); Earl Latham, *The Communist Controversy in Washington from the New Deal to McCarthy* (Cambridge, MA: Harvard University Press, 1966); M. J. Heale, *American Anticommunism: Combating the Enemy Within, 1830–1970* (Baltimore, MD: Johns Hopkins University Press, 1990); and Caute, *Great Fear*.

58. John D'Emilio, *Making Trouble: Essays on Gay History, Politics and the University* (New York: Routledge, 1992), 57–73.

59. D'Emilio, *Sexual Politics*, 49–51. See also Neil Miller, *Sex-Crime Panic: A Journey to the Paranoid Heart of the 1950s* (Los Angeles: Alyson Books, 2002), 105–11.

60. Lawrence M. Goldwyn, "Legal Ideology and the Regulation of Homosexual Behavior" (PhD diss., Stanford University, 1979), 23–47.

61. Mark Blasius and Steve Phelan, eds., *We Are Everywhere: A Historical Source Book of Gay and Lesbian Politics* (New York: Routledge, 1997), 274–75.

62. Andre Gide, *The Immoralist* (New York: Vintage, 1954), and Lewis MacAdams, *The Birth of Cool: Beat, Bebop, and the American Avant-Garde* (New York: Free Press, 2001).

63. NBC CART 9 March 1954, folder 7, box 1, NBC Files.

64. A swirl of controversy engulfed Maugham's novel *Cakes and Ale* when it was first published in 1930. It is a wicked satire on contemporary literary poseurs and the amorality of Great Britain's vaunted literary elite.

65. A week later, *Variety* observed the program "gave TV a grown-up stature and produced a lively sometimes crisp discussion." Qtd. in NBC CART 9 March 1954.

66. Stephen Tropiano, *The Prime Time Closet: A History of Gays and Lesbians on TV* (New York: Applause Theatre and Cinema, 2002), 1–5.

67. Ibid., ix, 4, and NBC CART 15 August 1956, folder 2, box 153, NBC Files. The program "Homosexuals and the Problems They Present" was seen as an episode of the Los Angeles–produced program *Confidential File* on 25 April 1954. A comparable treatment was broadcast by the New York–based show *The Open Mind* hosted by Dick Heffner on 4 August 1956. Similar shows followed in *The Open Mind* series. After one of *The Open Mind* discussion shows on homosexuality, a laudatory Helffrich wrote, "From a Continuity Acceptance point of view, it seems to me the picture looks bright [on discussing difficult, adult subjects on television.] At least there is a departure from the head-in-the-sand attitude [on this show that] TV can do without."

68. Tropiano, *Prime Time Closet*, 3. This was another title in the *Confidential File* series from 1955.

69. Ibid. This sensationally titled show was seen on WTVS-TV, Detroit, 1958.

70. Helffrich also acted as a free agent in this conspiracy of silence and in 1955 was at it again, noting that he deleted "an entire sequence [of *The Adventures of the Abbots*], which would have featured a swishy gent on a reception committee." NBC CART, 17 May 1955, folder 1, box 153, NBC Files.

71. William J. Mann, *Behind the Screen: How Gays and Lesbians Shaped Hollywood, 1910–1969* (New York: Viking Press, 2001), 335–37.

72. Ibid. Mann is quoting from an *Inside Story* piece from September 1964. No page number given.

73. NBC CART, 27 August 1958, folder 4, box 153, NBC Files.

74. Marilyn Yalom, *A History of the Breast* (New York: Ballantine, 1997), 177.

75. Maura Spiegel and Lithe Sebesta, *The Breast Book: An Intimate and Curious History* (New York: Workman, 2002), 279–82. "The big breasts that symbolized patriotism [in WWII]," write the authors, "would be come a well-loved hallmark of the All-American girl." In addition, say the authors, Freudians suggested that displaced breast, penis, and other sex fetishisms could also be detected in the American obsession with gargantuan, chrome-adorned automobiles of the 1950s. Along with large, eroticized

female mammaries, these befinned, swollen, gas-guzzlers were also enduring metaphors of industrial abundance, material waste, and sexual fixation that characterized the age.

76. NBC CART, 7 May 1959, folder 5, box 153, NBC Files.

77. Spiegel and Sebesta, *Breast Book*, 160.

78. Karal Ann Marling, *As Seen on TV: The Visual Culture of Everyday Life in the 1950s* (Cambridge, MA: Harvard University Press, 1996), 9.

79. "Dictator by Demand," *Time*, 4 March 1957, 34. See also Jane Dorner, *Fashion in the Forties and Fifties* (New Rochelle, NY: Arlington House, 1975), 28.

80. Marling, *As Seen on TV*, 12.

81. Carolyn Latteier, *Breasts: The Women's Perspective on an American Obsession* (New York: Harrington Park, 1998), 37–38.

82. Yalom, *History of the Breast*, 90.

83. Ibid., 9–12, 49, 91, 105, 147, 159.

84. Mick LaSalle, *Complicated Women: Sex and Power in Pre-Code Hollywood* (New York: St. Martin's Griffin, 2000), 8, 155. LaSalle writes that Shearer's "near transparent gown she wore in *A Free Soul* . . . still incites gasps at repertory houses."

85. Louis Chunovic, *One Foot on the Floor: The Curious Evolution of Sex on Television from* I Love Lucy *to* South Park (New York: TV Books, 2000), 28–30; Harry Castleman and Walter J. Podrazik, *Watching TV: Four Decades of American Television* (New York: McGraw Hill, 1982), 48; and Penny Stallings, *Forbidden Channels: The Truth They Hide from* TV Guide (New York: Harper Perennial, 1991), 75.

86. For a discussion of TV-manufactured fame, see Daniel Boorstin's classic, *The Image: A Guide to Pseudo-Events in America* (1961; repr., New York: Vintage, 1992), 45–61.

87. NBC CART, 30 November 1950, folder 3, box 1, NBC Files.

88. Castleman and Podrazik, *Watching TV*, 48.

89. NBC CART, 27 November 1950, folder 3, box 1, NBC Files.

90. "Boston Prelate Blasts TV Comics for 'Committing (Video) Suicide,'" *Variety*, 28 February 1951, 26.

91. Stallings, *Forbidden Channels*, 75; and Brooks and Marsh, *Complete Directory of Prime Time Network and Cable TV Shows*, 137–38.

92. After *Broadway Open House*, Dagmar had her own brief (four-month) network show, *Dagmar's Canteen*, and was a frequent guest panelist on the NBC-TV game show *Masquerade Party*. Virginia Ruth Egnor, the woman remembered as "Dagmar," died in 2001 at the age of seventy-nine. Dennis McClellan, "Comic Actress, Dagmar, Dies at 79," *Los Angeles Times*, 12 October 2001, 54.

93. NBC CART, 7 December 1951, folder 4, box 1, NBC Files.

94. NBC CART, 28 December 1951, folder 4, box 1, NBC Files.

95. NBC CART, 13 August 1951, folder 4, box 1, NBC Files.

96. NBC CART, 28 February 1951, folder 4, box 1, NBC Files.

97. NBC CART, 27 November 1951, folder 4, box 1, NBC Files.

98. NBC CART, 7 October 1952, folder 5, box 1, NBC Files.

99. NBC CART, 8 February 1952, folder 5, box 1, NBC Files.

100. NBC CART, 2 December 1952, folder 5, box 1, NBC Files.

101. NBC CART, 23 January 1952 and 2 February 1952, folder 5, box 1, NBC Files.

102. "Censorship Invades the Animal Kingdom," *TV Guide*, 4 January 1958, 12–15.

103. *The Hank McCune Show* had only a four-month run, September to December 1950, on NBC-TV; after that, it went into syndication. Brooks and Marsh, *Complete*

Directory of Prime Time Network and Cable TV Shows, 431; and McNeil, *Total Television*, 357.

104. NBC CART, 16 November 1950, folder 3, box 1, NBC Files.

105. Ibid. See also NBC CART, 5 November 1954, folder 7, box 1, NBC Files.

106. Elaine Tyler May, *Homeward Bound*, 93–94.

107. Alan Nadel, *Containment Culture: American Narrative, Postmodernism, and the Atomic Age* (Durham, NC: Duke University Press, 1995), 117.

108. Philip Wylie, *Generation of Vipers* (New York: Pocket Books, 1942, 1955), 184–96; and Donna Penn, "The Sexualized Woman: the Lesbian, the Prostitute, and Containment of Female Sexuality in Postwar America," in Joanne Meyerowitz, ed., *Not June Cleaver: Women and Gender in Postwar America, 1945–1960* (Philadelphia, PA: Temple University Press, 1994), 358–81.

109. See T. J. Jackson Lears, "Power, Culture and Memory," *Journal of American History* 75, no. 1 (June 1988): 137–40; George Lipsitz, *Time Passages: Collective Memory and American Popular Culture* (Minneapolis: University of Minnesota Press, 1990); Joanne Meyerowitz, "Beyond the Feminine Mystique: A Reassessment of Popular Mass Culture, 1946–1958," in Meyerowitz, *Not June Cleaver*, 229–62.

110. Meyerowitz, "Beyond the Feminine Mystique," 4, 231.

111. May, *Homeward Bound*, 93.

112. Walter Kendrick, *The Secret Museum: Pornography in Modern Culture* (Berkeley: University of California Press, 1987), 242.

113. NBC CART, 18 June 1957, folder 3, box 153, NBC Files.

114. The dancer's real names were Meta Krahn and Otto Ulbricht; both studied in Zurich and Berlin and were proficient in tap, mime, acrobatics, and ballet. See Ted Sennett, *Your Show of Shows* (New York: Leonard, 2002), and Sonny Watson, *Dance History Archives*, 1999, http://www.streetswing.com/histmai2/d2matah1.htm (accessed 9 November 2002).

115. Watson, *Dance History Archives*.

116. NBC CART, 15 May 1951, folder 4, box 1, NBC Files.

117. Ibid.

118. NBC CART, 5 October 1951, folder 4, box 1, NBC Files. The viewer is referring to the 9 September 1951 Mata and Hari dance on *Your Show of Shows*.

119. NBC CART, 31 October 1951, folder 4, box 1, NBC Files. The reference is to the 9 September 1951 Mata and Hari dance on *Your Show of Shows*.

120. NBC CART, 27 November 1951, folder 4, box 1, NBC Files.

121. NBC CART, 15 November 1951, folder 4, box 1, NBC Files. The reference is to the 8 November 1951 *Ford Festival Show*.

122. NBC CART, 5 March 1953, folder 6, box 1, NBC Files.

123. NBC CART, 6 October 1950, folder 3, box 1, NBC Files.

124. Ibid.

125. NBC CART, 8 July 1955, folder 1, box 153, NBC Files.

126. Carter was the first host of the DuMont broadcasting network's *Cavalcade of Stars* but was quickly snapped up by NBC-TV. For an overview of Carter's career, see David Weinstein, *The Forgotten Network: DuMont and the Birth of American Television* (Philadelphia, PA: Temple University, 2004), 114. See also James Van Schilling, *The Magic Window: American Television, 1939–1953* (New York: Hayworth, 2003), 133–35.

127. NBC CART, 31 October 1951, folder 4, box 1, NBC Files.

128. Pat Weaver and Thomas M. Coffey, *The Best Seat in the House: The Golden Years of Radio and Television* (New York: Knopf, 1994), 211.

129. Lawrence W. Levine, *Highbrow Lowbrow: The Emergence of Cultural Hierarchy in America* (Cambridge, MA: Harvard University Press, 1988), 85–107, 210, 254. "Sacralized culture" might best be understood as the assertion that classical art, dance, music, and the like bring human beings closer to God.

5. Gagging the Gags

1. "As We See It," *TV Guide*, 5 June 1953, 2.

2. *TV Digest*, 8 August 1953, 12.

3. "As We See It," *TV Guide*, 6 September 1958, 2.

4. *TV Digest*, 8 August 1953, 12.

5. NBC CART, 28 December 1948, folder 1, box 1, NBC Files; and NBC CART, 14 December 1949, folder 2, box 1, NBC Files.

6. NBC CART, 8 December 1949, folder 2, box 1, NBC Files.

7. References to profane speech can be found throughout NBC CART reports from 1948 to 1958.

8. NBC CART, 17 January 1949, folder 2, box 1, NBC Files.

9. H. L. Mencken, *The American Language, an Inquiry into the Development of English in the United States* (New York: Knopf, 1937), 300–18.

10. NBC CART, 22 December 1949, folder 2, box 1, NBC Files.

11. John C. Burnham, *Bad Habits: Drinking, Smoking, Taking Drugs, Gambling, Sexual Misbehavior and Swearing in American History* (New York: New York University Press, 1993), 210.

12. William L. O'Neil, *American High: The Years of Confidence, 1945–1960* (New York: Free Press, 1986), 212.

13. Ibid.

14. Qtd. in Robert S. Ellwood, *1950: Crossroads of American Religious Life* (Louisville, KY: Westminster John Knox Press, 2000), 11. See also David Morgan, "The Image of Religion in American *Life*, 1936–1951," in Erika Doss, ed., *Looking at* Life *Magazine* (Washington, DC: Smithsonian, 2001), 139–57.

15. Ellwood, *1950*, 11.

16. *The Swift Show* was a combination musical-variety-game show sponsored by the meat-processing concern Swift and Company, the corporation that pioneered daytime television. Swift then moved its show to prime time on NBC-TV, Thursday nights, 8:30–9:00 P.M. from 1948 to 1949. See also Brooks and Marsh, *Complete Directory of Prime Time Network and Cable TV Shows*, 1004.

17. NBC CART, 21 September 1948, folder 1, box 1, NBC Files.

18. NBC CART, 5 February 1954, folder 7, box 1, NBC Files.

19. NBC CART, 9 June 1955, folder 1, box 153, NBC Files.

20. William Harmon, C. Hugh Holman, and William Flint, *A Handbook to Literature*, 9th ed. (New York: Prentice Hall, 2002), 428.

21. Donald Pizer, *Realism and Naturalism* (Carbondale: Southern Illinois University Press, 1966), 3, 10–11; and Emory Elliott, *Columbia Literary History of the United States* (New York: Columbia University Press, 1988), 502–4, 599.

22. NBC CART, 9 June 1955, folder 1, box 153, NBC Files.

23. Ibid.

24. Frederick Lewis Allen, *Only Yesterday, An Informal History of the Nineteen Twenties* (New York: Harper and Row, 1964), 90–94; 209–10.

25. Burnham, *Bad Habits*, 216, 220. See also Paul S. Boyer, *Purity in Print: Book Censorship in America from the Gilded Age to the Computer Age*, 2nd ed. (Madison: University of Wisconsin Press, 2002), 143–51.

26. Brooks and Marsh, *Complete Directory of Prime Time Network and Cable TV Shows*, 182.

27. See Francis M. Nevins, *Bar-20: The Life of Clarence E. Mulford, Creator of Hopalong Cassidy* (Jefferson, NC: McFarland, 1993).

28. NBC CART, 26 April 1950, folder 3, box 1, NBC Files.

29. Gene Autry, "Gene Autry's Cowboy Code," *Gene Autry Entertainment*, 2009, http://www.geneautry.com/geneautry/geneautry_cowboycode.html.

30. NBC CART, 9 June 1955, folder 1, box 153, NBC Files.

31. NBC CART, 12 December 1956, folder 2, box 153, NBC Files.

32. NBC CART, 15 May 1958, folder 4, box 153, NBC Files.

33. NBC CART, 16 February 1955, folder 1, box 153, NBC Files.

34. NBC CART, 10 April 1957, folder 3, box 153, NBC Files.

35. NBC CART, 13 February 1953, folder 6, box 1, NBC Files.

36. Ibid.

37. Brooks and Marsh, *Complete Directory of Prime Time Network and Cable TV Shows*, 875–76, and McNeil, *Total Television*, 700–701.

38. NBC CART, 13 February 1953, folder 6, box 1, NBC Files.

39. Ibid.

40. NBC CART, 25 October 1955, folder 1, box 153, NBC Files; NBC CART, 14 June 1950, folder 3, box 1, NBC Files.

41. NBC CART, 10 November 1948, folder 1, box 1, NBC Files. The gesture was cut from the 2 November show, starring Milton Berle.

42. NBC CART, 17 October 1951, folder 4, box 1, NBC Files.

43. NBC CART, 5 March 1953, folder 6, box 1, NBC Files.

44. Peter N. Stearns, *Battleground of Desire: The Struggle of Self-Control in Modern America* (New York: New York University Press, 1999), 13–29.

45. Burges Johnson, *The Lost Art of Profanity* (Indianapolis, IN: Bobbs-Merrill, 1948), 30–35; also "Profanity: A Lost Art," *Atlantic Monthly*, 1912, 570–72; and "Are We Growing Profane?" *Literary Digest*, 1918, 33–34.

46. NBC CART, 15 November 1951, folder 4, box 1, NBC Files.

47. NBC CART, 31 October 1951, folder 4, box 1, NBC Files.

48. Ibid.

49. "Autos Flying Confederate Flags Barred from Parking at Capitol," *New York Times*, 9 November 1951, 1.

50. "*The* Flag, Suh! Confederacy's Banner Reaches a New Popularity," *Life*, 16 October 1951, 65–66.

51. NBC CART, 15 February 1952, folder 5, box 1, NBC Files.

52. NBC CART, 17 May 1955, folder 1, box 153, NBC Files.

53. NBC CART, 6 November 1952, folder 5, box 1, NBC Files. See also "The U.S. Flag Code," Public Law 829, 77th Cong., 2nd sess. (1941–42).

54. NBC CART, 17 May 1955, folder 1, box 153, NBC Files.

55. Brooks and Marsh, *Complete Directory of Prime Time Network and Cable TV Shows*, 1024.

56. NBC CART, 13 February 1953, folder 6, box 1, NBC Files.

57. See also Robert Bellah, Richard Madsen, William M. Sullivan, Ann Swidler, and Steven M. Tipton, *Habits of the Heart: Individualism and Commitment in American Life* (Berkeley: University of California Press, 1985).

58. Larry King, ed., *Love Stories of World War II* (New York: Crown, 2001), 4–5.

59. J. R. Poppele, "Moral Responsibility Cited as Challenge to Television, *Variety*, 28 July 1948, 28.

60. Briller, "Conscience of the Industry," 52–57.

61. Stallings, *Forbidden Channels*, 156. "When Lucy learns that she's going to have a baby, she tries to find the right way to tell this to Ricky," in the *I Love Lucy* episode titled "Lucy Is *Enceinte*," which first aired on December 8, 1952, for episode 10 of season 2. "I Love Lucy: Lucy Is *Enceinte* (1952)," *IMDB.com*, http://www.imdb.com/title/tt0609265/.

62. Louis Chunovic, *One Foot on the Floor: The Curious Evolution of Sex on Television from* I Love Lucy *to* South Park (New York: TV Books, 2000), 34; Castleman and Podrazik, *Watching TV*, 75; and Glenn C. Altschuler and David I. Grossvogel, *Changing Channels: America in* TV Guide (Urbana: University of Illinois Press, 1992), 13.

63. McNeil, *Total Television*, 524.

64. NBC CART, 16 November 1948, folder 1, box 1, NBC Files. See also Brooks and Marsh, *Complete Directory of Prime Time Network and Cable TV Shows*, 651.

65. NBC CART, 6 June 1958, folder 4, box 153, NBC Files.

66. Aurthur, Serling, Tunick, et al., *The Relation of the Writer to Television*, 16.

67. Tad Mosel, "Aristotle Live from New York," *Amherst Alumni Magazine*, Winter 1955, 14–19.

68. NBC CART, 29 November 1949, folder 2, box 1, NBC Files.

69. NBC CART, 17 December 1951, folder 4, box 1, NBC Files.

70. NBC CART, 31 May 1950, folder 3, box 1, NBC Files.

71. NBC CART, 21 September 1951, folder 4, box 1, NBC Files.

72. NBC CART, 23 March 1950, folder 3, box 1, NBC Files.

73. NBC CART, 13 December 1955, folder 1, box 153, NBC Files; and NBC CART, 5 November 1954, folder 7, box 1, NBC Files.

74. Terry Galanoy, Tonight: *An Anecdotal History of America's Favorite Talk Show* (Garden City, NY: Doubleday, 1972), 113–18.

75. "Helffrich: Where Do I Fit In?" *Variety*, 17 February 1960, 19.

76. Jim Windolf, "Directing Dave (Part 1)," http://www.icriticus.com/lsn-archive/lsn-012797.text (accessed 12 March 2002). Windolf notes the director of the show, Hal Gurnee, recalls NBC-TV later interrupted the playback of Paar's joke "with a seemingly gratuitous newsbreak."

77. Galanoy, Tonight: *An Anecdotal History*, 113–18.

78. Ibid. See also James Van Hise, *Forty Years at Night: The Story of the* Tonight Show (Las Vegas, NV: Pioneer Books, 1992), 37–41.

79. "Helffrich: Where Do I Fit," 19.

80. George Rosen, "Webs a Flop in Talent Dealings," *Variety*, 17 February 1960, 19, 36.

81. Richard N. Goodwin, *Remembering America: A Voice from the Sixties* (Boston: Little, Brown, 1988), 43–65; and Joseph Stone and Tim Yohn, *Prime Time and Misdemeanors:*

Investigating the 1950s TV Quiz Scandal—A D.A.'s Account (New Brunswick, NJ: Rutgers University Press, 1992), 319–20; Lewis L. Gould, ed., *Watching Television Come of Age:* The New York Times *Reviews by Jack Gould* (Austin: University of Texas Press, 2002), 139–58.

82. Stone and Yohn, *Prime Time and Misdemeanors*, 26–45.

83. "Helffrich: Where Do I Fit," 19.

84. Jackie Austin, interview by author, 11 January 1999, Madison, WI.

85. See Gerald N. Grob, *The Mad among Us: A History of the Care of America's Mentally Ill* (New York: Free Press, 1994).

86. Briller, "Conscience of the Industry," 56.

87. NBC CART, 4 May 1950, folder 3, box 1, NBC Files.

88. NBC CART, 27 July 1951 and 5 October 1951, folder 4, and 12 January 1953, folder 6, box 1, and 17 May 1955, 12 January 1956, and 6 April 1956, folder 1, and 11 June 1956, folder 2, box 153, NBC Files. The above is not an exhaustive list. References to "nuts" and "crazy" may be found numerous times and in many sections in the CARTs.

89. NBC CART, 23 March 1950, folder 3, box 1, NBC Files.

90. NBC CART, 27 July 1953, folder 6, box 1, NBC Files. The proposed anthology series *Your Jeweler's Showcase* was never produced.

91. NBC CART, 12 December 1956, folder 2, box 153, NBC Files.

92. Ibid.

93. NBC CART, 4 April 1958, folder 4, box 153, NBC Files.

94. NBC CART, 8 January 1957, folder 3, box 153, NBC Files.

95. NBC CART, 6 October 1950, folder 3, box 1, NBC Files.

96. Ibid.

97. NBC CART, 4 April 1958, folder 4, box 153, NBC Files.

98. NBC CART, 7 January 1958, folder 4, box 153, NBC Files.

99. NBC CART, 8 February 1951, folder 4, box 1, NBC Files.

100. Over 650 productions were broadcast from 1955 to 1958. See McNeil, *Total Television*, 531.

101. NBC CART, 7 January 1958, folder 4, box 153, NBC Files.

102. NBC CART, 12 March 1958, folder 4, box 153, NBC Files.

103. NBC CART, 20 September 1955, folder 1, box 153, NBC Files.

104. Qtd. in NBC CART, 26 August 1953, folder 6, box 1, NBC Files.

105. NBC CART, 18 November 1959, folder 5, box 153, NBC Files.

106. Brooks and Marsh, *Complete Directory of Prime Time Network and Cable TV Shows*, 1112–13. See also Jon Krampner, *The Man in the Shadows: Fred Coe and the Golden Age of Television* (New Brunswick, NJ: Rutgers University Press, 1997), 31, 37.

107. Bruce Nemerov, music specialist, The Center for Popular Music, Middle Tennessee State University, interview by author, 29 May 2002.

108. NBC, CART, 11 November 1951, box 1, folder 4, NBC Files.

109. "Video Censorship," *Broadcasting-Telecasting* 40, no. 10 (5 March 1951): 56.

110. "To Establish a National Citizens Advisory Board on Radio and Television," Senate Bill 1579, 82nd Cong., 1st sess., *Congressional Record*, 97, pt. 5 (1951): 5872. Also called the "Benton Bill" (S. 1579); see pt. 13, A 3169–A 3170, where U.S. Senator William Benton of Connecticut imagined the board comprising eleven private citizens from religious, cultural, civic, education, and communication groups. The yearly programming report issued by the group would determine to what extent the broadcasting industry was actually serving the public interest.

111. NBC CART, 6 November 1951, folder 4, box 1, NBC Files.

112. Brooks and Marsh, *Complete Directory of Prime Time Network and Cable TV Shows*, 1159; also see McNeil, *Total Television*, 936.

113. NBC CART, 7 December 1951, folder 4, box 1, NBC Files.

114. NBC CART, 27 November 1951, folder 4, box 1, NBC Files.

115. NBC CART, 7 December 1951, folder 4, box 1, NBC Files.

116. NBC CART, 17 December 1951, folder 4, box 1, NBC Files.

117. NBC CART, 27 November 1951, folder 4, box 1, NBC Files.

118. Ibid.

119. "Bannister Flays Code Critics," *Broadcasting-Telecasting* 41, no. 21 (19 November 1951): 78.

120. Donald Clarke, *The Rise and Fall of Popular Music* (New York: St. Martin's Griffin, 1995), 308–9.

121. NBC CART, 17 December 1951, folder 4, box 1, NBC Files.

122. Barry R. Litman, *The Vertical Structure of the Television Broadcasting Industry: The Coalescence of Power* (East Lansing: Michigan State University Press, 1979), 24.

123. Senate Committee on Interstate and Foreign Commerce, *Television Network Practices, Staff Report*, 85th Cong., 1st sess., 1957, 6.

6. TV Violence

1. George Comstock, "Television and Human Behavior," in Richard P. Adler, ed., *Understanding Television: Essays on Television as a Social and Cultural Force* (New York: Praeger, 1981), 35.

2. Douglas Cater, "Television and Thinking People," in Adler, *Understanding Television*, 11.

3. Barnouw, *Image Empire*, 65–80; *Television Factbook 1960, Supplement to Television Digest* (Radnor, PA: Triangle, 1960), 18; Cobbert Steinberg, *TV Facts* (New York: Facts on File, 1985), 85–86.

4. Merle Curti, *Probing Our Past* (New York: Harper, 1955), 172. See also Heywood Broun and Margaret Leech, *Anthony Comstock: Roundsman of the Lord* (New York: Literary Guild of America, 1927), 187; Paul Boyer, *Purity in Print: Book Censorship in America from the Gilded Age to the Computer Age*, 2nd ed. (Madison: University of Wisconsin Press, 2002), 1–22.

5. In 1928, the Payne Fund, a philanthropic group from Cleveland, Ohio, granted the Reverend William Short and his Motion Picture Research Council $200,000 to study the influences of movies on children. Seven universities and nineteen psychologists were involved, publishing eleven volumes of research findings. Short intended to use the Payne Fund studies as a weapon in the cultural struggle for social control of movies by the moral guardians. For a discussion of the Payne studies, see Black, *Hollywood Censored*, 151–55.

6. There were actually four iterations of the comic-book code. The first (and briefest) written in 1948 was followed by the heavily restrictive 1954 code, which was updated 1971 and again in 1989. Amy Kiste Nyberg, *Seal of Approval: The History of the Comics Code* (Jackson: University Press of Mississippi, 1998), 164–79; and David Hajdu, *The Ten-Cent Plague: The Great Comic Book Scare and How It Changed America* (New York: Farrar, Straus, and Giroux, 2008), 274–304.

7. "TV's Hottest Problem: Public Relations," *Sponsor*, 16 June 1952, 27–29. The *Sponsor* article also chides that only 30 of 428 House members were on the floor to vote for

the resolution. Gathings himself was not a member of the seven-person subcommittee but did act as its "star witness."

8. House Committee on Interstate and Foreign Commerce, *Investigation of Radio and Television Programs*, 82d Cong., 2d sess., 1952, House Report 2509, 10, 12, 30–73.

9. Keisha L. Hoerrner, "The Forgotten Battles: Congressional Hearings on Television Violence in the 1950s," *Web Journal of Mass Communication Research* 2, no. 3 (June 1999), http://www.scripps.ohiou.edu/wjmcr/vol02/2-3a.HTM (accessed 15 November 2000). Hoerrner also notes there was "a significant amount of symbolic congressional action from 1950 to 1999 in the area of television violence, but only two public laws enacted."

10. See Murray Edelman, *The Symbolic Uses of Politics* (Urbana: University of Illinois Press, 1970).

11. NBC CART, 27 September 1950, folder 3, box 1, NBC Files; NBC CART, 11 May 1956, folder 2, box 153, NBC Files. *TV Guide* reported that Phyllis Van Orman was head of ABC-TV continuity in 1956. See "To Cut or Not to Cut: Some Problems Faced by TV Film Editors," *TV Guide*, 28 July 1956, 10–11.

12. Jack Mabley, "TV's Holiday Fare for Kids: It's Murder," *Chicago Daily News*, 27 December 1952, 1.

13. Jack Mabley, correspondence with the author, 20 October 2002.

14. Jack Mabley, "Four-Day Total: 77 Killings, Poisonings, Fist Fights, Kidnappings Add Up to a Juvenile Bloodbath," *Chicago Daily News*, 29 December 1952, 1.

15. Jack Mabley, "Four Stations Show 2,500 TV Crimes a Year to Kids Here: Parents Alarmed as Tots Learn Violence Settles Everything," *Chicago Daily News*, 30 December 1952, 1.

16. Jack Mabley, "Some at Sets All Day Long: Get Punch Drunk from Killings, Kidnappings, Other Gun Violence," *Chicago Daily News*, 31 December 1952, 1.

17. Ibid.

18. Mabley, correspondence.

19. Ibid.

20. Jack Mabley, "Why Not Classify TV Shows?" *Chicago Daily News*, 2 January 1951, 17.

21. Jack Mabley, "Well, If We Must Get Rough," *Chicago Daily News*, 23 December 1952, 19.

22. Jack Mabley, "TV Kills 93 in Week on Child Programs," *Chicago Daily News*, 3 January 1953, 1.

23. Jack Mabley, "Crime Programs on TV Stir Storm of Protests by Parents," *Chicago Daily News*, 2 January 1953, 3.

24. Jack Mabley, "City Council Orders Probe of Crime on Kids' TV Shows," *Chicago Daily News*, 8 January 1953, 1.

25. Ibid.

26. Mabley, "Some at Sets All Day Long," 1.

27. Jack Mabley, "Predicts Cleanup in TV Crime," *Chicago Daily News*, 5 January 1953, 23.

28. Jack Mabley, "Educators Join War on TV Crime, *Chicago Daily News*, 31 December 1952, 1.

29. Jack Mabley, "TV Cowboys Start to Bite Dust," *Chicago Daily News*, 5 March 1953, 47. Rating figures represent the percentage of all television sets tuned to a given program.

30. NBC CART, 31 March 1953, folder 6, box 1, NBC Files; Jack Mabley, "City May Ask TV to Police Self," *Chicago Daily News*, 23 March 1953, 31.

31. NBC CART, 31 March 1953, folder 6, box 1, NBC Files.

32. Mabley, "City May Ask," 31.

33. Hoerrner, "The Forgotten Battles." Hoerrner's examples are not local government but the U.S. Congress. The principles of "symbolic discussion" nonetheless remain.

34. See Edelman, *The Symbolic Uses of Politics*, 1–21.

35. The show's title, *Chevrolet on Broadway*, after a few months was changed to *Chevrolet Tele-Theatre*. See Brooks and Marsh, *Complete Directory of Prime Time Network and Cable TV Shows*, 183; McNeil, *Total Television*, 822.

36. NBC CART, 30 September 1948, folder 1, box 1, NBC Files.

37. NBC CART, 7 October 1948, folder 1, box 1, NBC Files. Reperformances were uncommon in the days of live network television. Rod Serling's 1955 Emmy-winning teleplay "Patterns," about the character and ethics of big business, was also restaged. It was broadcast 16 January 1955 on NBC-TV's *Kraft Television Theatre* to rave reviews and was reperformed the following month. See Joel Engle, *Rod Serling, The Dreams and Nightmares of Life in the Twilight Zone* (Chicago: Contemporary, 1989), 112; Jack Gould, "Patterns Is Hailed as Notable Triumph," *Watching Television Come of Age: The New York Times Reviews by Jack Gould*, ed. Gould (Austin: University of Texas Press, 2002), 45–46.

38. NBC CART, 28 November 1949, folder 2, box 1, NBC Files.

39. NBC CART, 23 March 1950, folder 3, box 1, NBC Files.

40. Ibid.

41. NBC CART, 15 November 1951, folder 4, box 1, NBC Files.

42. *We, the People* was a popular radio program that began in the mid-1930s. It moved to television in 1948, becoming the first interview show to be simulcast by both NBC-TV and radio. Brooks and Marsh, *Complete Directory of Prime Time Network and Cable TV Shows*, 1113; and McNeil, *Total Television*, 899.

43. NBC CART, 27 November 1951, folder 4, box 1, NBC Files.

44. Ibid.

45. Tad Mosel, "Aristotle Live from New York," *Amherst Alumni Magazine*, winter 1995, 14–19.

46. NBC CART, 28 February 1951, folder 4, box 1, NBC Files.

47. Those who advertised on the emerging medium told extraordinary success stories. See Aurthur, Serling, Tunick, et al., *The Relation of the Writer to Television*, 7; and Barnouw, *Sponsor*, 47.

48. NBC CART, 8 December 1949, folder 2, box 1, NBC Files.

49. Stephen Bottomore, "The Panicking Audience? Early Cinema and the 'Train Effect,'" *Historical Journal of Film, Radio and Television* 19, no. 2 (1999): 177–216.

50. Ibid., 215.

51. Robert C. Toll, *The Entertainment Machine: American Show Business in the Twentieth Century* (New York: Oxford, 1982), 194.

52. Linda Williams, *Hard Core: Power, Pleasure, and the 'Frenzy of the Visible'* (Berkeley: University of California Press, 1989), 51–53.

53. See Rolf Wiggerhaus and Michael Robertson, *The Frankfurt School: Its History, Theories, and Political Significance* (Cambridge, MA: MIT Press, 1995). Frankfurt

School social philosophers and sociologists, distrusted mass culture and saw firsthand how corrupt leaders, like Adolf Hitler, could manipulate popular media for purposes of propaganda.

54. NBC CART, 13 October 1953, folder 6, box 1, NBC Files. The Winchell column to which Helffrich refers was printed in the *Daily Mirror* on 30 September 1953. Winchell could not have been referencing the NBC-TV production of *Peter Pan* starring Mary Martin; it did not air until the 1955–56 season. Winchell may well have used the anecdote to illustrate the effects of printed mass media on young children and paint television as an even bigger threat for dangerous mimicry.

55. NBC CART, 14 May 1955, folder 1, box 153, NBC Files.

56. *Responsibility*, 13–23.

57. Ibid., see also NBC CART, 16 February 1955, folder 1, box 153, NBC Files.

58. Ibid.

59. NBC CART, 1 April 1954, folder 7, box 1, NBC Files.

60. Ibid.

61. NBC CART, 13 October 1953, folder 6, box 1, NBC Files.

62. NBC CART, 1 April 1954, folder 7, box 1, NBC Files.

63. "House built" is how Helffrich classified television or radio shows that were NBC-TV produced, rather than ad-agency produced. NBC CART, 20 April 1950, folder 3, box 1, NBC Files.

64. NBC CART, 28 February 1951, folder 4, box 1, NBC Files.

65. Ibid.

66. Wilbur Schramm, Jack Lyle, and Edwin Parker, *Television in the Lives of Our Children* (Stanford, CA: Stanford University Press, 1961), 1; J. Michael Sproule, *Communication Today* (New York: Scott Foresman, 1981). See also Joseph Klapper, *The Effects of Mass Communication* (New York: Free Press, 1960). Many mass-communications scholars point to Klapper's work as one that indurated the minimal-effects hypothesis.

67. Schramm, Lyle, and Parker, *Television in the Lives of Our Children*, 1.

68. See Horace Newcomb and Paul M. Hirsch, "Television as a Cultural Form," in John Hartley and Roberta E. Pearson, eds., *American Cultural Studies: A Reader* (New York, Oxford, 2000), 163–73.

69. Helffrich, personal papers, author's collection. Helffrich spoke on television-programming responsibility at the behest of NBC-TV's "speakers bureau"—part of the network's public relations effort. See also NBC CARTs, 13 October 1953, 5 November 1954, and 5 May 1954, folder 7, box 1, NBC Files. Tennessee U.S. Senator Estes Kefauver was chair of the U.S. Senate Subcommittee on the Judiciary, which in 1955–56 investigated juvenile delinquency and comic books in the United States.

70. NBC CARTs, 17 October 1949, folder 2, box 1; 10 September 1952, folder 5, box 1; 11 June 1952, folder 5, box 1; 1 September 1954, folder 7, box 1; and 13 December 1955, folder 1, box 153, NBC Files.

71. NBC CART, 7 January 1958, folder 4, box 153, NBC Files.

72. NBC CART, 26 January 1950, folder 3, box 1, NBC Files.

73. "The Letter," NBC-TV Masterbook 93, box 32 (19 January 1950–26 January 1950). Library of Congress Film and Television Archive, Washington, DC.

74. See Black, *Hollywood Censored*, 305; *Responsibility*, 6–7; and "The Television Code of the NARTB," *The 1953 Television Yearbook* (New York: Radio and Daily, 1953), 809.

75. NBC CART, folder 2, box 1, 25 February 1949, NBC Files.

76. George Gallup, "The Gallup Poll Air Waves Share Blame," *Washington Post and Times-Herald*, 21 November 1954, 1A.

77. Ellen Wartella and Sharon Mazzarella, "A Historical Comparison of Children's Use of Leisure Time," in Richard Butsch, ed., *For Fun and Profit: The Transformation of Leisure into Consumption* (Philadelphia, PA: Temple University Press, 1990), 173–94.

78. James Gilbert, *A Cycle of Outrage: America's Reaction to the Juvenile Delinquent of the 1950s* (New York: Oxford University Press, 1986), 13–14, 25–28, 77–78.

79. In 1954, the Democrats won control of Congress, and Estes Kefauver replaced Robert Hendrickson, a Republican, as chair when the Subcommittee on Juvenile Delinquency reconvened in 1955.

80. Senate Subcommittee to Investigate Juvenile Delinquency, Committee on Judiciary, *Juvenile Delinquency (Television Programs)*, 83rd Cong., 2d sess., 1954, S. Rept. 1064, 1.

81. Ibid., 396.

82. Ibid., 182. The subcommittee produced three discreet volumes: *Juvenile Delinquency (Motion Pictures)*, *Juvenile Delinquency (Comic Books)*, and *Juvenile Delinquency (Television Programs)*.

83. NBC CART, 28 February 1951, folder 4, box 1, NBC Files.

84. NBC CART, 13 October 1953, folder 6, box 1, NBC Files.

85. NBC CART, 18 November 1959, folder 5, box 153, NBC Files.

86. Nyberg, *Seal of Approval*, 56, 59–66, 73–75, 80, 119–20, 56, 59–66, 73–75, 80, 119–20; David Hajdu, *The Ten-Cent Plague: The Great Comic Book Scare and How It Changed America* (New York: Farrar, Straus, and Giroux, 2008), 251–55.

87. NBC CART, 1 September 1954, folder 7, box 1, NBC Files.

88. Ibid.

89. Ibid.

7. Postwar Racial Discourse

1. Jerrold M. Packard, *American Nightmare: The History of Jim Crow* (New York: St. Martin's, 2002), 62–84. See also Pete Daniel, *Lost Revolutions: The South in the 1950s* (Chapel Hill: University of North Carolina Press, 2000), and Howard Beeth and Cary D. Wintz, eds., *Black Dixie: Afro-Texan History and Culture in Houston* (College Station: Texas A&M University Press, 1992).

2. C. Vann Woodward, *American Counterpoint: Slavery and Racism in the North and South* (New York: Smith, 1971), 43; William E. Barnhart and Eugene F. Schlickman, *Kerner: The Conflict of Intangible Rights* (Urbana: University of Illinois Press, 1999). See also Michael A. Fletcher, "Kerner Prophecy on Race Relations Came True, Report Says Despite Progress, Foundation Finds 'Separate and Unequal' Societies More Deeply Rooted," *Washington Post*, 1 March 1998, A6.

3. Alonzo L. Hamby, *Man of the People: A Life of Harry S. Truman* (New York: Oxford University Press, 1995), 434.

4. "Negro Talent Coming into Own on TV without Using Stereotypes: A Sure Sign That Television Is Free of Racial Barriers," *Variety*, 3 May 1950, 30, 40.

5. "Can TV Crack America's Color Line?" *Ebony*, May 1951, 58–65.

6. J. Fred MacDonald, *Blacks and White TV: African Americans in Television since 1948* (Chicago: Nelson-Hall, 1992), 3–10; Donald Bogle, *Primetime Blues: African Americans on Network Television* (New York: Farrar, Straus, and Giroux, 2001), 13–19.

7. Bogle, *Primetime Blues*, 13.

8. David Sarnoff, *Looking Ahead: The Papers of David Sarnoff* (New York: McGraw-Hill, 1968), 97.

9. Oakley, *God's Country*, 95; Barnouw, *Sponsor*, 47–58.

10. NBC CART, 20 April 1950, folder 3, box 1, NBC Files.

11. NBC CART, 6 October 1950, folder 3, box 1, NBC Files. The specific policy may be found in *Responsibility*, 5–12.

12. NBC CART, 17 January 1949, folder 2, box 1, NBC Files. Horn and Hardt was a postwar automat cafeteria in New York City.

13. Jackie Austin (Helffrich's daughter), interview by author, 11 January 1999, Madison, WI. See also Stockton Helffrich, FBI file, 1950.

14. "Counting Noses: NBCers Agree with Helffrich," "Top NBCer Says: Biggest Network Whitecollarites Need Guild," *White Collar Mike*, 1 August 1946, 1. See also Briller, "Conscience of the Industry," 52–57; and Stockton Helffrich, interview by Jackie Austin, 1 March 1987, Helffrich residence, Jackson Heights, New York.

15. Stockton Helffrich, interview by Austin.

16. NBC CART, 26 July 1950, box 1, folder 3, NBC Files.

17. Stephen C. Foster, *My Old Kentucky Home, Good Night* (New York: Firth, Pond, 1853).

18. Stephen C. Foster, *Old Folks at Home* (New York: Firth, Pond, 1851).

19. Stephen C. Foster, *Massa's in de Cold Ground* (New York: Firth, Pond, 1852).

20. NBC CART, 23 February 1950, box 1, folder 3, NBC Files.

21. NBC CART, 6 October 1950, box 1, folder 3, NBC Files.

22. Ibid.

23. NBC CART, 20 April 1950, folder 3, box 1, NBC Files.

24. For a detailed discussion of African Americans' postwar social goals, see John B. Kirby, *Black Americans in the Roosevelt Era: Liberalism and Race* (Knoxville: University of Tennessee Press, 1980).

25. NBC CART, 6 October 1950, box 1, folder 3, NBC Files.

26. NBC CART, 9 November 1950, box 1, folder 3, NBC Files.

27. "The Forgotten 15,000,000," *Sponsor*, October 1949, 24–25, 54–55. See also "Selling the Negro Market," *Tide*, 20 July 1951, 30; "Can TV Crack America's Color Line?" *Ebony*, May 1951, 58.

28. NBC CART, 28 January 1951, box 1, folder 4, NBC Files. The offensive epithet is defined as "a trick or drawback, especially if deliberately concealed; something inconsistent or out of place" and/or "an unacknowledged black forebearer of a white person, with 'woodpile' a slang for 'family tree.'" It is unclear how or in what context Senator Mundt used the phrase. See J. E. Lighter, J. O'Connor, and J. Ball, eds., *Random House Historical Dictionary of American Slang: A-G (Random House Historical Dictionary of American Slang, Vol. 1)* (New York: Random, 1994), 916.

29. *The American Forum of the Air*, originating from Washington, D.C., was seen on NBC-TV from 1950 to 1957. The talk show began on radio in 1937. See McNeil, *Total Television*, 40; and Brooks and Marsh, *Complete Directory of Primetime Network and Cable TV Shows*, 41.

30. NBC CART, 28 January 1951, box 1, folder 4, NBC Files.

31. Stepin Fetchit was the stage name of Lincoln Perry, an actor who became known for his stereotyped portrayals in early cinema of black men. His caricature usually

painted blacks as lazy, easily frightened, chronically idle, and inarticulate. See Donald Bogle, *Toms, Coons, Mulattoes, Mammies, and Bucks: An Interpretive History of Blacks in American Film* (New York: Continuum, 1989).

32. NBC CART, 19 February 1951, box 1, folder 4, NBC Files.

33. NBC CART, 21 November 1951, box 1, folder 4, NBC Files.

34. Robert J. Donovan, *Conflict and Crisis: The Presidency of Harry S. Truman* (New York: Norton, 1977), 333–34; and Hamby, *Man of the People*, 364–66.

35. NBC CART, 21 November 1951, box 1, folder 4, NBC Files.

36. "(TV Code) The Television Code of the NARTB," rept. in *Radio/Television Daily: 1953 Television Year Book, Sixteenth Annual Edition* (New York: Radio Daily, 1953), 813.

37. See Eileen Southern, *The Music of Black Americans: A History* (New York: Norton, 1983); Douglas Gilbert, *American Vaudeville: Its Life and Times* (New York: Dover, 1940). See also Robert C. Allen, "Vaudeville and Film 1895–1915: A Study in Media Interaction," (PhD diss., University of Iowa, 1977).

38. John E. DiMeglio, *Vaudeville USA* (Bowling Green, OH: Bowling Green University Popular Press, 1973), 25; Joe Laurie Jr., *Vaudeville: From the Honky-Tonk to the Palace* (New York: Holt, 1953), 3. See also Susan Kattwinkel, *Tony Pastor Presents: Afterpieces from the Vaudeville Stage* (Phoenix, AZ: Abbey, 1998).

39. Michael Rogin, *Blackface, White Noise: Jewish Immigrants in the Hollywood Melting Pot* (Berkeley: University of California Press, 1996). Rogin argues blackface was the most popular American form of entertainment, so immigrant groups, especially the Irish and Jews, adopted it as a means of assimilation into the dominant American culture.

40. See Eric Lott, *Love and Theft: Blackface Minstrelsy and the American Working Class* (New York: Oxford University Press, 1993).

41. Herbert G. Goldman, biographer to Jolson and Cantor, notes that a performer's use of "blackface, though lending accent to broader facial expressions, was often said to inhibit the rendering of subtler emotions." *Banjo Eyes: Eddie Cantor and the Birth of Modern Stardom* (New York: Oxford, 1997), 68.

42. Herbert G. Goldman, *Jolson: The Legend Comes to Life* (New York: Oxford University Press, 1988), 170–71. See also Goldman, *Banjo Eyes*, 57–77.

43. By 1935, the legendary Palace Theatre, once flagship to a six-hundred-theater vaudeville circuit, had become a movie house with no vaudeville acts at all. Most historians agree vaudeville died as the result of changing entertainment economics brought about by the popularity of radio, talking movies, and the impact of the Great Depression. Robert W. Synder, *The Voice of the City: Vaudeville and Popular Culture in New York* (New York: Oxford University Press, 1989), 155–61.

44. Sam Brylawski, "Thanks for the Memory: New Bob Hope Gallery Opens at Library," *Information Bulletin* 59, no. 6 (June 2000), *Library of Congress*, http://www.loc.gov/loc/lcib/0006/hope.html (accessed 15 May 2001).

45. In addition to Eddie Cantor, *The Colgate Comedy Hour*'s revolving hosts included William Abbott and Lou Costello, Dean Martin and Jerry Lewis, Ed Wynn, Donald O'Connor, Ethel Merman, and Frank Sinatra. Other stars hosting only a few episodes included Bob Hope, Tony Martin, Jimmy Durante, and Fred Allen. See McNeil, *Total Television*, 171; and Brooks and Marsh, *Complete Directory of Prime Time Network and Cable TV Shows*, 202.

46. Cantor also christened the polio-fighting charity fund the "March of Dimes." See Goldman, *Banjo Eyes*, 195–96, 269.

47. NBC CART, 27 September 1951, folder 4, box 1, NBC Files.

48. NBC CART, 5 October 1951, folder 4, box 1, NBC Files.

49. For a discussion of ideology and social reproduction, see John B. Thompson, *Ideology and Modern Culture: Critical Social Theory in the Era of Mass Communication* (Stanford, CA: Stanford University Press, 1990), 85–97.

50. Brooks and Marsh, *Complete Directory of Prime Time Network and Cable TV Shows*, 202.

51. NBC CART, 6 November 1951, folder 4, box 1, NBC Files.

52. NBC CART, 31 October 1951, folder 4, box 1, NBC Files.

53. NBC CART, 10 September 1952, folder 5, box 1, NBC Files.

54. Ibid.

55. NBC CART, 2 December 1952, folder 5, box 1, NBC Files.

56. NBC CART, 12 January 1953, folder 6, box 1, NBC Files. See also NBC CART, 23 July 1952, folder 5, box 1, NBC Files; and NBC CARTs, 7 February 1953, 13 February 1953, and 5 May 1954, folder 6, box 1, NBC Files.

57. NBC CART, 16 February 1955, folder 1, box 153, NBC Files.

58. NBC CART, 5 February 1954, folder 7, box 1, NBC Files.

59. Goldman, *Banjo Eyes*, 378.

60. NBC CART, 5 February 1954, folder 7, box 1, NBC Files.

61. Goldman, *Banjo Eyes*, 378.

62. Thomas Cripps, "*Amos 'n' Andy* and the Debate over American Racial Integration," in John E. O'Connor, ed., *American History/American Television: Interpreting the Video Past* (New York: Ungar, 1983), 38. Cripps also mentions NBC-TV's "integration without identification" policy and the network's hiring of a black public-relations firm.

63. *TV Digest*, 23 August 1952, 10.

64. Horton qtd. in NBC CART, 12 January 1953, folder 6, box 1, NBC Files.

65. NBC CART, 26 September 1952, folder 5, box 1, NBC Files; *TV Digest*, 23 August 1952, 10; NBC CART, 12 January 1953 and 5 March 1953, folder 6, box 1, NBC Files.

66. Daniel, *Lost Revolutions*, 191.

67. Daniel, *Lost Revolutions*, 196. See also Stephen J. Whitfield, *A Death in the Delta: The Story of Emmett Till* (New York: Free Press, 1988), 2–6.

68. See James N. Upton, *A Social History of 20th Century Urban Riots* (Bristol, IN: Wyndham Hall, 1984).

69. NBC CART, 10 September 1951, folder 4, box 1, NBC Files.

70. NBC CART, 5 March 1953, folder 6, box 1, NBC Files.

71. NBC CART, 16 November 1953, folder 6, box 1, NBC Files.

72. NBC CART, 22 June 1951, folder 4, box 1, NBC Files.

73. Three black actresses played the role of Beulah over the course of its television run from October 1950 to September 1953: Ethel Waters, Hattie McDaniel (who appeared in only a few episodes before falling ill), and Louise Beavers. McNeil, *Total Television*, 90; and Brooks and Marsh, *Complete Directory of Prime Time Network and Cable TV Shows*, 96.

74. Jannette L. Dates and William Barlow, eds., *Split Image: African Americans in the Mass Media* (Washington, DC: Howard University Press, 1990); Elizabeth Kolbert, "From Beulah to Oprah: The Evolution of Black Images on TV," *New York Times*, 15 January 1993; MacDonald, *Blacks and White TV*, 23–24, 46, 118; Bogle, *Primetime Blues*,

19–26; Mary Ann Watson, *Defining Visions: Television and the American Experience since 1945* (Orlando, FL: Harcourt Brace, 1989), 23–31.

75. McNeil, *Total Television*, 44; Brooks and Marsh, *Complete Directory of Prime Time Network and Cable TV Shows*, 46.

76. Melvin P. Ely, *The Adventures of Amos 'n' Andy: A Social History of an American Phenomenon* (New York: Free Press, 1991); Bart Andrews and Arghus Julliard, *Holy Mackerel! The Amos 'n' Andy Story* (New York: Dutton, 1986). See also W. T. Lhamon, *Raising Cain: Blackface Performance from Jim Crow to Hip Hop* (Cambridge, MA: Harvard University Press, 1998).

77. U.S. Commission on Civil Rights, *Window Dressing on the Set: Women and Minorities in Television*, 1977, 4–5.

78. Ibid.

79. Cripps, "*Amos 'n' Andy*," 43–49.

80. Ely, *Adventures of Amos 'n' Andy*, 216.

81. Cripps, "*Amos 'n' Andy*," 43–49.

82. Darrell Y. Hamamoto, *Nervous Laughter: Television Situation Comedy and Liberal Democratic Ideology* (New York: Praeger, 1989) 43. For a grounding discussion of the era, see also Mary L. Dudziak, *Cold War Civil Rights: Race and the Image of American Democracy* (Princeton, NJ: Princeton University Press, 2000), 3–17.

83. Cripps, "*Amos 'n' Andy*," 39.

84. NBC-TV's owned-and-operated New York station had several call-letter iterations. It was WNBT, then WRCA, and as of May 1960, WNBC-TV. See Joseph H. Udelson, *The Great Television Race: A History of American Industry, 1925–1941* (Tuscaloosa, AL: University of Alabama Press, 1982).

85. NBC CART, 5 November 1954, folder 7, box 1, NBC Files.

86. Ibid.

87. NBC CART, 12 January 1953 folder 6, box 1, NBC Files.

88. *Sponsor*, October 1949, 24–25, 54–55. See also *Tide*, 20 July 1951, 30.

89. NBC CART, 10 September 1959, folder 5, box 153, NBC Files.

90. Patrick Garry, *An American Paradox: Censorship in a Nation of Free Speech* (Westport, CT: Praeger, 1993), 88, 128. See also Nat Hentoff, *Free Speech for Me—but Not for Thee: How the American Left and Right Relentlessly Censor Each Other* (New York: HarperCollins, 1992).

91. William Clotworthy, telephone interview by the author, Murfreesboro, TN, 10 August 2004. For a discussion on NBC-TV censorship during this period (albeit before Clotworthy's tenure, 1979–90), see Robert George Pekurny, "Broadcast Self-Regulation: A Participant-Observation Study of the National Broadcasting Company's Broadcast Standards Department" (PhD diss., University of Minnesota, 1977).

8. Of Truth and Toilet Paper

1. Barnouw, *Golden Web*, 285.

2. Michael Ritchie, *Please Stand By: A Prehistory of Television* (Woodstock, NY: Overlook, 1994), 99. Survey data estimates about 170,000 domestic television receivers in 1947 and a total U.S. population of 144,988,938.

3. Barnouw, *Golden Web*, 286.

4. James L. Baughman, *The Republic of Mass Culture: Journalism, Filmmaking, and*

Broadcasting in America since 1941, 2nd ed. (Baltimore, MD: Johns Hopkins University Press, 1997), 43.

5. Baughman, *Republic of Mass Culture*, 53.

6. Baughman, *Republic of Mass Culture*, 43. By 1947, NBC pioneered a coaxial network linking four eastern stations: New York City, Philadelphia, Schenectady, New York, and Washington, D.C. Next, AT&T developed more expensive microwave technology for long-distance television transmission, installing repeater stations every twenty-five miles. On September 25, 1950, AT&T opened a microwave relay system between New York and Chicago; in 1951, the system reached the west coast. See also Steven Lubar, *InfoCulture: The Smithsonian Book of Information Age Inventions* (Boston: Houghton Mifflin, 1993), 136.

7. The seven stations on the air in New York City in 1952 were WCBS-TV, channel 2; WNBT (later WRCA, then WNBC-TV), channel 4; WABD, channel 5; WJZ (later WABC-TV), channel 7; WOR-TV, channel 9; WPIX, channel 11; and WATV, channel 13. Barnouw, *Golden Web*, picture, 282–83.

8. Susan Smulyan, *Selling Radio: The Commercialization of American Broadcasting, 1920–1934* (Washington, DC: Smithsonian, 1994), 70. See also Alfred N, Goldsmith and Austin C. Lescarboura, *This Thing Called Broadcasting* (New York: Holt, 1930), 48; Paul Schubert, *The Electric World: The Rise of Radio* (New York: Macmillan, 1928), 219.

9. Gary A. Steiner, *The People Look at Television: A Study of Audience Attitudes* (New York: Knopf, 1963), 219. See also *Television Digest*, 7 March 1960, 11, 212–13.

10. NBC CART, 28 September 1948, folder 1, box 1, NBC Files.

11. Marjorie Heins, *Not in Front of the Children: "Indecency," Censorship, and the Innocence of Youth* (New York: Hill and Wang, 2001), 92.

12. Steiner, *People Look at Television*, 213.

13. NBC CART, 28 September 1948, folder 1, box 1, NBC Files.

14. NBC CART, 26 January 1949, folder 2, box 1, NBC Files.

15. NBC CART, 2 November 1949, folder 2, box 1, NBC Files. See also NBC CART, 8 March 1950, folder 3, box 1, NBC Files.

16. NBC CART, 15 February 1950, folder 3, box 1, NBC Files.

17. NBC CART, 8 March 1950, folder 3, box 1, NBC Files. See also Pat Weaver and Thomas M. Coffey, *Best Seat in the House.*

18. Brooks and Marsh, *Complete Directory of Prime Time Network and Cable TV Shows*, 348; and McNeil, *Total Television*, 282.

19. Cary O'Dell, *Women Pioneers in Television: Biographies of Fifteen Industry Leaders* (Jefferson, NC: McFarland, 1997), 81–92.

20. Val Adams, "Glamour Girl of the Television Screen," *New York Times*, 19 February 1950, 11.

21. See "Faye's Décolleté Makes TV Melee," *Life*, 10 April 1950, 87; and "Faye Joins List of Ten Best-Dressed," *Los Angeles Daily News*, 1 January 1951.

22. "Transition," *Newsweek*, 21 March 1993, 82.

23. C. E. Butterfield, "Those Plunging Necklines Worry Video Studios," *New York Times*, 19 March 1950, in Frederic S. Lane, *The Decency Wars: The Campaign to Cleanse American Culture* (Amherst, NY: Prometheus, 2006), 28.

24. NBC CART, 4 May 1950, folder 3, box 1, NBC Files.

25. See Lewis L. Gould, ed., *Watching Television Come of Age:* The New York Times *Reviews by Jack Gould* (Austin: University of Texas Press, 2002), 95, 115.

26. *Sponsor*, 8 May 1950, qtd. in NBC CART, 16 May 1950, folder 3, box 1, NBC Files.

27. NBC CART, 27 October 1950, folder 3, box 1, NBC Files.

28. *Responsibility*, 6.

29. NBC CART, 25 November 1957, folder 3, box 153, NBC Files.

30. NBC CART, 27 January 1960, folder 5, box 153, NBC Files.

31. Beth Bailey, "Sexual Revolutions," in David Farber, ed., *The Sixties: From Memory to History* (Chapel Hill: University of North Carolina, 1994), 235–62.

32. Paul F. Lazarsfeld and Harry Field, *The People Look at Radio: Report on a Survey Conducted by the National Opinion Research Center* (Chapel Hill: University of North Carolina Press, 1946), 29–31.

33. NBC CART, 2 February 1949, folder 2, box 1, NBC Files.

34. Ibid.

35. NBC CART, 15 August 1950, folder 3, box 1, NBC Files.

36. NBC CART, 8 March 1950, folder 3, box 1, NBC Files.

37. NBC CART, 8 February 1951, folder 4, box 1, NBC Files.

38. The women's chat program was seen on WNBT-TV from 1 May 1950 to 9 October 1951. McNeil, *Total Television*, 447.

39. NBC CART, 16 May 1950, folder 3, box 1, NBC Files.

40. NBC CART, 20 April 1950, folder 3, box 1, NBC Files.

41. NBC CART, 9 November 1950, folder 3, box 1, NBC Files.

42. NBC CART, 22 June 1951, folder 4, box 1, NBC Files.

43. NBC CART, 3 June 1954, folder 7, box 1, NBC Files.

44. Margaret Visser, *The Rituals of Dinner: The Origins, Evolution, Eccentricities, and Meaning of Table Manners* (New York: Grove Weidenfeld, 1991), 69–70.

45. Peter N. Stearns, *Battleground of Desire: The Struggle of Self-Control in Modern America* (New York: New York University Press, 1999), 3. See also Ellen Rothman, "Sex and Self-Control: Middle Class Courtship in America, 1780–1870," *Journal of Social History* 15 (1982): 409–25; and C. Dallett Hemphill, *Bowing to Necessities: A History of Manners in America, 1620–1860* (New York: Oxford University Press, 1999), 70–71, 132.

46. NBC CART, 15 December 1953, folder 6, box 1, NBC Files.

47. NBC CART, 14 December 1949, folder 2, box 1, NBC Files.

48. NBC CART, 2 November 1949, folder 2, box 1, NBC Files.

49. NBC CART, 26 August 1953, folder 6, box 1, NBC Files.

50. NBC CART, 1 July 1954, folder 7, box 1, NBC Files.

51. NBC CART, 17 October 1949, folder 2, box 1, NBC Files.

52. NBC CART, 10 September 1951, folder 4, box 1, NBC Files.

53. NBC CART, 5 May 1954, folder 7, box 1, NBC Files.

54. Brooks and Marsh, *Complete Directory of Prime Time Network and Cable TV Shows*, 665, and McNeil, *Total Television*, 538.

55. McNeil, *Total Television*, 538. Helffrich does not specifically write about this episode but does mention "advance publicity on some upcoming *Medic* [shows] worried a few." NBC CART, 25 October 1955, folder 1, box 153, NBC Files.

56. NBC CART, 14 April 1955, folder 1, box 153, NBC Files.

57. Julie L. Horan, *The Porcelain God: A Social History of the Toilet* (Toronto, Ontario: Carol, 1997), 81.

58. Milton Berle with Haskel Frankel, *Milton Berle: An Autobiography* (New York: Applause Theatre and Cinema, 2002), 280.

59. NBC CART, 8 March 1950, folder 3, box 1, NBC Files.

60. NBC CART, 8 February 1951, folder 4, box 1, NBC Files.

61. NBC CART, 1 November 1954, folder 7, box 1, NBC Files.

62. Scott Paper Company qtd. in Horan, *Porcelain God*, 145.

63. NBC CART, 9 February 1956, folder 2, box 153, NBC Files.

64. NBC CART, 23 December 1959, folder 5, box 153, NBC Files.

65. NBC CART, 19 November 1950, folder 3, box 1, NBC Files.

66. NBC CART, 15 May 1951, folder 4, box 1, NBC Files.

67. NBC CART, 16 February 1955, folder 1, box 153, NBC Files.

68. NBC CART, 5 January 1951, folder 4, box 1, NBC Files.

69. NBC CART, 3 May 1953, folder 6, box 1, NBC Files.

70. NBC CART, 16 January 1951, folder 4, box 1, NBC Files.

71. NBC CART, 28 September 1948, folder 1, box 1, NBC Files.

72. NBC CART, 10 November 1948, folder 1, box 1, NBC Files.

73. NBC CART, 6 August 1954, folder 7, box 1, NBC Files.

74. NBC CART, 1 July 1954, folder 7, box 1, NBC Files.

75. NBC CART, 1 April 1954, folder 7, box 1, NBC Files.

76. NBC CART, 16 February 1955, folder 1, box 153, NBC Files.

77. NBC CART, 31 May 1950, folder 3, box 1, NBC Files.

78. NBC CART, 6 October 1950, folder 3, box 1, NBC Files.

79. Briller, "Conscience of the Industry," 55.

80. NBC CART, 7 February 1949, folder 2, box 1, NBC Files.

81. NBC CART 25 February 1949, folder 2, box 1, NBC Files.

82. NBC CART, 16 January 1951, folder 4, box 1, NBC Files.

83. NBC CART, 14 September 1949, folder 2, box 1, NBC Files.

84. NBC CART, 18 August 1949, folder 2, box 1, NBC Files.

85. NBC CART, 16 January 1950, folder 3, box 1, NBC Files.

86. NBC CART, 19 September 1950, folder 3, box 1, NBC Files.

87. Briller, "Conscience," 55.

88. NBC CART, 18 September 1956, folder 2, box 153, NBC Files.

89. Briller, "Conscience," 55.

90. Ibid. See also NBC CART, 18 September 1956, folder 2, box 153, NBC Files.

91. *Broadcasting Yearbook* (Washington, DC: Broadcasting, 1950), 16.

92. Richard W. Pollay and Timothy Dewhirst, "Marketing Cigarettes with Low Machine-Measured Yields," in Donald R. Shopland, ed., *Risks Associated with Smoking Cigarettes with Low Machine-Measured Yields of Tar and Nicotine. Smoking and Tobaccos Control Monograph No. 13* (Bethesda, MD: U.S. Department of Health and Human Services, 2001), 199.

93. NBC CART, 30 September 1948, folder 1, box 1, NBC Files.

94. McNeil, *Total Television*, 584-85.

95. Reuven Frank, *Out of Thin Air: The Brief, Wonderful Life of Network News* (New York: Simon and Schuster, 1991), 42.

96. Steve Craig and Terry Moellinger, "So Rich, Mild, and Fresh": A Critical Look at Cigarette Commercials, 1948-1971" (unpublished paper, University of North Texas, Denton, 2000).

97. Frank, *Out of Thin Air*, 33.

98. NBC CART, 13 February 1953, folder 6, box 1, NBC Files.

99. Qtd. in Pollay and Dewhirst, "Marketing Cigarettes," 203.

100. NBC CART, 13 February 1953, folder 6, box 1, NBC Files.

101. NBC CART, 7 October 1948, folder 1, box 1, NBC Files.

102. NBC CART, 25 July 1949, folder 2, box 1, NBC Files.

103. NBC CART, 26 July 1950, box 1, folder 3, NBC Files.

104. NBC CART, 18 September 1951, box 1, folder 4, NBC Files.

105. NBC CART, 26 January 1950, box 1, folder 3, NBC Files.

106. NBC CART, 5 January 1951, folder 4, box 1, NBC Files.

107. NBC CART, 16 November 1950, box 1, folder 3, NBC Files.

108. NBC CART, 16 May 1950, folder 3, box 1, NBC Files.

109. See Larry C. White, *Merchants of Death: The American Tobacco Industry* (New York: Morrow, 1988), passim.

110. Karen S. Miller, *The Voice of Business: Hill and Knowlton and Postwar Public Relations* (Chapel Hill: University of North Carolina Press, 1999), 121. Miller does an excellent job tracing the history of big tobacco's 1950s public-relations campaign on 121–45.

111. NBC CART, 15 December 1953, folder 6, box 1, NBC Files.

112. Qtd. in Pollay and Dewhirst, "Marketing Cigarettes," 201.

113. Ibid. See also Larry C. White, "Cigarettes on Trial: The Public Health Balancing Act," *American Council on Science and Health*, 1 October 1991, http://www.acsh.org/publications/pubID.808/pub_detail.asp (accessed 22 September 2002).

114. Miller, *Voice of Business*, 121–45.

115. Sophia "Maxie" Helffrich, interview with the author, 11 March 2000, Helffrich apartment, New York.

116. NBC CART, 16 May 1950, folder 3, box 1, NBC Files.

117. NBC CART, 11 December 1950, folder 3, box 1, NBC Files.

118. NBC CART, 26 July 1950, box 1, folder 3, NBC Files.

119. NBC CART, 5 January 1949, folder 2, box 1, NBC Files.

120. NBC CART, 2 February 1949, folder 2, box 1, NBC Files.

121. NBC CART, 21 December 1948, folder 1, box 1, NBC Files.

122. Mary F. Corey, *The World through a Monocle:* The New Yorker *at Midcentury* (Cambridge: Harvard University Press, 1999), 198.

123. NBC CART, 22 June 1951, folder 4, box 1, NBC Files.

124. NBC CART, 7 June 1951, folder 4, box 1, NBC Files.

125. NBC CART, 28 December 1951, folder 4, box 1, NBC Files.

126. NBC CART, 3 June 1954, folder 7, box 1, NBC Files.

127. NBC CART, 17 May 1955, folder 1, box 153, NBC Files.

128. Barnouw, *Tower in Babel*, 158.

129. NBC CART, 3 May 1953, folder 6, box 1, NBC Files.

130. NBC CART, 2 February 1949, folder 2, box 1, NBC Files.

131. NBC CART, 20 September 1955, folder 1, box 153, NBC Files.

132. NBC CART, 15 February 1949, folder 2, box 1, NBC Files. See also NBC CARTs, 14 December 1949 and 2 February 1949, folder 2, box 1, NBC Files.

133. NBC CART, 15 February 1949, folder 2, box 1, NBC Files.

134. See "Advertising and Marketing Code," *Beer Institute*, http://www.beerinstitute.org/tier.asp?bid=249 (accessed 5 October 2002). The Beer Institute is an industry lobbying group.

135. John C. Burnham, *Bad Habits: Drinking, Smoking, Taking Drugs, Gambling,*

Sexual Misbehavior, and Swearing in American History (New York: New York University Press, 1993), 69–70.

136. Keisha L. Hoerrner, "The Forgotten Battles: Congressional Hearings on Television Violence in the 1950s," *Web Journal of Mass Communication Research* 2, no. 3 (June 1999), http://www.scripps.ohiou.edu/wjmcr/vol02/2-3a.HTM (accessed 5 October 2002).

137. NBC CART, 11 January 1954, folder 7, box 1, NBC Files.

138. Thomas C. Cochran, *The Pabst Brewing Company: The History of an American Business* (New York: New York University Press, 1948), 380–81.

139. Burnham, *Bad Habits*, 63.

140. Cochran, *Pabst*, 385. Cochran writes Pabst began targeting women as drinkers in 1933, the year beer first appeared as a packaged grocery item.

141. NBC CART, 8 January 1957, folder 3, box 153, NBC Files.

142. Barnouw, *Image Empire*, 65.

143. Harold Mehling, *The Great Time-Killer* (Cleveland, OH: World, 1962), 257.

144. NBC CART, 12 December 1957, folder 3, box 153, NBC Files. See also Stockton Helffrich, "Self-Regulation by Networks." *Journal of Broadcasting*, 1, no. 2 (Spring 1957), 124–28. In this article, Helffrich reveals, "Over three dozen people . . . scattered from coast to coast" devoted themselves to CA efforts on behalf of NBC-TV.

145. Stockton Helffrich, "Broadcasting Codes at the Crossroads?" *Variety*, 8 January 1964, 115–24; Stockton Helffrich, "Self-Regulation in TV Advertising," *Television Quarterly* 3, no. 3 (Summer 1964): 74–77.

146. Stockton Helffrich, "Censorship for TV," in Irving Settle and Norman Glenn, eds., *Television Advertising and Production Handbook* (New York: Crowell, 1953), 271.

Conclusion: A Prescient Vision

1. The colorful line "more 'Steinbeckian' than 'Marxian'" is taken from Christine A. Spivey, who is referring to folk singer Woody Guthrie, but also aptly describes Helffrich and many others in the Popular Front at the time. Christine A. Spivey, "This Land Is Your Land, This Land Is My Land: Folk Music, Communism, and the Red Scare as a Part of the American Landscape," *Student Historical Journal, Loyola University* 28 (1996–97): 3, http://chn.loyno.edu/history/journal/1996-7/documents/ThisLandisYourLandThisLandisMyLand_FolkMusicCommunismandtheRedScareasPartoftheAmericanLandsc.pdf (accessed 17 March 2005). See also Wayne Hampton, *Guerilla Minstrels: John Lennon, Joe Hill, Woody Guthrie, Bob Dylan* (Knoxville, TN: University of Tennessee Press, 1986), 130, 146; Cedric Belfrage, *The American Inquisition: 1945–1960* (Indianapolis, IN: Bobbs-Merrill, 1973), 101–3; Stockton Helffrich, private papers, author's collection. See also David K. Dunnaway, *How Can I Keep from Singing: Pete Seeger* (New York: Basic, 1981), 63.

2. Crossman, *God That Failed*, 2. 3, 5.

3. Richard M. Fried, *Nightmare in Red: The McCarthy Era in Perspective* (New York: Oxford, 1990), 37.

4. Lillian Berman, interview by Jackie Austin, 7 October 1987, Oregon, WI.

5. Crossman, *God That Failed*, 21.

6. See Spigel's discussion of Victorian domestic ideals and family amusements in Spigel, *Make Room For TV*, 11–35. See also Stephanie Coontz, *Marriage, a History: From Obedience to Intimacy, or How Love Conquered Marriage* (New York: Viking, 2005), 232, 235.

7. NBC CART, 27 January 1960, folder 5, box 153, NBC Files.

8. NBC CART, 10 February 1959, folder 5, box 153, NBC Files.

9. NBC CART, 23 December 1959, folder 5, box 153, NBC Files.

10. NBC CART, 6 June 1959, folder 5, box 153, NBC Files.

11. NBC CART, 27 January 1960, folder 5, box 153, NBC Files.

12. Jeff Kisseloff, *The Box: An Oral History of Television, 1920–1961* (New York: Penguin, 1997), xii.

13. Lynda M. Maddox and Eric J. Zanot, "The Suspension of the National Association of Broadcasters' Code and Its Effects on the Regulation of Advertising" (paper presented at the sixty-sixth annual meeting of the Association for Education in Journalism and Mass Communication, Corvallis, OR, August 6–9, 1983); Keith Adler, *Advertising Resource Handbook.* (East Lansing, MI: Advertising Resources, 1989). See also Alfred R. Schneider with Kaye Pullen, *The Gatekeeper: My 30 Years as a TV Censor* (Syracuse, NY: Syracuse University Press, 2001), 82.

14. See, among others, David P. Mackey, "The National Association of Broadcasters: Its First Twenty Years" (PhD diss., Northwestern University, 1961); Leslie Jackson Turner, "How Far Is Too Far? The Evolution of Prime-Time Standards at the Broadcast Television Networks from 1970–1995" (PhD diss., Florida State University, 1996); Matthew Murray, "Broadcast Content Regulation and Cultural Limits, 1920–1962" (PhD diss., University of Wisconsin, 1996).

15. Briller, "Conscience of the Industry," 52–57.

17. Michael J. Copps, "Commissioner Michael J. Copps Calls for Re-Examination of FCC's Indecency Definition, Analysis of Link between Media Consolidation and Race to the Bottom," *Federal Communications Commission*, Washington, DC, 21 November 2002, http://www.fcc.gov/commissioners/copps/statements2002.html (accessed 14 April 2003). The second program causing heavy complaints was the two-part mini series *Master Spy*, a drama on the alleged espionage activities of Robert Hanssen, seen on CBS-TV, November 10 and 17, 2001.

18. "Morality in Media interview: Federal Communications Commissioner Michael J. Copps," http://www.moralityinmedia.org/ (accessed 4 December 2001).

19. L. Brent Bozell III, "'Nip/Tuck' Knows No Bounds," *Parents Television Council, 1998–2009* http://www.parentstv.org/ptc/shows/main.asp?shwid=1726 (accessed 21 September 2004).

20. "Episode List for Nip/Tuck, Season 1," *IMDB*, http://www.imdb.com/title/tt0361217/episodes.

21. "Nip/Tuck," Online Public Access Catalog, *Irwindale Library*, http://64.60.154.124/FullDisp?itemid=30003561 (accessed 21 September 2004).

22. NBC CART, 7 October 1948, folder 1, box 1, NBC Files; NBC CART, 28 November 1949, folder 2, box 1, NBC Files.

23. "Episode List for Nip/Tuck, Season 1."

24. Betsy R. Armstrong, *The Avalanche Book* (Golden, CO: Fulcrum, 1992).

25. Melinda Newman, "The Nipple Ripple Effect," *Billboard* 116, 25 December 2004, 17.

26. "Shorts: Janet's Titillation Becomes Tivo's Greatest Hit," *Media Life*, http://www.medialifemagazine.com/news2004/feb04/feb02/2_tues/news7tuesday.html.

27. "Super Bowl Ratings Up Slightly over 2003," *SI.com*, 2 February 2004, http://sportsillustrated.cnn.com/2004/football/nfl/specials/playoffs/2003/02/02/bc.fbn.superbowlratings.ap/index.html (accessed 5 February 2004).

28. The fine is the largest ever levied against a U.S. television broadcaster.

29. John Eggerton, "CBS' Janet Jackson Fine Thrown Out: Third Circuit Court of Appeals Throws Out Fine against CBS Stations for Airing Janet Jackson Super Bowl Reveal," *Broadcasting and Cable*, 22 July 2008, http://www.broadcastingcable.com/index.asp?layout=articlePrint&articleID=CA6580012 (accessed 21 July 2008). See also *CBS Corporation et al. v. Federal Communication Commission*, 06–3575, U.S. Court of Appeals (3rd Cir. 2008), 97–99.

30. Sophia "Maxie" Helffrich, Helffrich's widow, interview by author, Helffrich residence, 11 March 2000, Jackson Heights, NY; Jackie Austin, interview by author, 11 January 1999, Madison, WI; Richard Finley Krauser, interview by author, Helffrich residence, 11 March 2000, Jackson Heights, NY. Other biographical information was gathered through family accounts, Helffrich's personal documents, and Federal Bureau of Investigation records. See Stockton Helffrich, FBI file. Helffrich's FBI file indicates he was a registered member of the American Labor Party in 1942 and was mentioned in the "records of the Queens County Communist Party" in May 1944. See Helffrich's FBI file, "Confidential Report," 4.

31. NBC CART, 27 January 1960, folder 5, box 153, NBC Files.

Index

About 'The Immoralist,' 85–87

Action on Smoking and Health (ASH), 181–82

"Adam and Eve" sketch, 9–10

Adams, David, 112

Addams, Jane, 36–37

ad-libbing, 10–11, 68, 101, 183

Adorno, Theodor W., 133

Adventures of Hopalong Cassidy, The, 102–3, 127

Adventure Time Theatre, 127

advertising, 17, 31–32, 161–62; to African Americans, 152; alcohol, 64–65, 182–86; brassieres and undergarments, 162–67, 199; cigarettes and tobacco, 109, 119, 177–82; Communist scare and, 52; congressional inquiries, 185–86; deodorants, 4, 167–70; depilatories and skin-care products, 174–76; extra time as compensation, 120–21; Kinsey Report and, 77; laxatives, toilets, and toilet paper, 170–74; negative strategies, 169, 175; plugola/payola, 183–84; race issues and, 6–8, 143–44, 146, 149, 152, 157; *Responsibility* manual, 64–68; self-regulation, 187–89; television as electronic marketing tool, 80–81; Television Code and, 71–72; truth in, 53, 67, 176–77, 178

Advertising Age, 157

African Americans: class issues, 157; as television characters, 6–9, 155–60; veterans, 145. *See also* race issues

alcohol: advertising, 64–65, 182–86; portrayal of, 59–60

Allen, Fred, 10–12

Allen, Frederick Lewis, 102

Allen, Steve, 16, 66

Ameche, Don, 9, 111

America, 25–26

America, postwar: affluence, 23–24, 44; anxiety, 23, 74–75, 94, 114; gender roles, 93–94; religious revival, 21–24; social culture of, 1–2, 43–45, 63–64, 73–75; women, stresses on, 93–94

American Broadcasting Corporation (ABC-TV), 165, 172, 175

American Business Consultants, 52

American Civil Liberties Union (ACLU), 11, 85, 194

American Forum of the Air, The, 147

American Labor Party, 40, 53, 191

American Mental Health Association, 53, 116

American System economic model, 32

American Telephone and Telegraph (AT&T), 161

American Television Society, 69

Amos 'n' Andy, 6–9, 18, 156–58

Anderson, Bill, 112

Anderson, Eddie, 7

Annie Get Your Gun (Berlin), 120

antiexploitation, 56, 70–71

anxiety: about Communism, 18–21, 50–51; about mental illness, 113–15; about sexuality, 74–75; postwar, 1, 13, 23, 94

Armstrong, Louis, 119

Arrow Show, The, 76, 83, 183

Arthur Murray Show, The, 29

Atmore, Joseph, 66

audience: advertising, response to, 162–66; imagined as white middle-class, 57; immigrant, 8; perceptions of, 6, 18–19, 31, 32, 57–58; race issues and, 150, 151, 153–54

audience warm-up activity, 84

Austin, Jackie, 42, 113

Autry, Gene, 103–4

Averil, Lawrence, 140

Bailey, Beth, 74, 167
Baker, Joseph, 147
Baldwin, James, 7
Ball, Lucille, 109
Bannister, Harry, 119
Baragrey, John, 48
Barnouw, Erik, 161
Baughman, James L., 58, 161
beer commercials, 184–85
Bell, Howard, 128
Bellah, Robert, 107–8
Bennett, Tony, 120
Benton, William, 27, 70, 118, 227n. 110
Bergen, Candice, 10
Bergen, Edgar, 9–10
Berle, Milton, 18, 66, 90, 172, 181, 182, 183
Berlin, Irving, 120
Berman, Lillian, 42
Berman, Murray, 40–41, 42, 191
Beulah, 126, 156, 158, 235n. 73
Bierly, Ken, 52
Bigelow Show, The, 66
blackface minstrelsy, 147–51, 234nn. 39, 41
blacklisting, 50, 52–54
Boddy, William, 18
bodily restraint, 169–70, 172–74
Bogle, Donald, 143
Bono, 3
Bottomore, Stephen, 131–32
Boyd, William, 102–3
Boyer, Charles, 86
Bozell, L. Brent, III, 195–96
Braren, Warren, 152
Brasselle, Keefe, 151
brassieres and undergarments, 162–67, 199
breakdown of society argument, 59
breasts, 3, 88–91, 92, 167, 221–22n. 75
Briller, Bert, 177
Brinkman, Paul D., 77
Broadcasting-Telecasting, 70
Broadway, 101
Broadway Open House, 90–91
Brooks, Tim, 102
Browder, Earl, 39
Brown, Andrew (Andy) *(Amos 'n' Andy)*, 7
Burke, Caroline, 79–80

Burnham, John C., 59, 100
Burrows, Abe, 86

Caesar, Sid, 186
Cakes and Ale (Maugham), 86
Camel News Caravan, The, 178–79
Camel Newsreel Theatre, The, 178
"Cancer by the Carton," 181
Cantor, Eddie, 10, 83–84, 147–49, 151, 234n. 46
Carlborg, Herb, 123
Carroll, Howard J., 29
Carson, Johnny, 66
Carter, Jack, 147
CART reports. *See* Continuity Acceptance Radio/Television (CART) reports
Castleman, Harry, 90
Catholic Church, 25–28; anti-Communism, 20–21; Legion of Decency (LOD), 10, 26–27, 28, 31; television code proposals, 28–31
cause and effect model, 132–35
censorship: "common sense," 14, 56; early-twenty-first-century return of, 2–3, 196–97; golden age of television, 1–3; as helpful, 80; to improve social conditions, 160; public calls for, 24–25; radio, 2–5; self-censorship, 67–68, 110–12, 241n. 144; vagueness of language, 56, 67
Chambers, Whitaker, 50
Chaplain, Charlie, 105
Chapman, Tom, 29
Chase, Ilka, 86, 90
Chevrolet on Broadway, 129, 138
Chevrolet Tele-Theatre, 103
Chicago television violence case study, 124–29
children, effects of television violence on, 133–36
Children's Advertising Review Unit, 194
children's programming, 4, 25, 55–57, 72, 177
City Council of Chicago, 125–26
civil rights movement, 9, 44
classic literature, editing of, 111–12, 137–38
Clock, The, 84, 111–12, 131
Clooney, Rosemary, 120

Clotworthy, William, 160, 236n. 91
coaxial cable, 161, 237n. 6
Cochran, Doris, 119
Cogley, John, 52
Cold War, 13, 18–21; sexual containment, 92–94. *See also* Communism
Colgate Comedy Hour, 84, 101, 147, 151, 234n. 45
Columbia Broadcasting System (CBS-TV), 45; bra commercials, 163–64; Communist scare and, 52–53; Janet Jackson incident, 196–98; race issues and, 155–58
"Come on-a My House" (song), 120
comic books, 133, 141
Comic Magazine Publishers, 122
Committee of Industrial Organizations (CIO), 45–46, 213n. 51
Communism, 190; blacklisting, 50, 52–54; fear of, 13, 18–21, 50–51; homosexuality linked to, 84–85. *See also* Cold War
Communist Party of the United States of America (CPUSA), 19, 37–41, 46–47, 53, 190–91
Como, Perry, 66
Comstock Laws, 62
Congress, 122–24
congressional inquiries, 25, 185–86, 228–29n. 7, 229n. 9
Congressional Record, 10
Constitution, U.S., 22–23
contunuity, as concept, 15
Continuity Acceptance Radio/Television (CART) reports, 14, 161–62; final report, 193, 199; language as issue in, 59, 110–12; parental responsibility addressed, 57, 134–35. *See also individual topics*
continuity editors, 14, 16
Cooney, Mrs. Leighton, 124
Coontz, Stephanie, 58–59
Copps, Michael J., 195
copycat behavior, 131
Corey, Mary F., 44, 59–60
Correll, Charles J., 7
Counterattack, the Newsletter of Facts on Communism, 52

"Counting Noses—NBCers Agree with Helffrich," 46
cow and udder jokes, 92
Cowboy Code, 103–4
Craig, Douglas, 4, 5
crazy, as term, 115
Cripps, Thomas, 157, 235n. 62
critics, 116–17, 119, 134, 156, 164–65
Crosby, John, 134, 156, 165
Crossman, Richard, 190
culture: cultural paradox, 24–28; mass culture, 139–41; of postwar America, 63–64, 73–75; television's role in summoning, 96–98; youth, 120, 139
Cushing, Richard J., 27, 90

Dagmar, 90–91
Daily News (Chicago), 125–27
Daniel, Pete, 153
Dear Phoebe, 141
Death Valley Days, 18
de la Ossa, Ernest, 146
Delta Sigma Theta, 155
D'Emilio, John, 77, 83
Denning, Michael, 37–38
Dennis, Peggy, 40
deodorants, 4, 167–70
depilatories and skin-care products, 174–76
Dewhirst, Timothy, 178
Diggins, John Patrick, 65
Ding Dong School, 109
Dior, Christian, 88–89
direct-effects model, 132–35
divorce, portrayal of, 4–5, 58–59
"Doing What Comes Natur'lly" (song), 120
Donna Reed Show, The, 16
"Double Door," 48
Dragnet, 137
DuMont Television Network, 70
Dunninger, Joseph, 66–67, 217n. 55
Dyke, Ken R., 11, 12, 48

Ebony, 142–43, 146
Eddie Cantor Story, The, 151
Edelman, Murray, 123, 129
Edgar, Paul G., 133

Edison, Thomas, 132
Egnor, Virginia Ruth, 90–91
Ehrenhalt, Alan, 21, 31, 63
Eiges, Syd, 146
Eighteenth Amendment, 5, 185
Eisenhower, Dwight D., 22, 85, 107
Eisler, Benita, 62
Ellwood, Robert S., 23, 100
Emerson, Faye, 90, 164–65
Every Day's a Holiday (West), 10
Executive Order 10450, 85

Faulkner, William, 20
Fay, Joey, 183–84
Federal Bureau of Investigation (FBI), 20, 46, 49–50, 152
federal censorship board recommendation, 90–91
Federal Communications Commission (FCC), 2, 10, 14, 118, 161, 197–98; *Public Service Responsibility of Broadcast Licensees*, 61–62
Federal Trade Commission, 176, 177
Fibber McGee and Molly, 7
Fifteen with Faye, 164–65
First Amendment, 123
Fish, Hamilton, 51
flags, 106–7
Flanders, Ralph, 22–23
Folsom, Frank, 152
Ford Star Review, 96
Ford Theatre, 105, 134
Foster, Stephen, 144–45
Four Star Playhouse, 157
Frankfurt School, 133, 230–31n. 53
Freud, Sigmund, 114
Fried, Richard M., 190
Frontiers of Faith, 94–95

Gaines, William, 141
Gallagher, Mike, 61
Gangbusters, 150
Garry, Patrick, 160
Gathings, Ezekial Chandler, 25, 122–23
Gene Autry, 127
GI Bill of Rights, 65
Gide, Andre, 85–87

Gilbert, James, 139–40
Glove, The (Somin), 48–50
G-man myth, 49
God That Failed, The (ed. Crossman), 47, 190
Goldbergs, The, 17
Goldwyn, Lawrence M., 85
Gordon, Linda, 64
Gornick, Vivian, 38–39, 40
Gosden, Freeman F., 7
Gould, Jack, 11, 116–17, 119, 156
Graham, Billy, 22
Gramsci, Antonio, 14
Grauer, Ben, 82, 86
Great Depression, 34–35, 38
Grey, Irving, 184

Haas, Francis J., 26
Hallmark Hall of Fame, 137
Hamamoto, Darrell Y., 157
Hamilton, Marybeth, 10
Hampton, Wayne, 190
Hank McCune Show, The, 92
Hari, Eugene, 95–96, 223n. 114
Harvey, Paul, 18
Havig, Alan, 10
Hays Commission code, 28, 57–58, 128, 209n. 78
Heale, M. J., 38
Heffernan, Joseph, 140
hegemony, 14
Heldenfels, R. D., 25
Helffrich, Charles, 34
Helffrich, Clara Denis, 41
Helffrich, Delores, 42, 114, 212n. 35
Helffrich, Richard, 42
Helffrich, Sophia "Maxie," 243n. 30
Helffrich, Stockton: cultural and historical context, 1–2, 13–14; as director of script adaptation, 44; early career, 15–17; early guidebook, 34; final CART report, 193, 199; on human dignity, 159; humanitarian awards, 114; as mediator, 188; as mid-level manager, 158–59; military service, 41–43; as page and guide, 33–34; placed at Continuity Acceptance Department, 47–48; Popular Front and

Communist Party years, 37–41, 144, 190–91; progressive approach, 53–54, 78, 190–91; public speaking, 15–16, 231n. 69; recants Communism, 47–48; social outlooks, 34–35, 190–92; as tour guide and artist, 35–36; undergoes psychoanalysis, 47, 114; union organizing effort, 45–47, 213n. 60; at Union Settlement Association, 36–37, 38, 40

Heller, Robert, 53

Hendershot, Heather, 17

Hendrickson, Robert, 140, 232n. 79

Henry, George W., 83

Herberg, Will, 47

Herbert, Jack, 171

Herring, Clyde, 10

Hey Mulligan, 137

Hileman, Donald B., 77

Hill and Knowlton, 181

Hilmes, Michele, 7, 8

Himmelweit, Hilde T., 23

Hiss, Alger, 19, 50

Hitler, Adolf, 39

Hoellen, John J., 125–26, 128

Hoerrner, Keisha L., 123, 128, 186, 229n. 9

Holiday in Las Vegas, 166

Hollywood blacklist, 50

"Home Life of a Buffalo," 129

homosexuality, 4, 50, 51, 192–93, 220n. 36, 221n. 67; gays and lesbians in television business, 87–88; laws forbidding, 73, 84–85; linked to Communism, 84–85; on postwar television, 83–87; WNBT-TV broadcasts, 85–87. See also sexuality

Honeymooners, The, 17–18

Hoover, J. Edgar, 20, 49–50, 141

Hope, Bob, 111, 147

Horan, Julie L., 172

Horkheimer, Max, 133

Horn and Hardt's Children's Hour, The, 144

Horton, Mildred McAfee, 152–53

House Subcommittee on Interstate and Foreign Commerce, 18

House Un-American Activities Committee (HUAC), 27, 50

Howard University, 155

Howdy Doody, 177

Howe, Irving, 5

Hull House, 36–37

humor, theories of, 78

Huntley, Chet, 6

hypodermic-needle model, 58, 132–33

"I Get Ideas" (song), 119–20

I Love Lucy, 109

Immoralist, The (Gide), 85–87

incongruity theories, 78

indecency fines, 197–98, 203nn. 3, 4

Inglis, Fred, 14

Irwin, Mary, 132

Isserman, Maurice, 39, 40

Jack Carter Show, 96, 97, 145

Jackson, Janet, 2–3, 196–97

Jahncke, Lee, 112

Jessel, George, 109–10

Jewish radio humor, 4–5

Johnson, Grace, 123, 165

Johnson, Harold Ogden "Chic," 83, 114

Jolson, Al, 147, 148, 149, 150

Jones, Amos (Amos 'n' Andy), 7

Jorgenson, Christine, 81–83

Judy Canova Show, The, 7

juvenile delinquency, 139–41, 232n. 79

J. Walter Thompson Agency, 12

Kate Smith Show, 150

Kathi Norris Show, The, 168, 174

Kaufman, Samuel, 33

Keenan, John, 52

Kefauver, Estes, 140, 231n. 69, 232n. 79

Kefauver Commission, 140–41, 231n. 69

Kellogg, Susan, 64

Kemble, Dorothy, 11

Kendrick, Walter, 94

King Solomon's Mines, 147

Kinsey, Alfred C., 62–64

Kinsey Report, 62–64, 75–78, 79, 82, 97

Kirkpatrick, Ted, 52

Kiss, The, 132

Kisseloff, Jeff, 157, 193

Kraft Television Theatre, 48–50, 83, 105–6, 130; race issues and, 150, 152

Kukla, Fran, and Ollie, 107

"Ladies in Retirement," 130
Lane, Thomas, 25, 27, 90, 118
Langford, Frances, 111
language: mental illness, portrayal of, 113–17; pregnancy, references to, 108–10; profanity, 99–102; taboos, 59; television writers and, 110–11; vagueness of in censorship, 56, 67; vulgarity, 102–8; "water closet" incident, 112–13; WWJ-TV, Detroit, 117–21
laxative ads, 170–71
"Lazy Bones" (song), 147
Lears, T. J. Jackson, 93
Leave It to Beaver, 16
LeBow, Guy, 24–25
Lee, Peggy, 119, 120
Legion of Decency (LOD), 10, 26–27, 28, 31
Leoncavallo, Ruggero, 111
Lester, Jerry, 90–91
Levine, Lawrence W., 97
Lewis, Fulton, Jr., 21
Lewis, Jerry, 84, 183
Liebman, Max, 111
Life with Luigi, 17
Lights Out, 117–18, 130, 134, 155
Lillie, Bea, 111
Lipsitz, George, 93
Litman, Barry R., 121
Lloyd, Jack, 87
Loren, Sophia, 88
Lovett, Robert Morse, 38
lowbrow culture, concept of, 17–18, 65–66, 105–6
loyalty oath, CBS, 53

Mabley, Jack, 124–28
Macbeth, 137
MacRorie, Janet, 3–4, 10
Mages, Morris, 126–27
"Man at the Crossroads Looking with Hope and High Vision to the Choosing of a New and Better Future" (Rivera), 35–36
Mann, William J., 87
Mannes, Marya, 81
Mansfield, Jayne, 166
Marling, Karal Ann, 89

marriage, portrayal of, 58–59
Marsh, Earle, 102
Martin, Dean, 84, 88, 183
Mary Kay and Johnny, 109
mass culture, 139–41
Masterpiece Playhouse, 79
Masterson, D. J., 28
Mata, Ruth, 95–96, 223n. 114
"Mata and Hari," 95–96
Matinee Theatre, 116
Maugham, W. Somerset, 86
May, Elaine Tyler, 19–20, 93
May, Mark, 140–41
Mazzarella, Sharon, 139
McCarthy, Joseph, 21, 51, 85
McConnell, Joseph H., 118–19
McCraw, Thomas K., 68
McLean, Albert F., Jr., 5
McLeon, Elizabeth, 9
McNinch, Frank, 10
Medic, 172
Menser, Clarence L., 11
mental illness, portrayal of, 43, 53, 113–17, 192, 227n. 88
Merman, Ethel, 120
Meyerowitz, Joanne, 93–94
Mickelson, Sig, 53
Miller, Burke, 95
Miller, Douglas T., 51
Miller, Karen S., 181
Mintz, Stephen, 64
Miracle Case, 26
Miranda Prorsus (Pius XII), 29–30
Miss America Pageant, 29
modernist realism, 101–2
Monro, D. H., 78
Morgan, Robert Shepherd, 69–70, 71–72
Morrison, Toni, 8
Mosel, Tad, 110, 130
Most Beautiful Girl in the World, The, 29
Motion Picture Production Code (Movie Code), 69–70
Motion Picture Research Council, 228n. 5
movies, 132; censorship codes, 69–70, 122; Communism in, 50–51; Hays Commission code, 28, 57, 128, 209n. 78; Legion of Decency (LOD) and, 10, 26–27, 28, 31

Muir, Jean, 52
Mulford, Edward, 102
Mundt, Karl, 147, 233n. 28
Murray, Matthew, 18, 31–32
Murrow, Edward R., 23
music, censorship of, 4, 117–20
My Little Margie, 115

Nadel, Alan, 93
National Association for the Advance-
    ment of Colored People (NAACP),
    145–46, 156–57
National Association of Broadcasters
    (NAB): Code Authority, 30, 194–97;
    Standards of Good Practices (Radio
    Code), 69, 71
National Association of Colored Women,
    152
National Association of Radio and Televi-
    sion Broadcasters (NARTB), 28; Code
    Review Board, 187; Television Code
    (TV Code), 69–72
National Broadcasting Corporation
    (NBC), 44; contribution to Television
    Code, 70–72; gags about, 11; as good
    public servant, 66; NBC radio Depart-
    ment of Continuity Acceptance, 3–4;
    race and hiring policy, 152–53; union
    organizing effort, 45–47. *See also*
    Continuity Acceptance Radio/Televi-
    sion (CART) reports; *Responsibility:
    A Working Manual of NBC Program
    Policies*
National Catholic Welfare Conference
    (NCWC), 27, 29
National Citizens Advisory Board, 27
National Council of Catholic Men
    (NCCM), 26, 27, 29
National Institute of Mental Health, 116
National Society of Television Producers
    (NSTP), 28
National Television Review Board pro-
    posal, 28–29
National Urban League (NUL), 146
NBC. *See* National Broadcasting Corpora-
    tion (NBC)
Negro Youth Leagues, 144

New Dealers, 38
New Yorker audience, 59–60
New York State Commission against Dis-
    crimination, 151
New York Times, 28, 116, 119, 164–65
Nichols, L. B., 49
Nip/Tuck, 195–96
nontelevision works, 44, 79–80
Norfleet, Barbara, 24
Norton, John H., Jr., 126
nose thumbing, 105–6
Nowak, Marion, 51
nuclear family: as anti-communist, 20;
    Catholic view of, 25–26
Nyren, Reuben T., 125

Oakley, J. Ronald, 22, 23, 62, 73
occult beliefs, 65–67
O'Connell, William, 4
O'Connor, Timothy J., 125, 128
Odets, Clifford, 37
O'Hara, John F., 29
Old Gold Amateur Hour, The, 145
Old Gold Show, 180
Olsen, John Siguard "Ole," 83, 114
O'Neal, Frederick, 151
"Operation Frontal Lobes," 96–97
Orr, Paul, 112
O'Shea, Daniel T., 52–53
Our Gang, 150
Ovaltine, 177
owned-and-operated stations (O&Os),
    162, 179
Ozzie and Harriet, 16, 126

Paar, Jack, 16, 112–13, 226n. 76
pages and guides, NBC, 33–34
Pagliacci (Leoncavallo), 111
panty raids, 25
Papal Encyclical, 29–30
Paramount Pictures, 10
parent monitoring, 124–25, 195–96
Parents Television Council, 195–96
Park, Ben, 154
paternalism, 58
Paul Winchell and Jerry Mahoney Show,
    105

Payne Fund studies, 122, 228n. 5
Peale, Norman Vincent, 22
Pearl Harbor, 41
Perry, Lincoln, 233–34n. 31
Perry Como Show, 166
Peter Pan, 133, 135
Philbrick, Herbert A., 51
Philco TV Playhouse, 130
Phillips, Barnet, 132
Pirandello, Luigi, 79–80, 138
Pius XI, 20
Pius XII, 29–30, 31
plugola/payola, 183–84
Podrazik, Walter, 90
Pollay, Richard W., 178
Poppele, J. R., 109
Popular Front, 37–41, 144, 190–91, 241n. 1
pregnancy, references to, 108–10
Printers' Ink, 157, 166
programming, 16–17, 216n. 36; children's
    programs, 4, 25, 55–57, 72, 177; crime-
    and-mystery category, 57–58, 122; early
    censorship guide, 55–64; early era,
    24–25; sports, 17; Television Code and,
    70–71; urban and ethnic, 17–18
public service announcements, 116
*Public Service Responsibility of Broadcast
    Licensees* (FCC "Blue Book"), 61–62

quiz-show scandals, 112, 183

race issues, 60–61, 144–46, 192, 233n. 28;
    advertising and, 6–8, 143–44, 149, 152,
    157; African American characters on
    television, 6–9, 155–60; audience re-
    sponse, 150, 151, 153–54; hiring policy,
    152–53; ignored by media, 7–9; inte-
    gration without identification policy,
    152–55; NBC-TV/RCA corporate poli-
    cy, 146–47, 149; radio era, 4–7; segrega-
    tion, 142. *See also* African Americans
race riots, 142, 153
racial stereotypes, 5–9, 60–61, 142–60,
    233–34n. 31; blackface minstrelsy, 41,
    147–51, 234n. 39
radio: *Amos 'n' Andy*, 4–5; censorship, 2–5;
    crime dramas, 122; Jewish humor, 4–5;

race issues and, 4–7; sexuality on, 4–5,
    9–10
Radio and Television Daily, 77
Radio City, 33
Radio Code, 69, 71
Radio Corporation of America (RCA),
    33–34; race and hiring policy, 152–53
Radio Guild, 45, 46
Radio News, 33
"Rain in the Morning," 116
ratings, 127
Reader's Digest, 181
realism, 101–2, 130–31, 137
*Red Channels: The Report of Communist
    Influence in Radio and Television*, 52–53
religion, 61; Catholic Church, 10, 20–21,
    25–28, 31; postwar renaissance, 100–
    101; revival, 1950s, 21–24
reperformances, 230n. 37
*Responsibility: A Working Manual of NBC
    Program Policies*, 55–71; on mentions of
    God, 99–100; on mentions of poisons,
    129–30; race issues and, 60–61; Section
    1: Program Content, 55–64; Section 2:
    Commercial Content, 64–68; Section 3:
    Operating Procedures, 68–69
Rice, John, 132
Rivera, Diego, 35–36
R. J. Reynolds Tobacco Company, 178
Robert Montgomery Presents, 105, 130
Rogers, Richard, 86
Rogin, Michael, 234n. 39
Rooney, Mickey, 137
Roosevelt administration, 39
Rosen, George, 113
Rosenbergs, Julius and Ethel, 19, 50
Rovere, Richard H., 21

Sanders, Julio Cesar A., 119
Sarnoff, David, 32, 68, 143, 198
Schramm, Wilbur, 134–35
Schrecker, Ellen, 38, 39, 40
Sebesta, Lithe, 88
Seduction of the Innocent (Wertham), 133
Senate Judiciary Committee on Internal
    Security, 27
Senate Labor Committee, 152

Senate Resolution 89, 140
Senate Subcommittee on the Judiciary, 140, 231n. 69
Serling, Rod, 230n. 37
Sexual Behavior in the Human Female (Kinsey), 62–63, 76–77
Sexual Behavior in the Human Male (Kinsey), 62–64, 75–76
sexuality: breasts, 3, 88–92, 167, 221–22n. 75; dancing, 94–96; Kinsey Report, 62–64; Kinsey Report on television, 75–78; perversion, fears of, 19–20; postwar attitudes, 73–75; on radio, 4–5, 9–10; sexual containment and censorship, 92–94; in television drama, 79–81; transgender and transsexual, 81–83. *See also* homosexuality
Sharkey, Sam, 115
Sheehy, Maurice, 10
Sheen, Fulton J., 13, 22
Shore, Dinah, 117, 120
Short, William, 228n. 5
Silvera, Frank, 6
Silvers, Phil, 76, 183
Sinatra, Frank, 101
situation comedies (sit-coms), 7, 17–18, 92
Six Characters in Search of an Author (Pirandello), 79–80
$64,000 Question, The, 29
Smythe, Dallas W., 140
Sneeze, The, 132
sneezing, portrayal of, 132, 175–76
Somin, W. O., 48–50
Soviet Union, 38–39
Spellman, Francis Joseph, 20–21, 26
Spiegel, Maura, 88
Spigel, Lynn, 18
Sponsor, 123, 146, 165
Stabile, James, 112–13
Stalin, Joseph, 39, 40
Standards of Good Practices (Radio Code), 69, 71
Stanton, Bob, 180
Stanton, Frank, 81, 155
Stark, Steven D., 18
Steffens, Lincoln, 38
"Stepin Fetchit" character, 147, 233–34n. 31

Stevenson, Adlai E., 21
stimulus-response (S-R) theory, 58
Stockton, Delores, 41
Stone, Abraham, 86
Stop Me If You've Heard This One, 83
Stromberg, Hunt, Jr., 87
substance abuse, portrayal of, 60
suicide, portrayal of, 4, 129–31
Sullivan, Ed, 142–43, 149
Supreme Court, 26
Swayze, John Cameron, 178–79
"Sweet Violets" (song), 117–19
Swift Show, The, 101, 224n. 16
swish, as term, 83–84
symbolic politics, 123, 128–29

Taft, Robert, 21
Tales of Wells Fargo, 104
Talmadge, Herman, 153
Tanner, Paul F., 29
taxicab drivers' strike of 1934, 37
television: as cultural centerpiece, 17–18; as cultural missionary, 96–98; effects of, 131–36; as invited guest in home, 26, 58, 71, 94, 109, 120, 140; as object of ridicule, 99; public space created by, 73; rate of diffusion, 2, 17; set sales, 17, 24, 44
Television Board of Directors, of the NARTB, 69
Television Broadcasters Association (TBA), 27–28
Television Code (TV Code), 69–70, 69–72; NBC's contribution to, 70–72
Television Program Standards Committee, of the NARTB, 69–70
Television Review Board (Archdiocese of Chicago), 28
Texaco Star Theatre, 105, 116, 181, 182–83
Tex and Jinx Show, 107
Thalberg, Irving G., 80
Thomas, Danny, 150
Timberlake, Justin, 196
Time, 20
Toast of the Town, 149
tobacco advertising, 109, 119, 177–82
Tobacco Institute Research Committee, 181

toilets and toilet paper, 171–73
Toll, Robert C., 132
Tollin, Anthony, 7
Tolson, Clyde, 49
Tonight Show, The, 16, 90, 112–13
To Secure These Rights, 147
Toynbee, Arnold, 13
Toynbee Hall, 36
train effect, 131–32
Trammel, Niles, 12
Trimpey, Betty, 108
Trimpey, Miles, 108
Tropiano, Stephen, 87
Truman, Harry S., 50, 60–61, 147, 180
Truman Doctrine, 18
"TV's Holiday Fare for Kids: It's Murder,"
    124

Uncle Sam's Story, 116
"Uncle Tom" character, 5, 7
union organizing, 39–40, 45–47
Union Settlement Association, 36–37, 38,
    40, 191
United Office and Professional Workers
    of America (UOPWA), 45–46
uses and gratifications model, 134–35

Van Horne, Harriet, 79
Vanishing Prairie, The, 92
Variety, 112–13, 142
vaudeville, 5, 147–51, 234n. 43
Victoria's Secret Fashion Show Special, 195
violence: Chicago television case study,
    124–29; effects of television on chil-
    dren, 133–36; first congressional probe,
    122–24; general, 136–38; juvenile de-
    linquency and Kefauver Commission,
    139–41; suicide, 129–31
Volsted Act (National Prohibition Act),
    182
vulgarity, 102–8

Waiting for Lefty (Odets), 37
Ward, Harry, 127, 150, 171–72

Warren, Carol, 43
Wartella, Ellen, 139
"water closet" incident, 112–13
Waters, Ethel, 156
Watson, Carl, 173–74, 177
Wayne King Show, The, 117–19
Weaver, Sylvester "Pat," 96–97, 146, 164,
    168, 171, 177
WENR-TV, Chicago, 126
Wertham, Frederic, 133
West, John, 146
West, Mae, 9
Westerns, 102–5, 127
We, the People, 130, 230n. 42
WHDH-TV, Boston, 90
White Collar Mike, 45–46
Williams, Linda, 132
Winchell, Paul, 66, 217n. 55
Winchell, Walter, 133, 231n. 54
Windolf, Jim, 226n. 76
WMCA, New York, 45
WNBQ-TV, Chicago, 124–27
WNBT-TV, New York, 15, 102, 168; broad-
    casts on homosexuality, 85–87
women, postwar stresses on, 93–94
Works Project Administration (WPA) 37
World Series, 1947, 18
World War II, 41–43
WRCA-TV, New York, 158
writers, taboo language and, 110–11
WTMJ-TV, Milwaukee, 30, 131
WWJ-TV, Detroit, 117–21
Wylie, Max, 133
Wynder, Ernst L., 181
Wynn, Ed, 183

You Asked for It, 25, 123
Young and Rubicam, 11, 52
Your Hit Parade, 119
Your Jeweler's Showcase, 115
Your Show of Shows, 95, 186
youth culture, 120, 139

Zachary, Beulah, 107

Robert Pondillo is an associate professor of electronic media communication at Middle Tennessee State University. His articles on early network TV censorship have appeared in the *Journal of Popular Film and Television* and numerous academic and popular publications. Pondillo is also an award-winning short-film writer-director.